Call
of
the
Night

〈5〉

KOTOYAMA

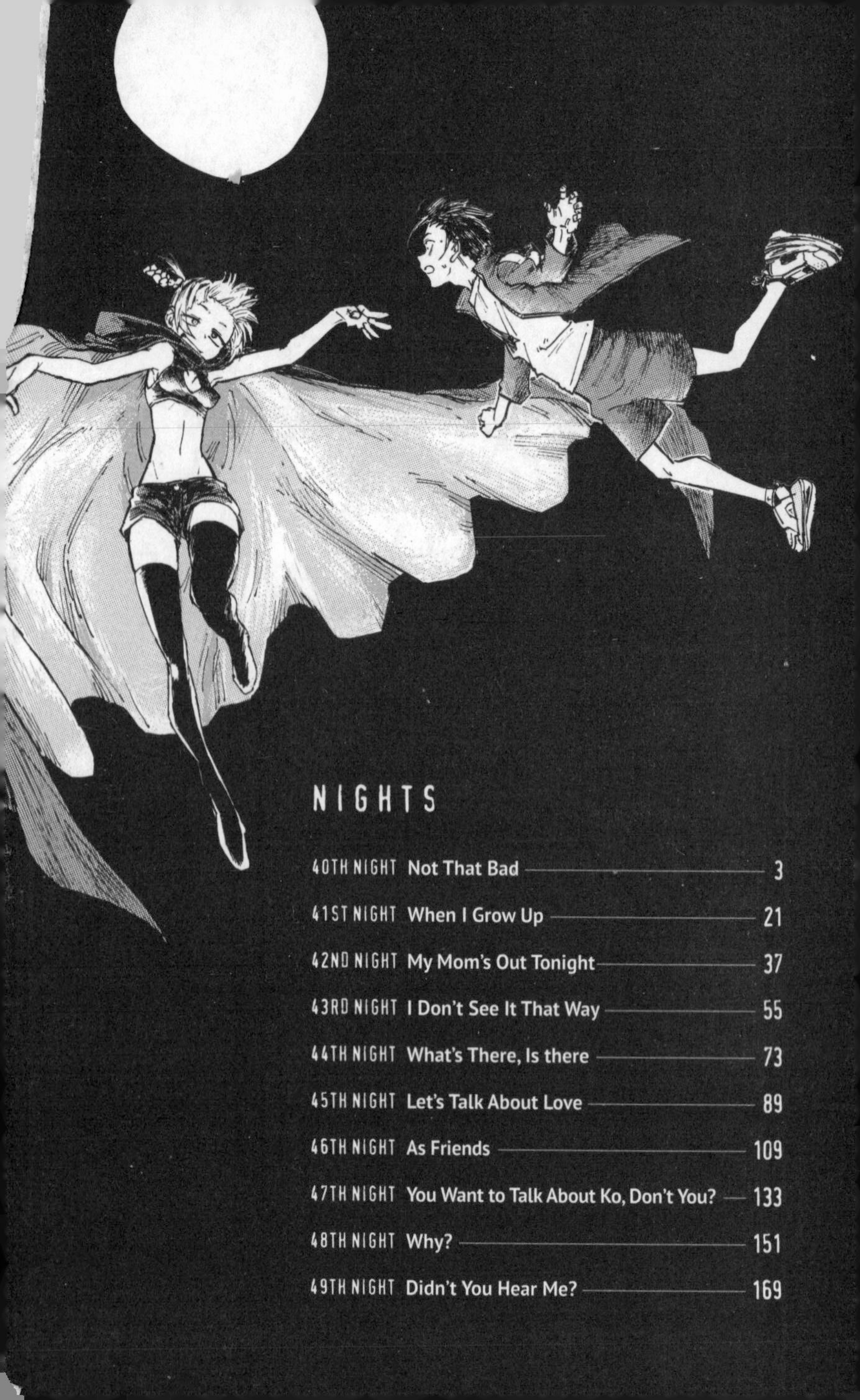

NIGHTS

NIGHT 40: NOT THAT BAD

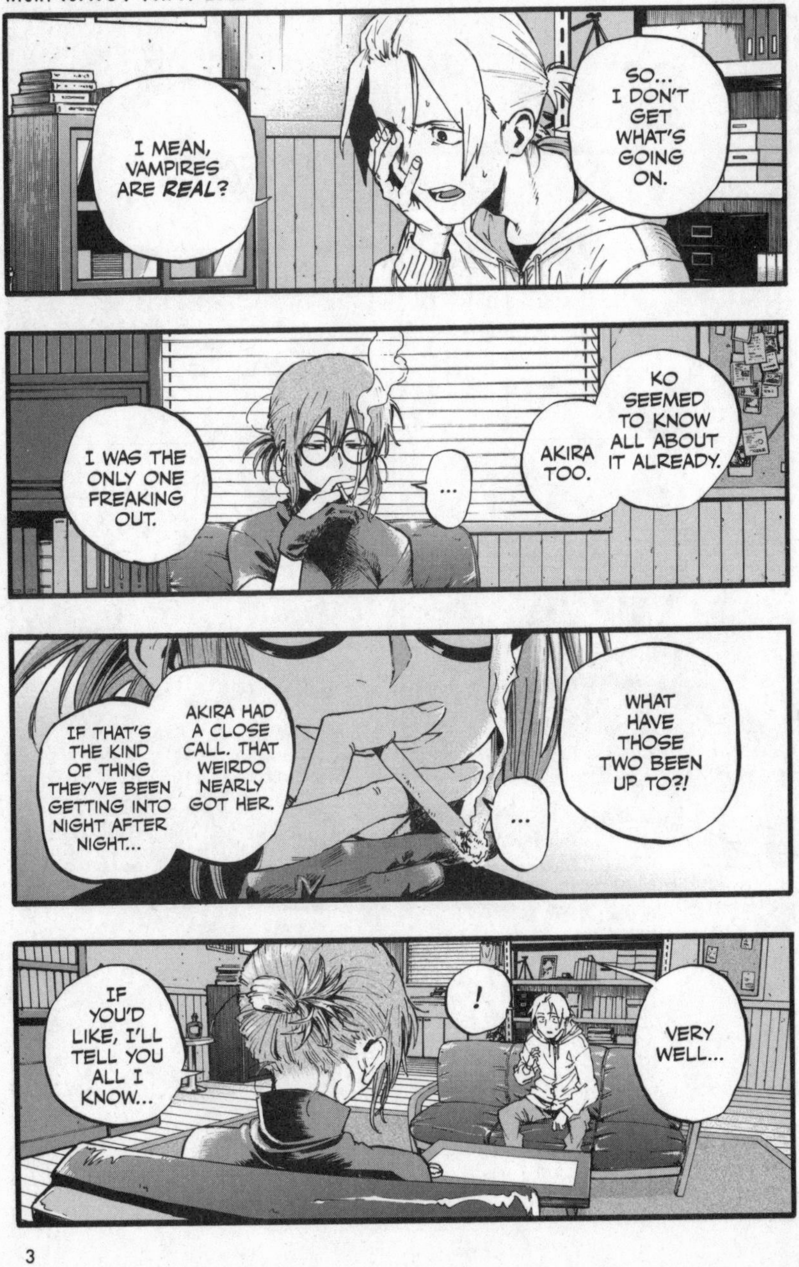
SO... I DON'T GET WHAT'S GOING ON.
I MEAN, VAMPIRES ARE *REAL*?
KO SEEMED TO KNOW ALL ABOUT IT ALREADY.
AKIRA TOO.
...
I WAS THE ONLY ONE FREAKING OUT.
WHAT HAVE THOSE TWO BEEN UP TO?!
...
AKIRA HAD A CLOSE CALL. THAT WEIRDO NEARLY GOT HER.
IF THAT'S THE KIND OF THING THEY'VE BEEN GETTING INTO NIGHT AFTER NIGHT...
VERY WELL...
!
IF YOU'D LIKE, I'LL TELL YOU ALL I KNOW...

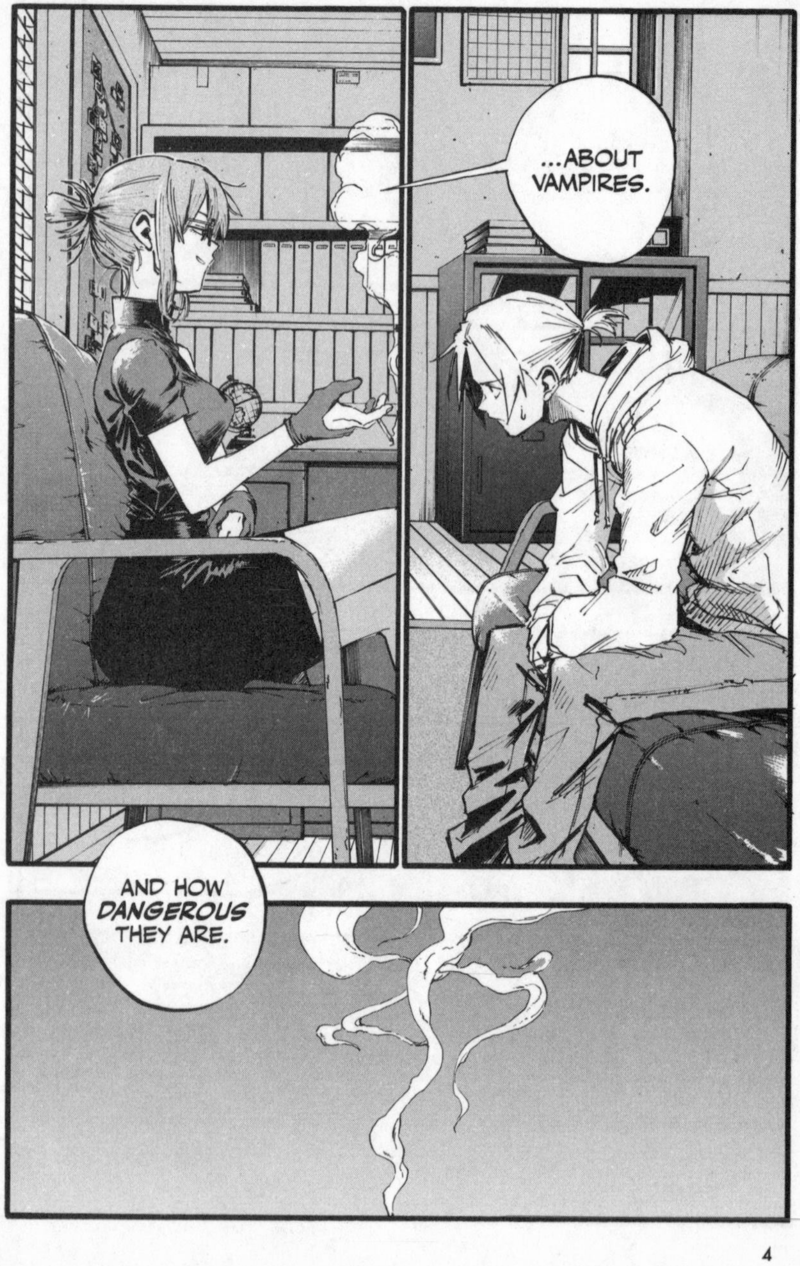
...ABOUT VAMPIRES.
AND HOW *DANGEROUS* THEY ARE.

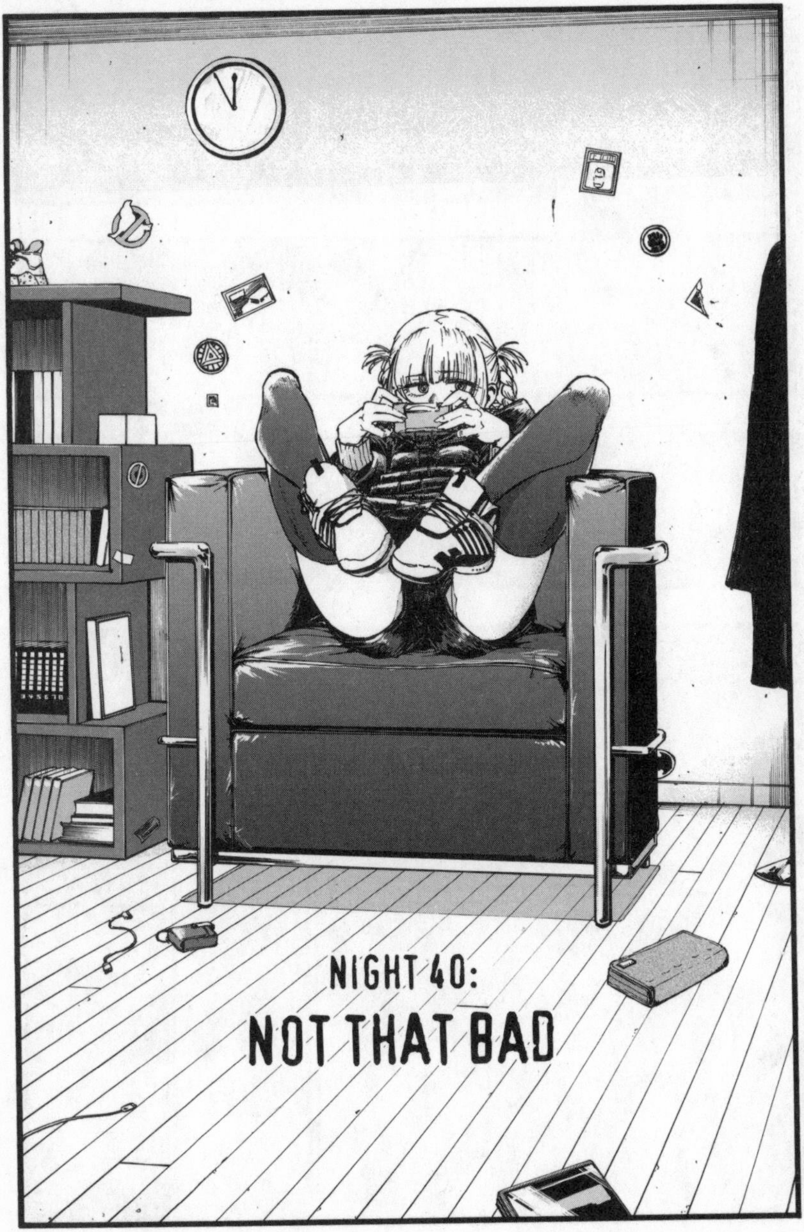
NIGHT 40:
NOT THAT BAD

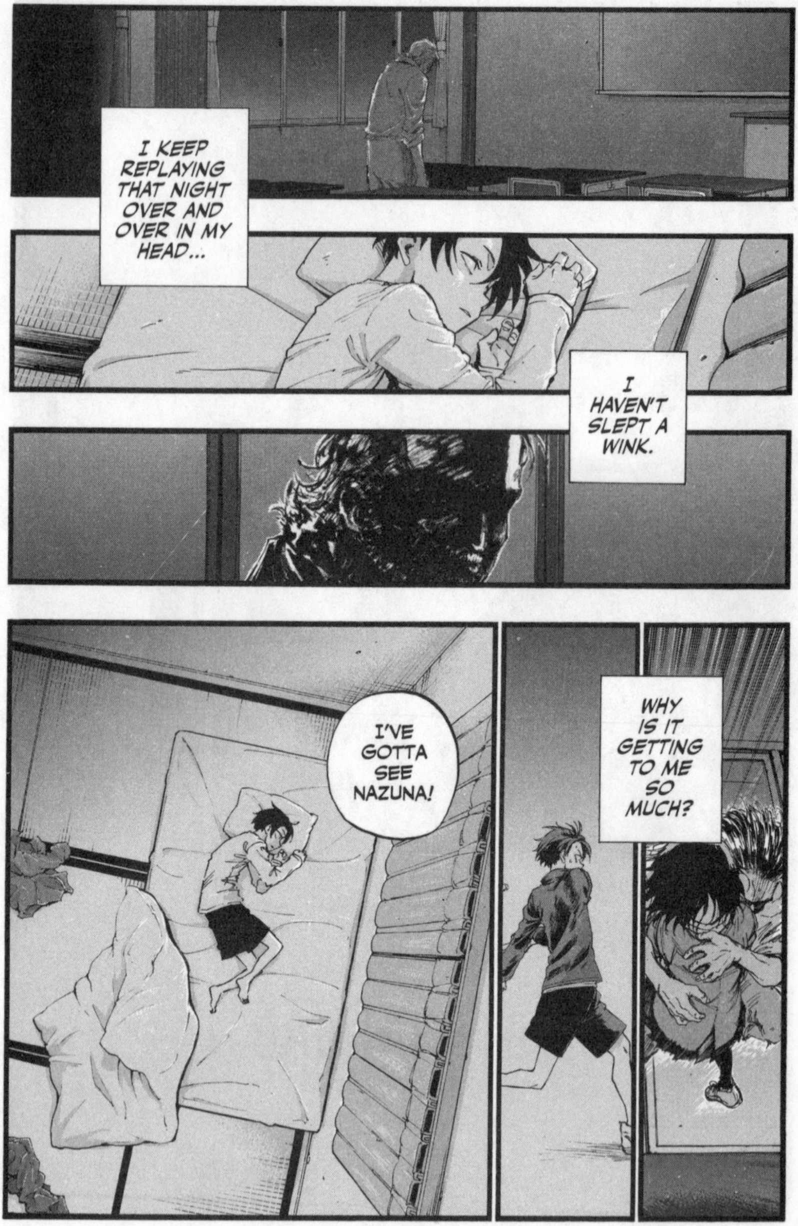
I KEEP REPLAYING THAT NIGHT OVER AND OVER IN MY HEAD...
I HAVEN'T SLEPT A WINK.
WHY IS IT GETTING TO ME SO MUCH?
I'VE GOTTA SEE NAZUNA!

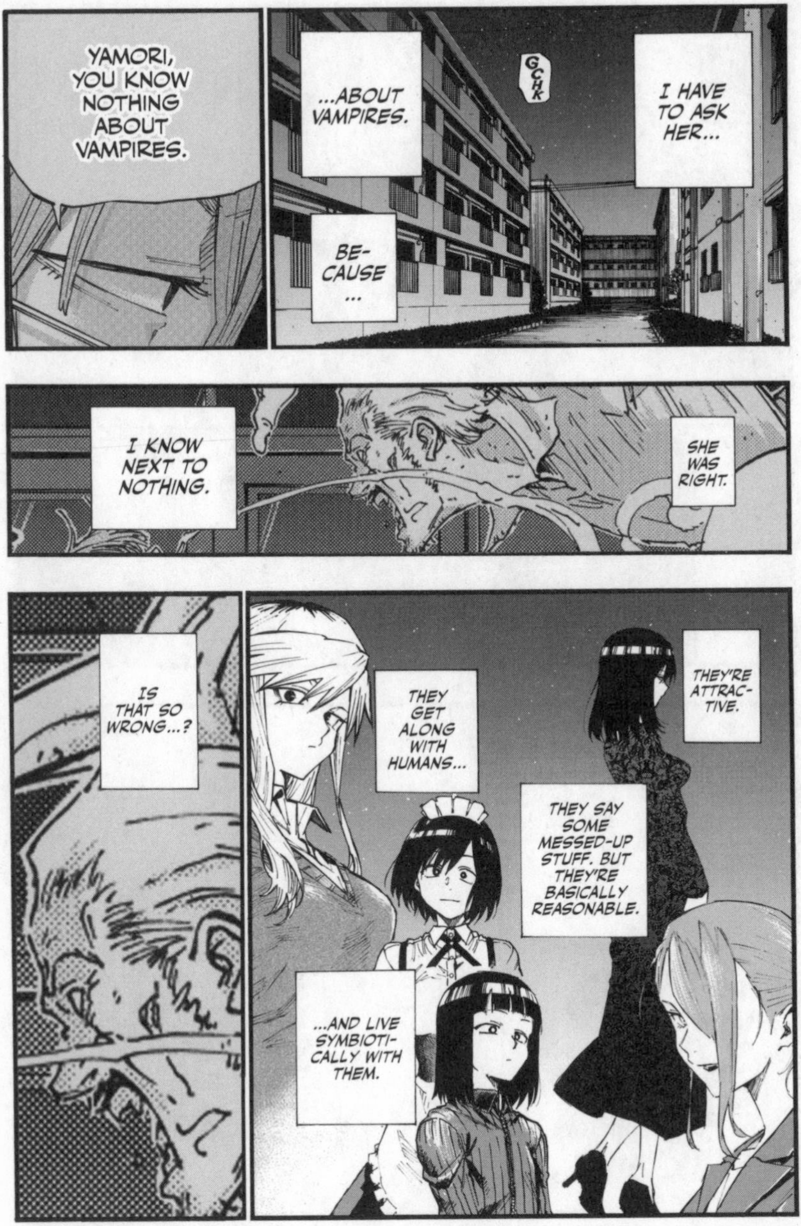
I HAVE TO ASK HER...
GCHK
...ABOUT VAMPIRES.
BE-CAUSE ...
YAMORI, YOU KNOW NOTHING ABOUT VAMPIRES.
SHE WAS RIGHT.
I KNOW NEXT TO NOTHING.
THEY'RE ATTRAC-TIVE.
THEY GET ALONG WITH HUMANS...
THEY SAY SOME MESSED-UP STUFF. BUT THEY'RE BASICALLY REASONABLE.
...AND LIVE SYMBIOTI-CALLY WITH THEM.
IS THAT SO WRONG...?

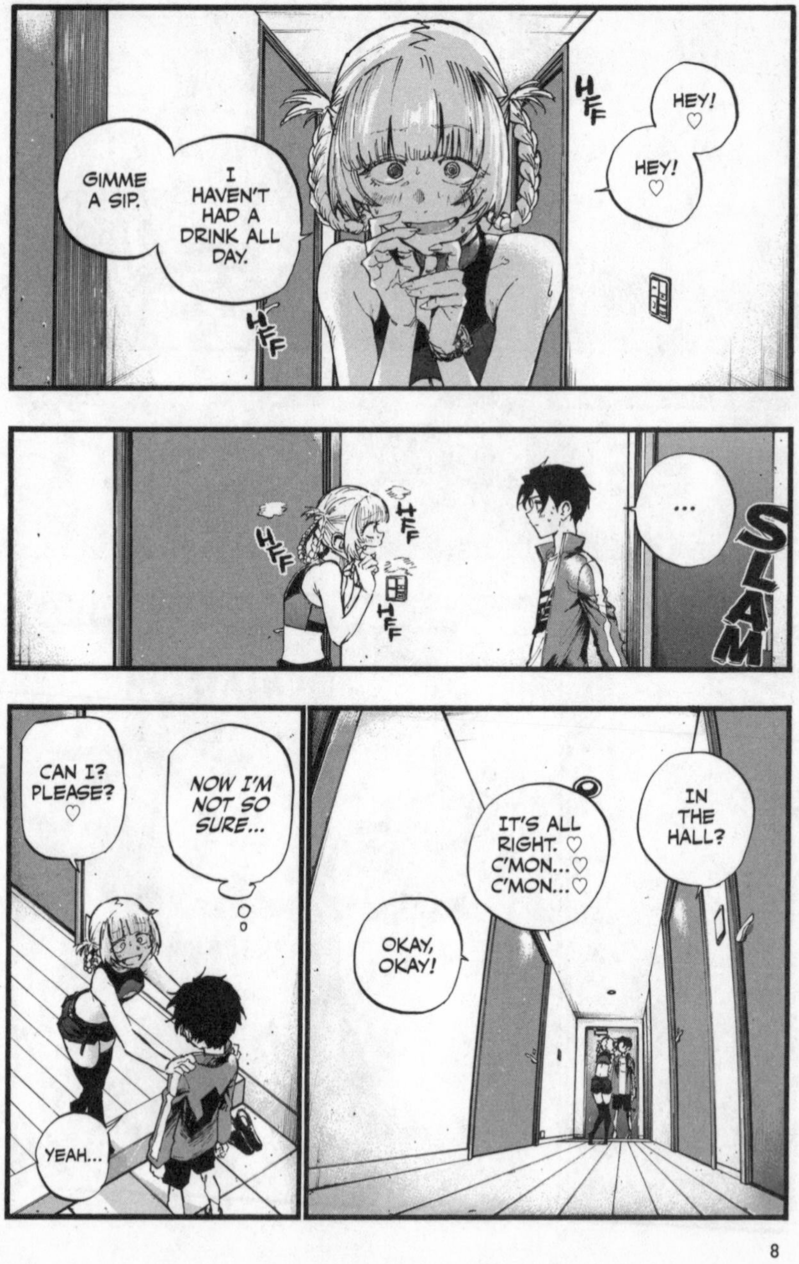
HEY! ♡
HEY! ♡
HFF
I HAVEN'T HAD A DRINK ALL DAY.
GIMME A SIP.
HFF
SLAM
...
HFF
HFF
HFF
IN THE HALL?
IT'S ALL RIGHT. ♡ C'MON...♡ C'MON...♡
OKAY, OKAY!
NOW I'M NOT SO SURE...
CAN I? PLEASE? ♡
YEAH...

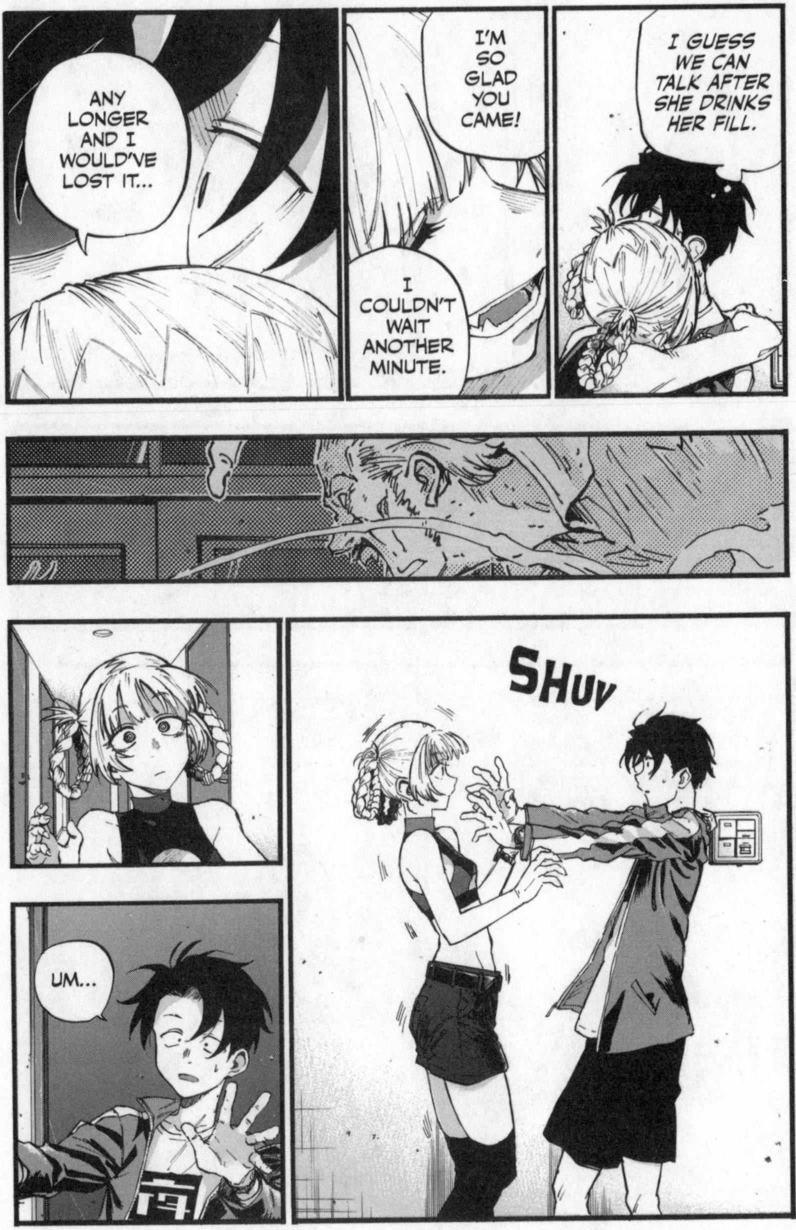
I GUESS WE CAN TALK AFTER SHE DRINKS HER FILL.
I'M SO GLAD YOU CAME!
I COULDN'T WAIT ANOTHER MINUTE.
ANY LONGER AND I WOULD'VE LOST IT...
SHUV
UM...

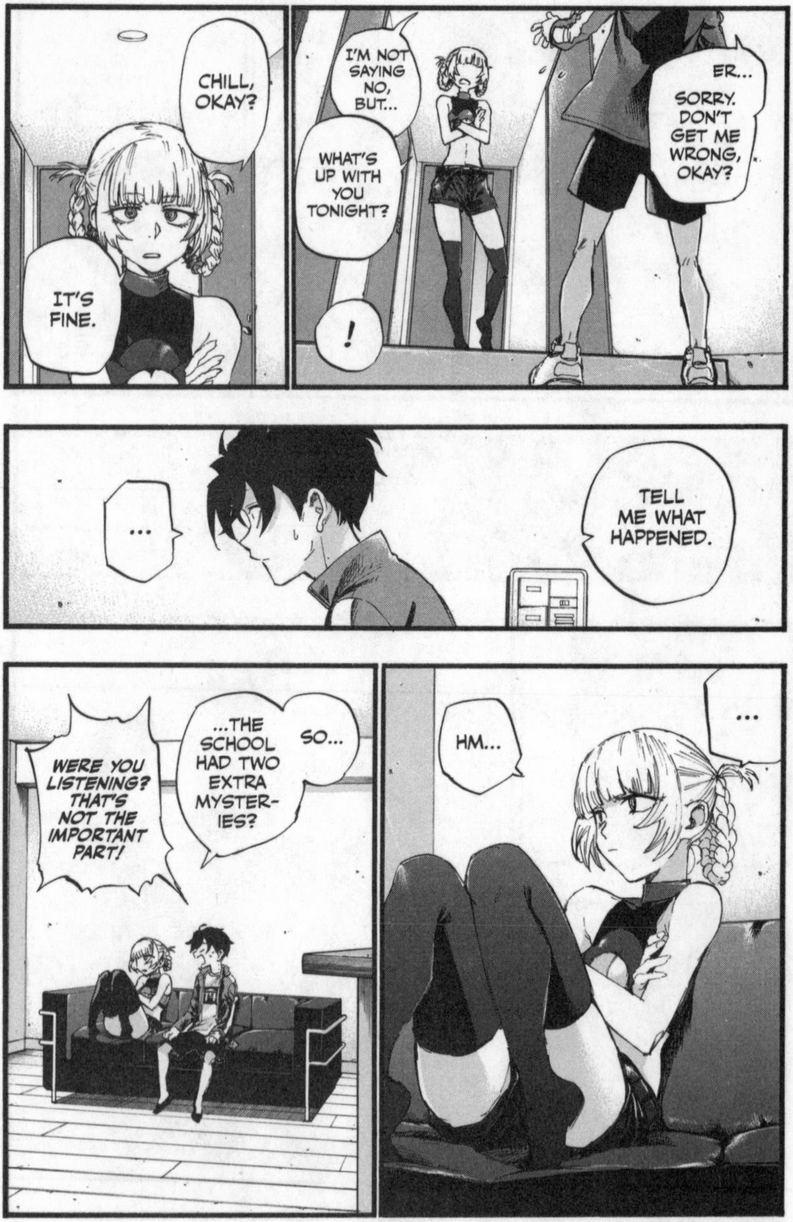
ER...
SORRY. DON'T GET ME WRONG, OKAY?
I'M NOT SAYING NO, BUT...
WHAT'S UP WITH YOU TONIGHT?
!
CHILL, OKAY?
IT'S FINE.
TELL ME WHAT HAPPENED.
...
...
HM...
SO...
...THE SCHOOL HAD TWO EXTRA MYSTERIES?
WERE YOU LISTENING? THAT'S NOT THE IMPORTANT PART!

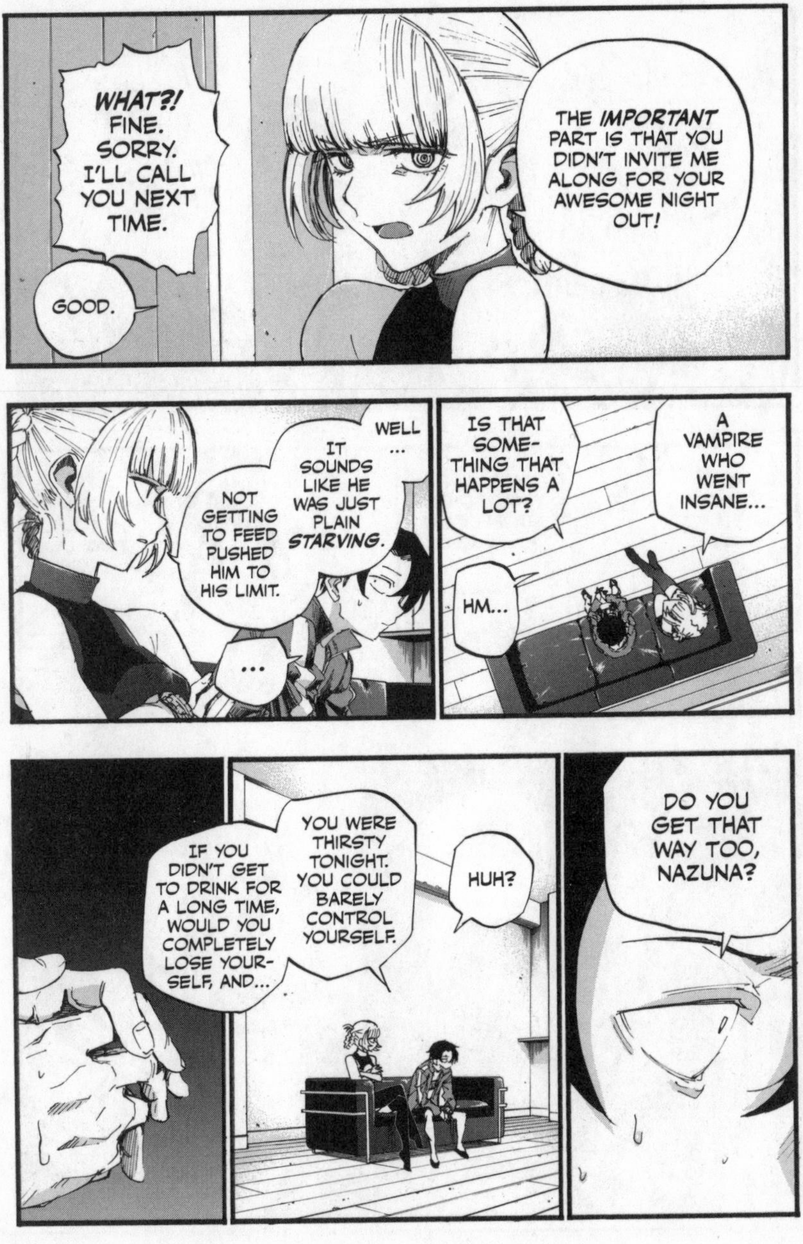
THE IMPORTANT PART IS THAT YOU DIDN'T INVITE ME ALONG FOR YOUR AWESOME NIGHT OUT!
WHAT?! FINE. SORRY. I'LL CALL YOU NEXT TIME.
GOOD.
A VAMPIRE WHO WENT INSANE...
IS THAT SOME-THING THAT HAPPENS A LOT?
HM...
WELL ...
IT SOUNDS LIKE HE WAS JUST PLAIN STARVING.
NOT GETTING TO FEED PUSHED HIM TO HIS LIMIT.
...
DO YOU GET THAT WAY TOO, NAZUNA?
HUH?
YOU WERE THIRSTY TONIGHT. YOU COULD BARELY CONTROL YOURSELF.
IF YOU DIDN'T GET TO DRINK FOR A LONG TIME, WOULD YOU COMPLETELY LOSE YOUR-SELF, AND...

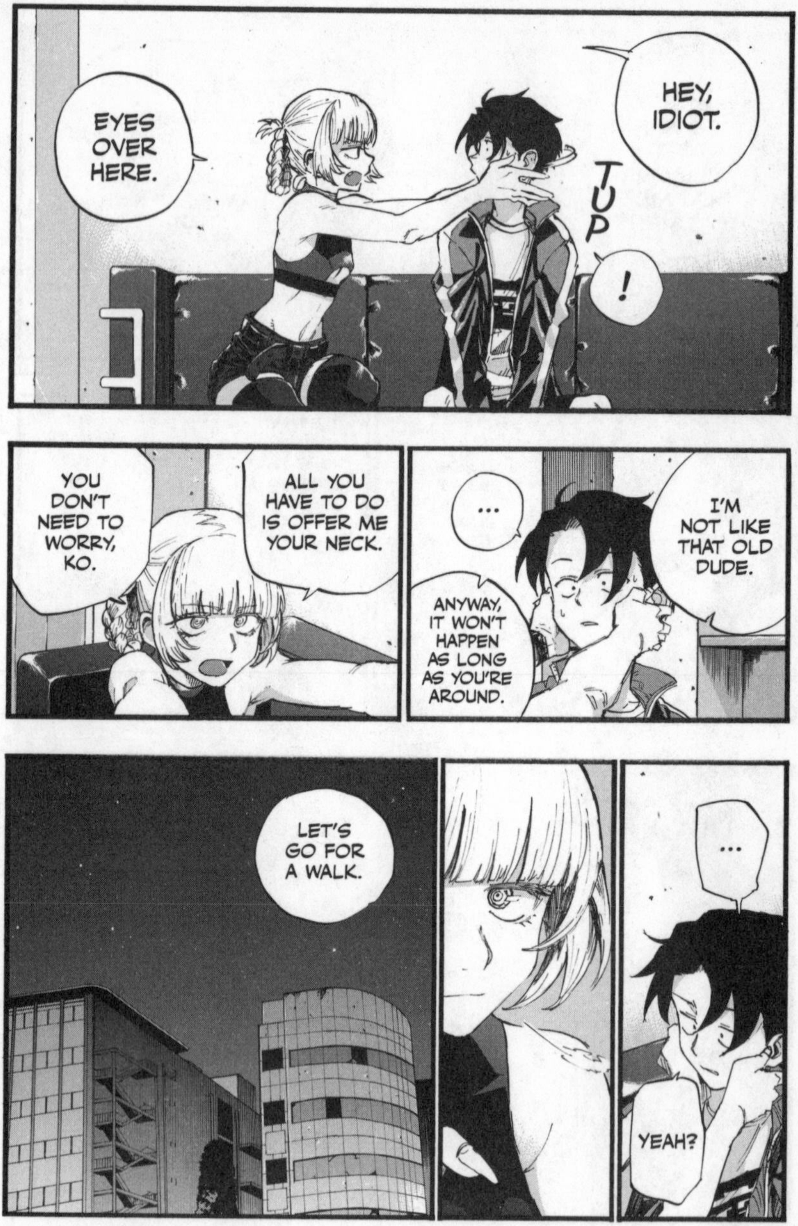
HEY, IDIOT.
TUP
!
EYES OVER HERE.
I'M NOT LIKE THAT OLD DUDE.
...
ANYWAY, IT WON'T HAPPEN AS LONG AS YOU'RE AROUND.
ALL YOU HAVE TO DO IS OFFER ME YOUR NECK.
YOU DON'T NEED TO WORRY, KO.
...
YEAH?
LET'S GO FOR A WALK.

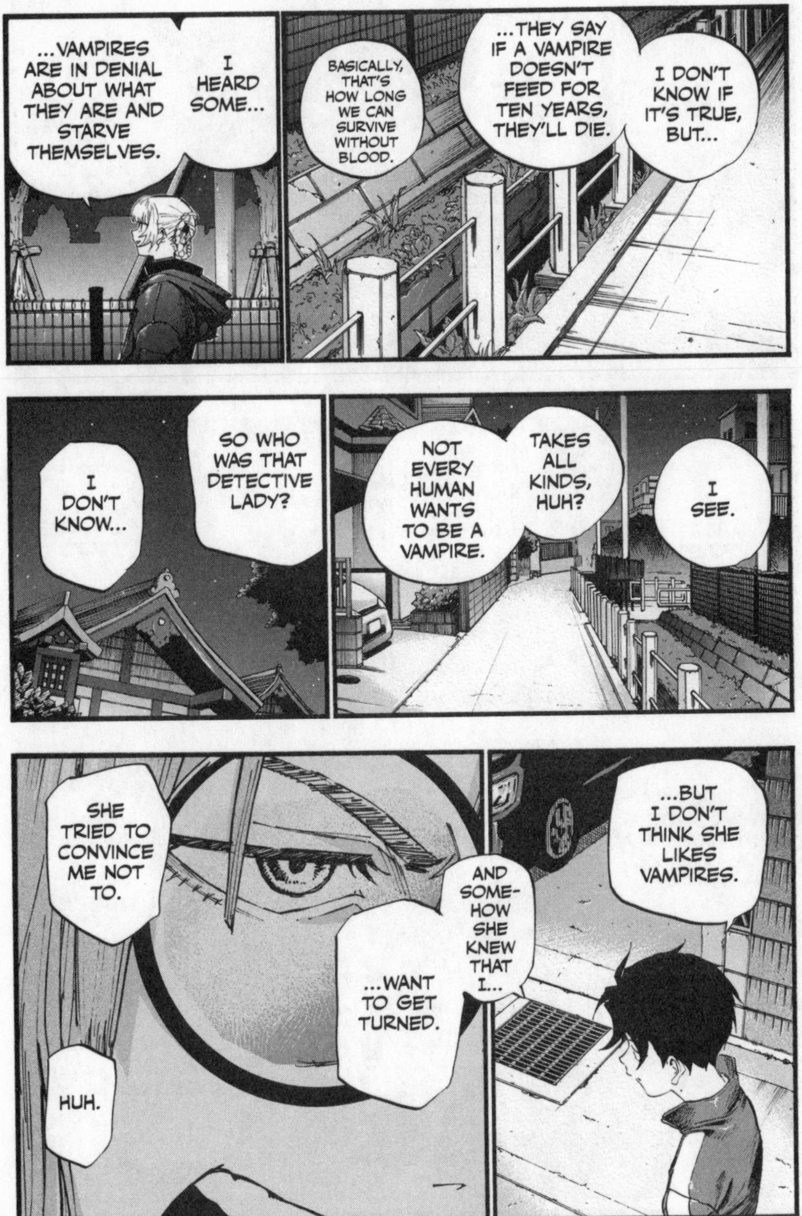
I DON'T KNOW IF IT'S TRUE, BUT...
...THEY SAY IF A VAMPIRE DOESN'T FEED FOR TEN YEARS, THEY'LL DIE.
BASICALLY, THAT'S HOW LONG WE CAN SURVIVE WITHOUT BLOOD.
I HEARD SOME...
...VAMPIRES ARE IN DENIAL ABOUT WHAT THEY ARE AND STARVE THEMSELVES.
I SEE.
TAKES ALL KINDS, HUH?
NOT EVERY HUMAN WANTS TO BE A VAMPIRE.
SO WHO WAS THAT DETECTIVE LADY?
I DON'T KNOW...
...BUT I DON'T THINK SHE LIKES VAMPIRES.
SHE TRIED TO CONVINCE ME NOT TO.
AND SOME-HOW SHE KNEW THAT I...
...WANT TO GET TURNED.
HUH.

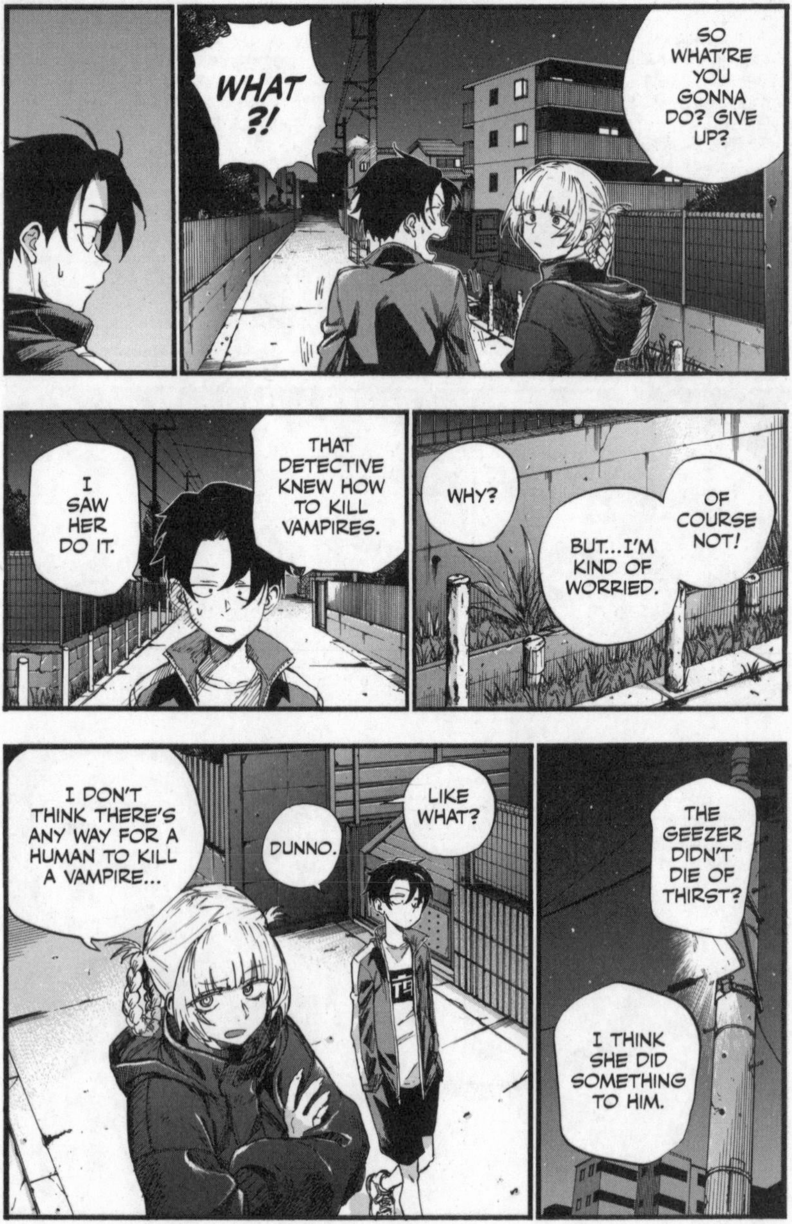
SO WHAT'RE YOU GONNA DO? GIVE UP?
WHAT ?!
OF COURSE NOT!
BUT...I'M KIND OF WORRIED.
WHY?
THAT DETECTIVE KNEW HOW TO KILL VAMPIRES.
I SAW HER DO IT.
THE GEEZER DIDN'T DIE OF THIRST?
I THINK SHE DID SOMETHING TO HIM.
LIKE WHAT?
DUNNO.
I DON'T THINK THERE'S ANY WAY FOR A HUMAN TO KILL A VAMPIRE...

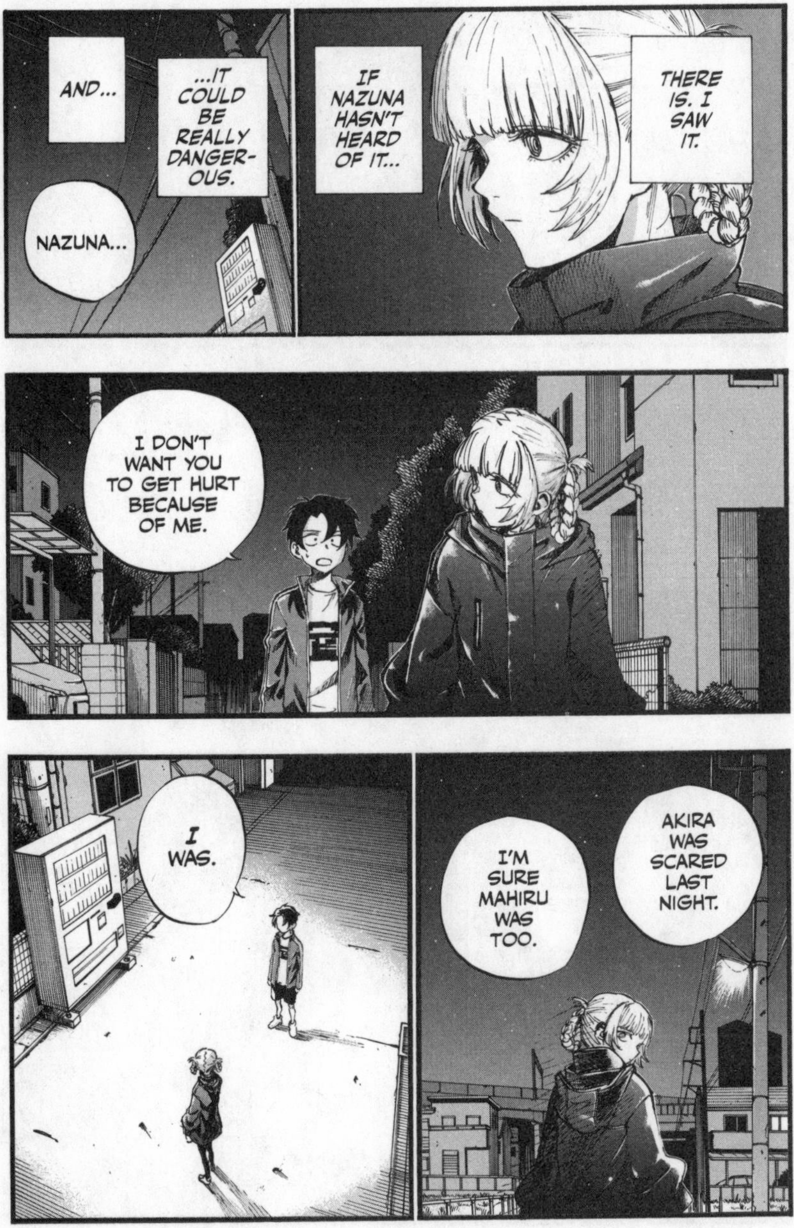
THERE IS. I SAW IT.
IF NAZUNA HASN'T HEARD OF IT...
...IT COULD BE REALLY DANGER-OUS.
AND...
NAZUNA...
I DON'T WANT YOU TO GET HURT BECAUSE OF ME.
AKIRA WAS SCARED LAST NIGHT.
I'M SURE MAHIRU WAS TOO.
I WAS.

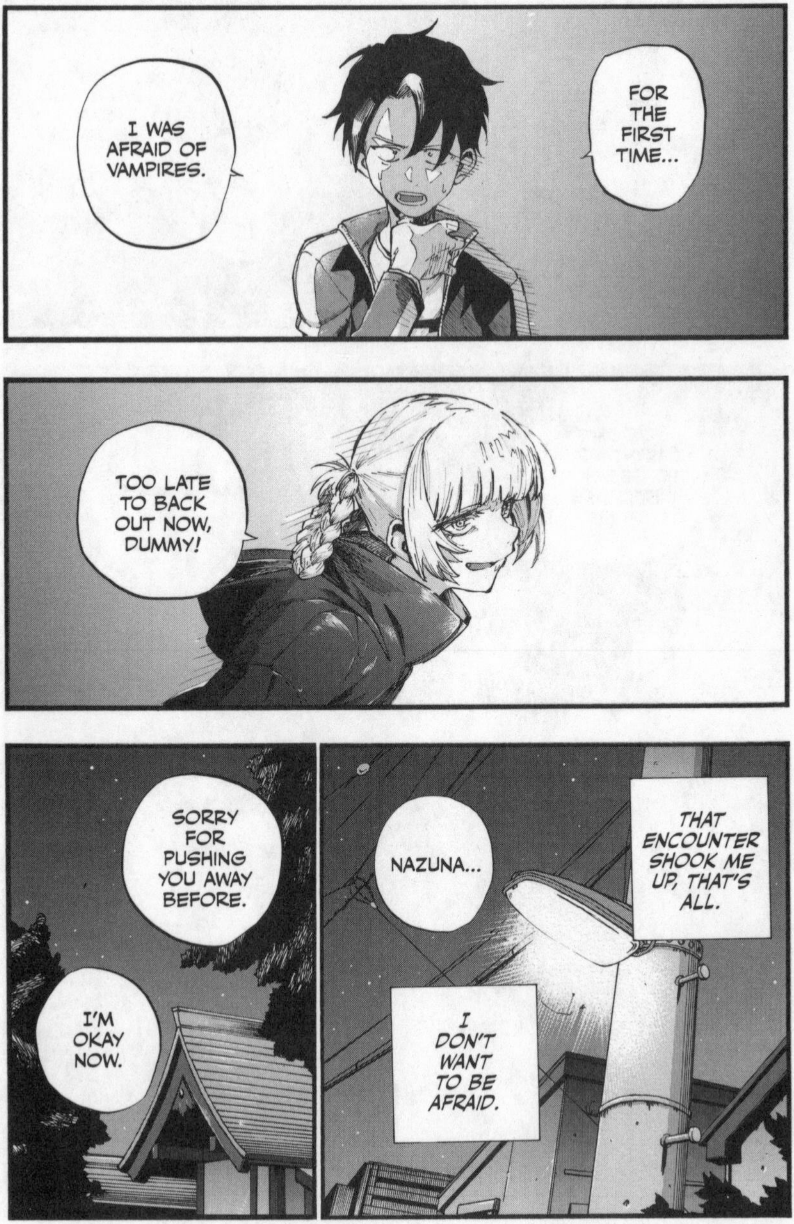
FOR THE FIRST TIME...
I WAS AFRAID OF VAMPIRES.
TOO LATE TO BACK OUT NOW, DUMMY!
THAT ENCOUNTER SHOOK ME UP, THAT'S ALL.
NAZUNA...
I DON'T WANT TO BE AFRAID.
SORRY FOR PUSHING YOU AWAY BEFORE.
I'M OKAY NOW.

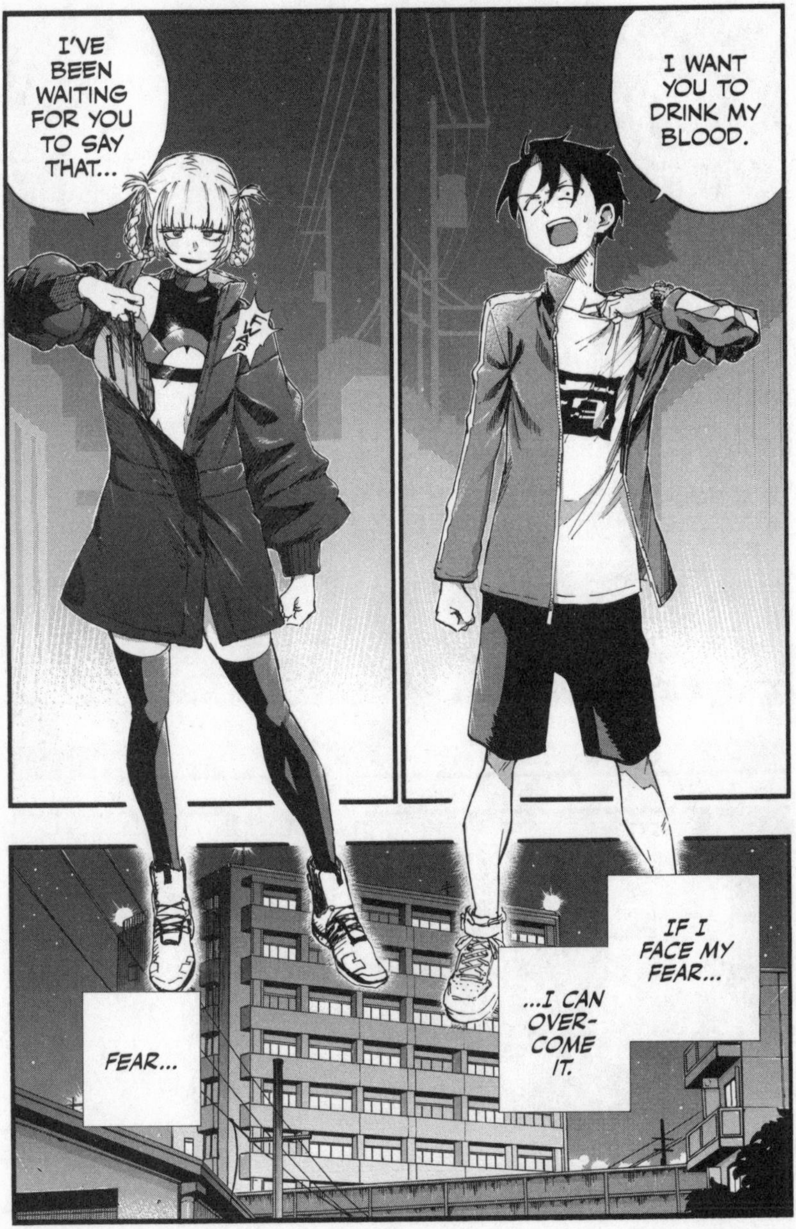
I WANT YOU TO DRINK MY BLOOD.
I'VE BEEN WAITING FOR YOU TO SAY THAT...
FWAP
IF I FACE MY FEAR...
...I CAN OVER-COME IT.
FEAR...

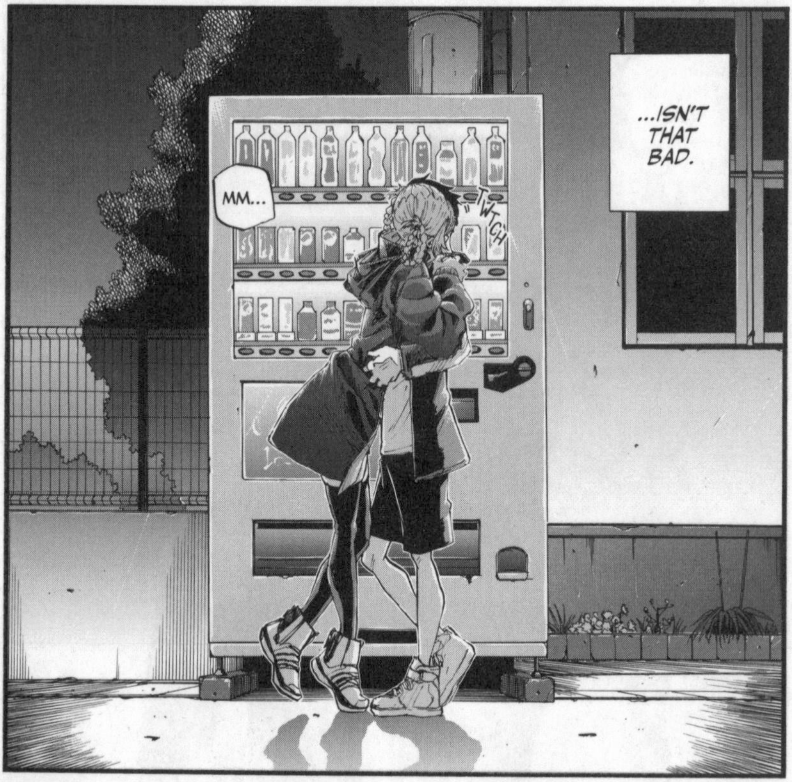
...ISN'T THAT BAD.
TWTCH
MM...
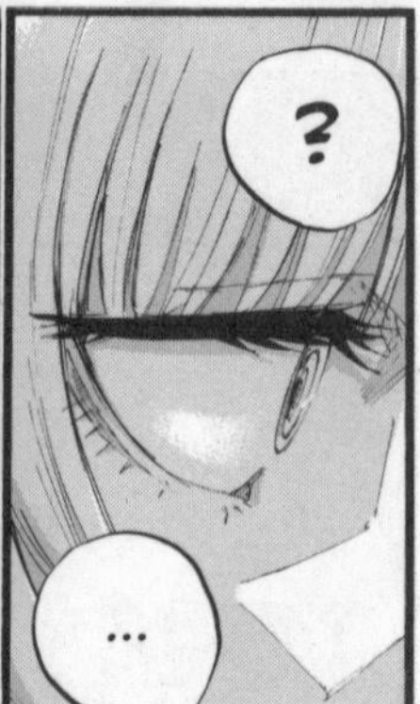
?
...
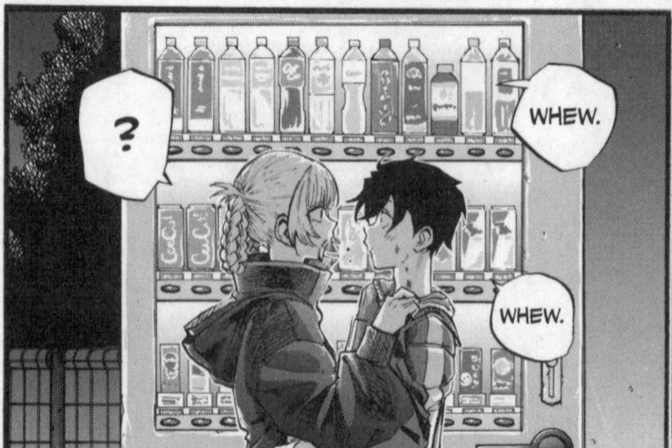
WHEW.
?
WHEW.

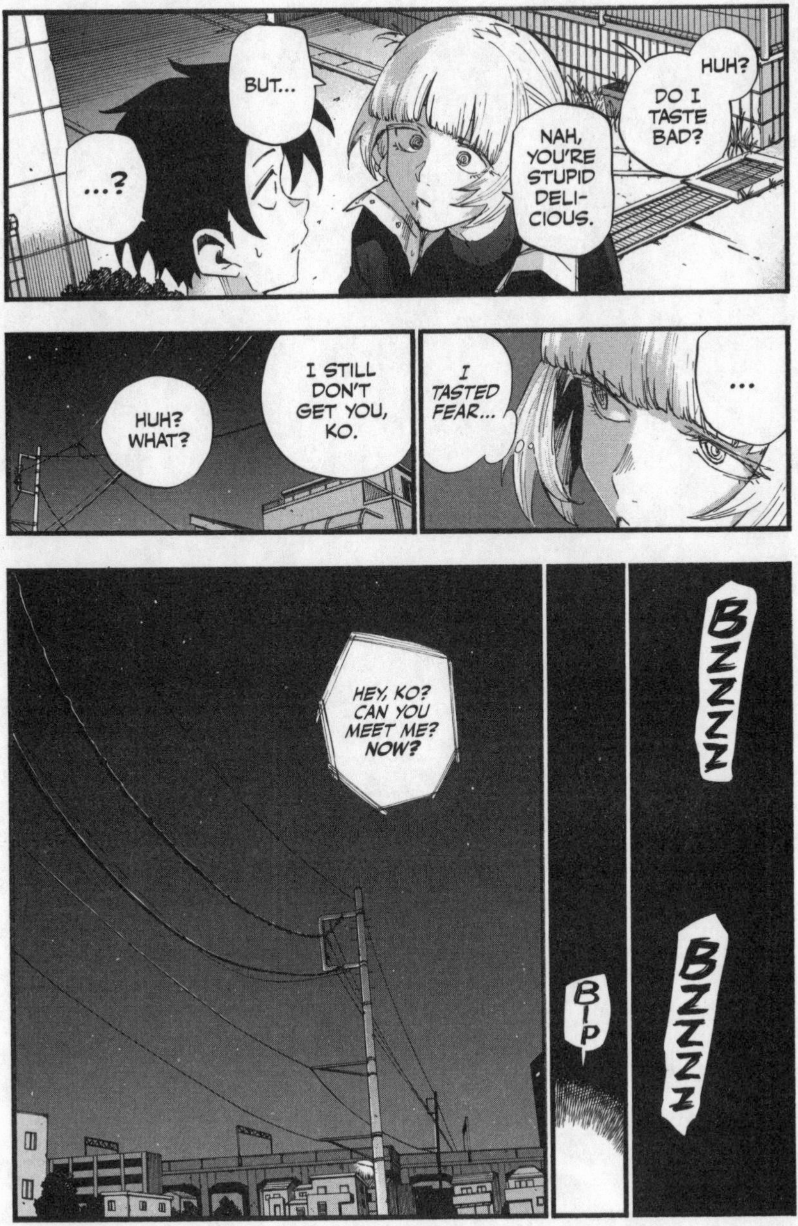
HUH? DO I TASTE BAD?
NAH, YOU'RE STUPID DELICIOUS.
BUT...
...?
...
I TASTED FEAR...
I STILL DON'T GET YOU, KO.
HUH? WHAT?
BZZZZ
BZZZZ
BIP
HEY, KO? CAN YOU MEET ME? NOW?

Call of the Night

NIGHT 41: WHEN I GROW UP

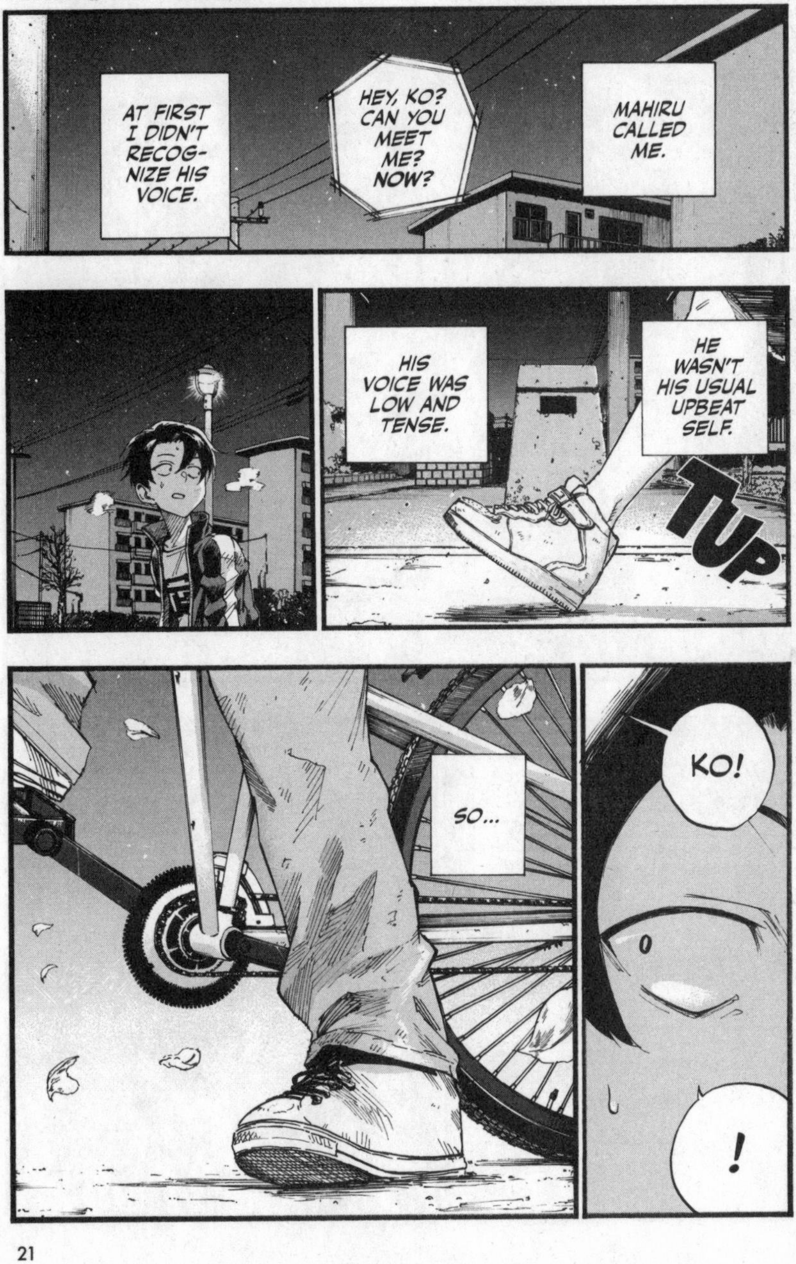
MAHIRU CALLED ME.
HEY, KO? CAN YOU MEET ME? NOW?
AT FIRST I DIDN'T RECOG-NIZE HIS VOICE.
HE WASN'T HIS USUAL UPBEAT SELF.
HIS VOICE WAS LOW AND TENSE.
TUP
KO!
!
SO...

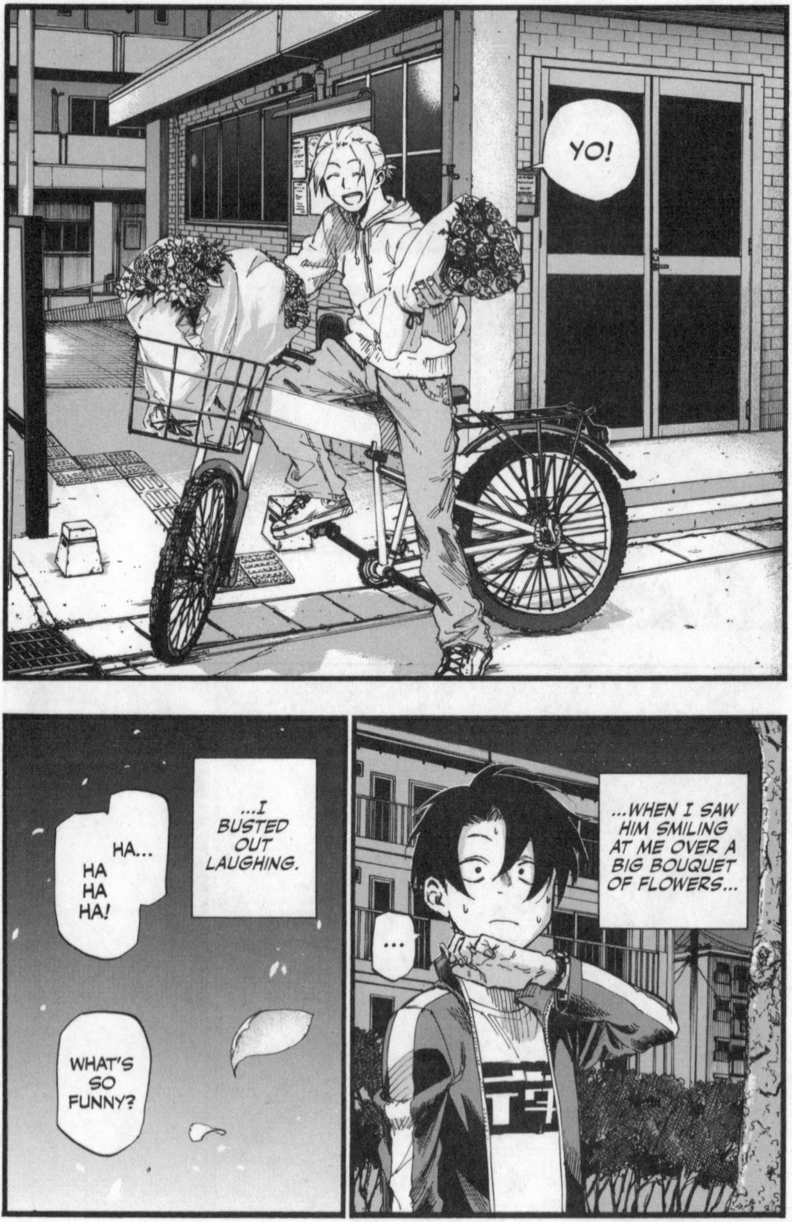
YO!
...WHEN I SAW HIM SMILING AT ME OVER A BIG BOUQUET OF FLOWERS...
...
...I BUSTED OUT LAUGHING.
HA... HA HA HA!
WHAT'S SO FUNNY?

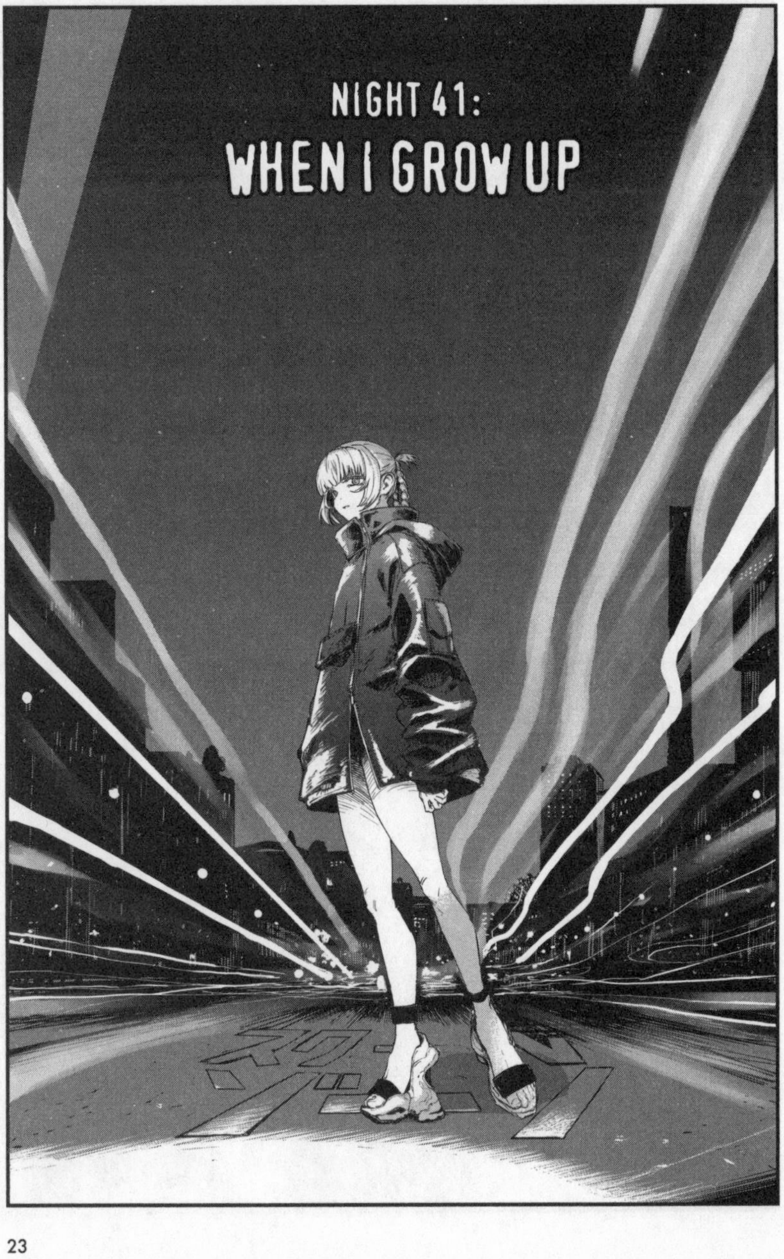
NIGHT 41:
WHEN I GROW UP

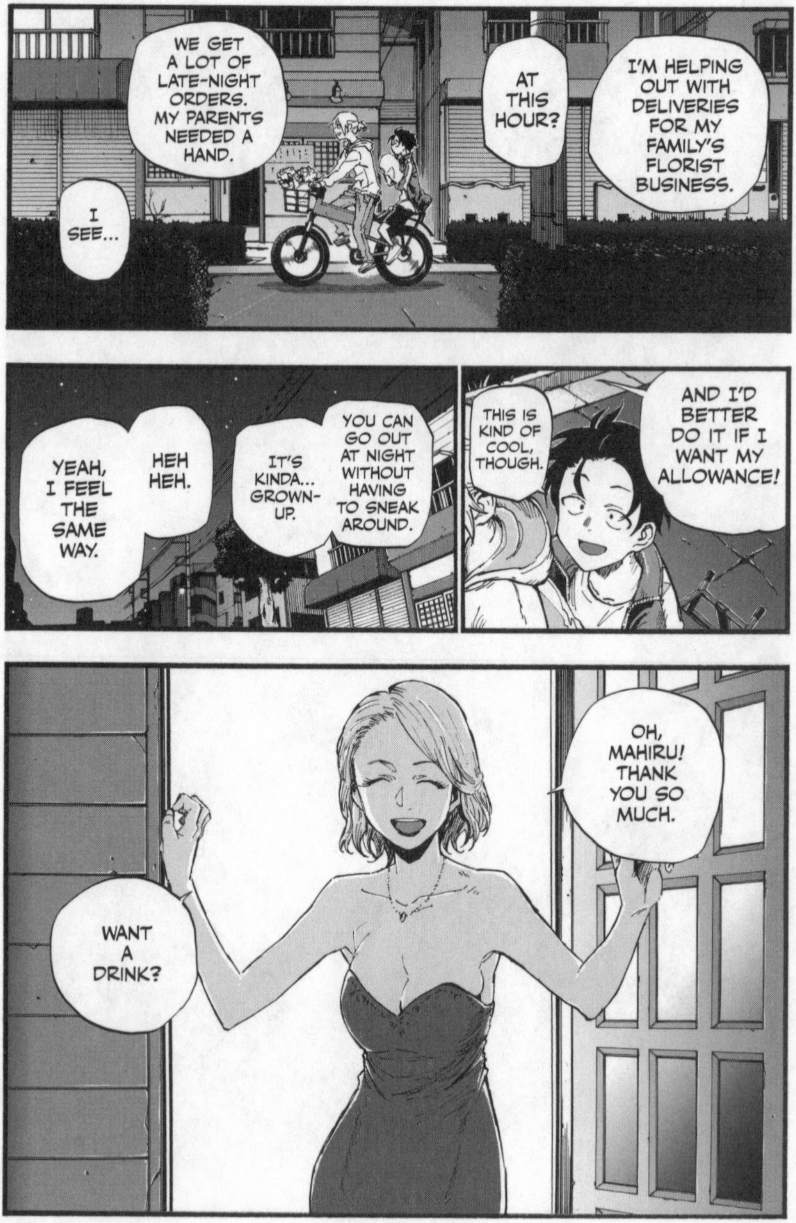
I'M HELPING OUT WITH DELIVERIES FOR MY FAMILY'S FLORIST BUSINESS.
AT THIS HOUR?
WE GET A LOT OF LATE-NIGHT ORDERS. MY PARENTS NEEDED A HAND.
I SEE...
AND I'D BETTER DO IT IF I WANT MY ALLOWANCE!
THIS IS KIND OF COOL, THOUGH.
YOU CAN GO OUT AT NIGHT WITHOUT HAVING TO SNEAK AROUND.
IT'S KINDA... GROWN-UP.
HEH HEH.
YEAH, I FEEL THE SAME WAY.
OH, MAHIRU! THANK YOU SO MUCH.
WANT A DRINK?

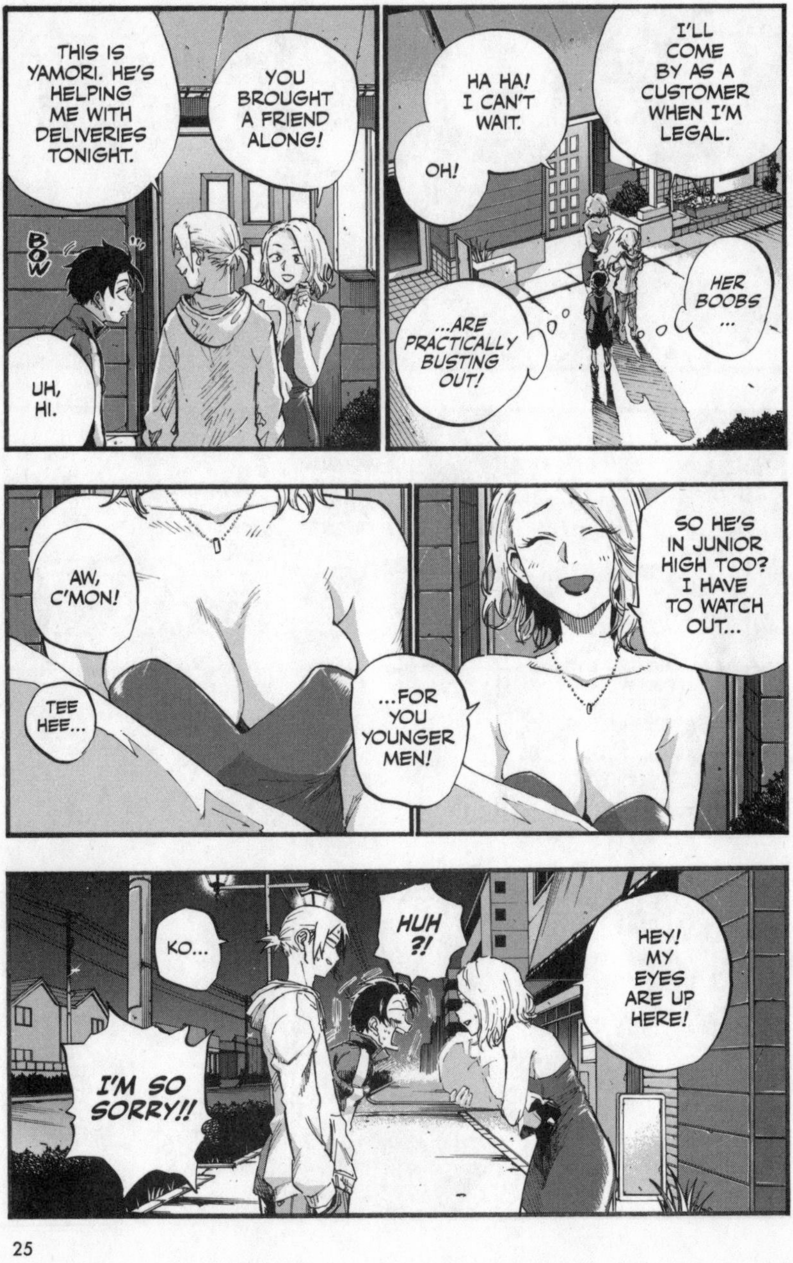
I'LL COME BY AS A CUSTOMER WHEN I'M LEGAL.
HA HA! I CAN'T WAIT.
OH!
HER BOOBS ...
...ARE PRACTICALLY BUSTING OUT!
YOU BROUGHT A FRIEND ALONG!
THIS IS YAMORI. HE'S HELPING ME WITH DELIVERIES TONIGHT.
BOW
UH, HI.
SO HE'S IN JUNIOR HIGH TOO? I HAVE TO WATCH OUT...
...FOR YOU YOUNGER MEN!
AW, C'MON!
TEE HEE...
HEY! MY EYES ARE UP HERE!
HUH ?!
KO...
I'M SO SORRY!!

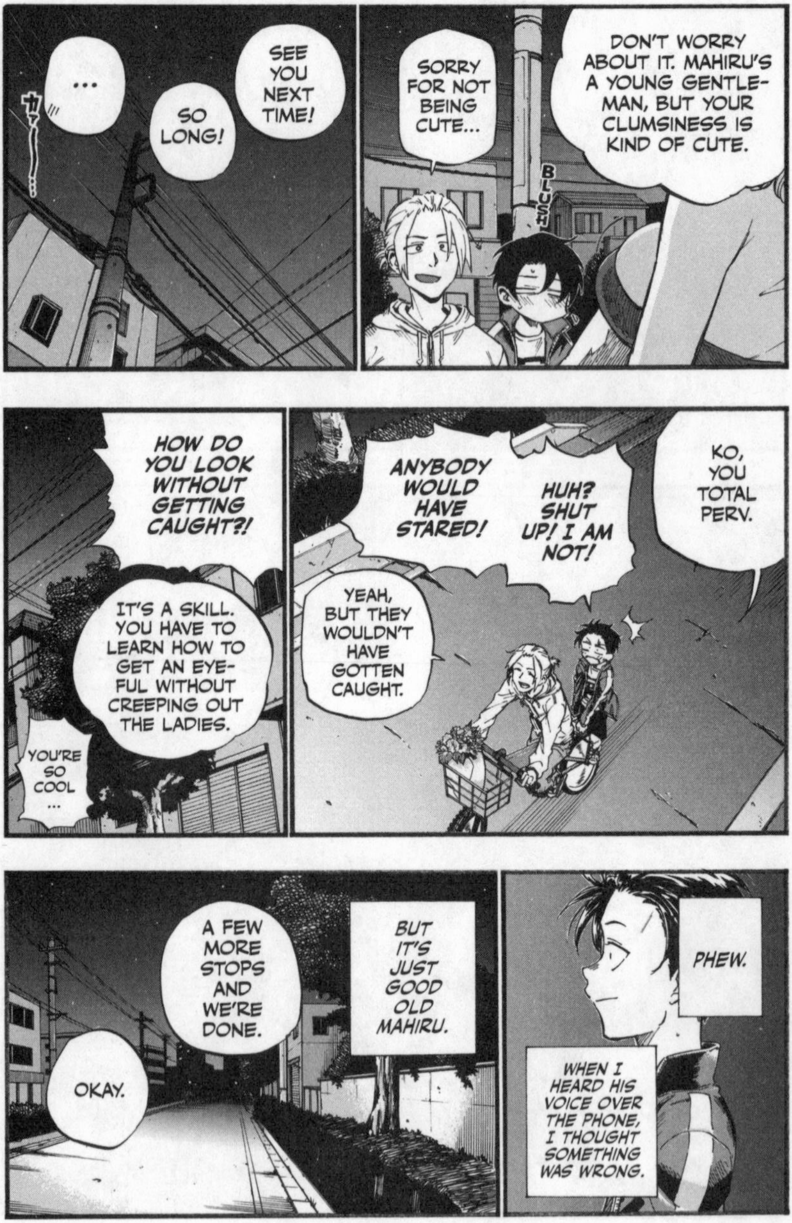
DON'T WORRY ABOUT IT. MAHIRU'S A YOUNG GENTLEMAN, BUT YOUR CLUMSINESS IS KIND OF CUTE.
SORRY FOR NOT BEING CUTE...
BLUSH
SEE YOU NEXT TIME!
SO LONG!
...
KO, YOU TOTAL PERV.
HUH? SHUT UP! I AM NOT!
ANYBODY WOULD HAVE STARED!
YEAH, BUT THEY WOULDN'T HAVE GOTTEN CAUGHT.
HOW DO YOU LOOK WITHOUT GETTING CAUGHT?!
IT'S A SKILL. YOU HAVE TO LEARN HOW TO GET AN EYEFUL WITHOUT CREEPING OUT THE LADIES.
YOU'RE SO COOL...
PHEW.
WHEN I HEARD HIS VOICE OVER THE PHONE, I THOUGHT SOMETHING WAS WRONG.
BUT IT'S JUST GOOD OLD MAHIRU.
A FEW MORE STOPS AND WE'RE DONE.
OKAY.

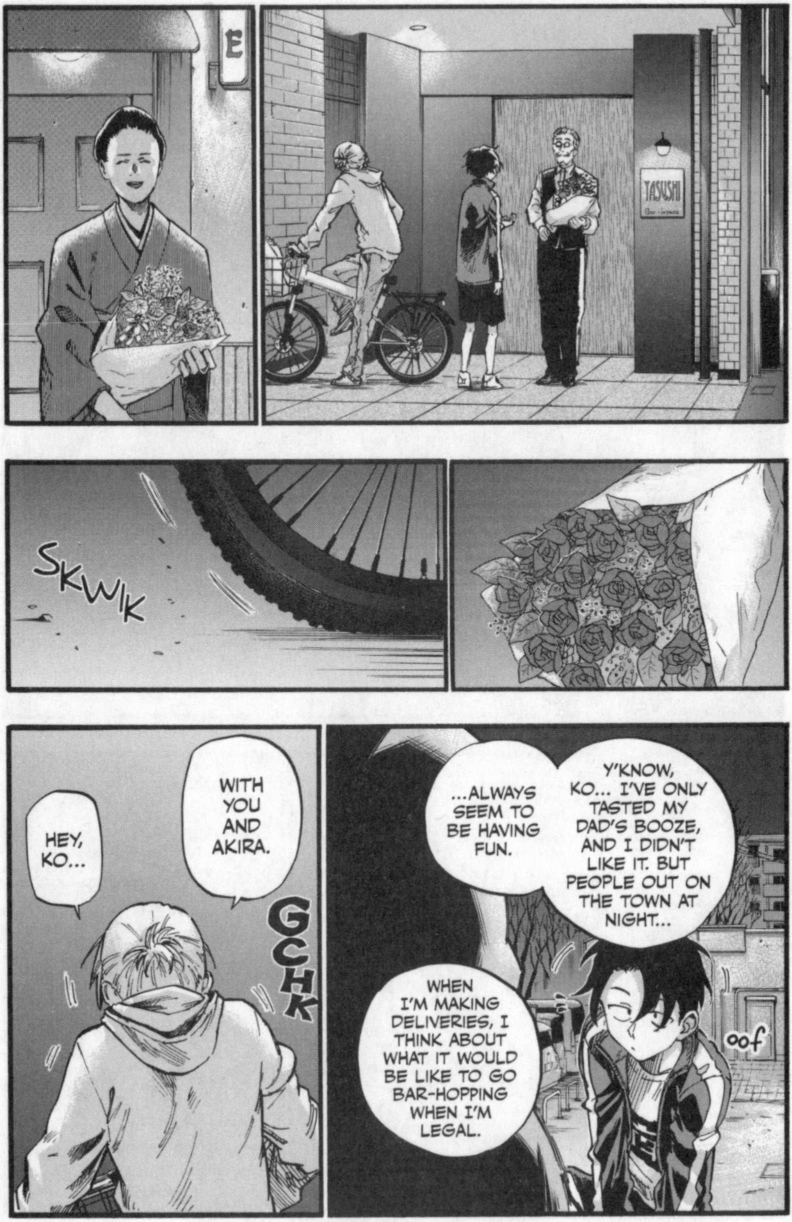
YASUSHI
E
SKWIK
Y'KNOW, KO... I'VE ONLY TASTED MY DAD'S BOOZE, AND I DIDN'T LIKE IT. BUT PEOPLE OUT ON THE TOWN AT NIGHT...
...ALWAYS SEEM TO BE HAVING FUN.
WHEN I'M MAKING DELIVERIES, I THINK ABOUT WHAT IT WOULD BE LIKE TO GO BAR-HOPPING WHEN I'M LEGAL.
oof
WITH YOU AND AKIRA.
GCHK
HEY, KO...

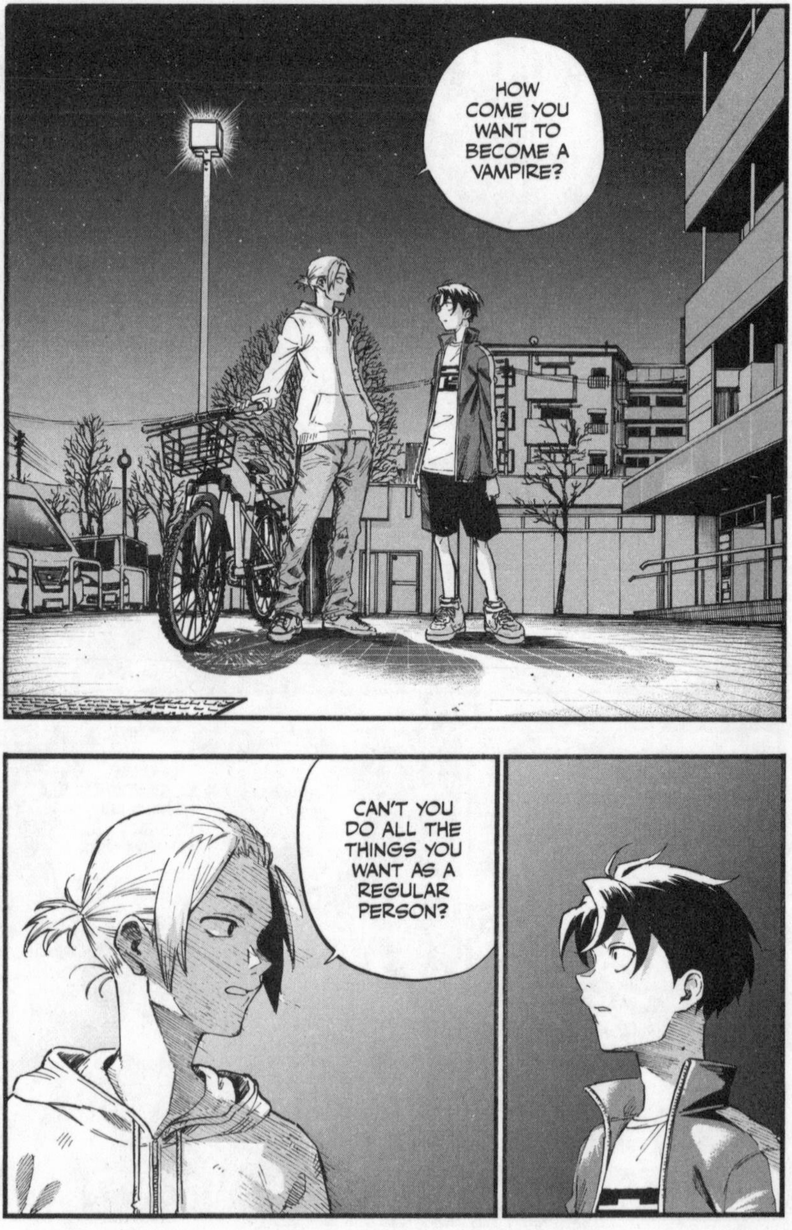
HOW COME YOU WANT TO BECOME A VAMPIRE?
CAN'T YOU DO ALL THE THINGS YOU WANT AS A REGULAR PERSON?

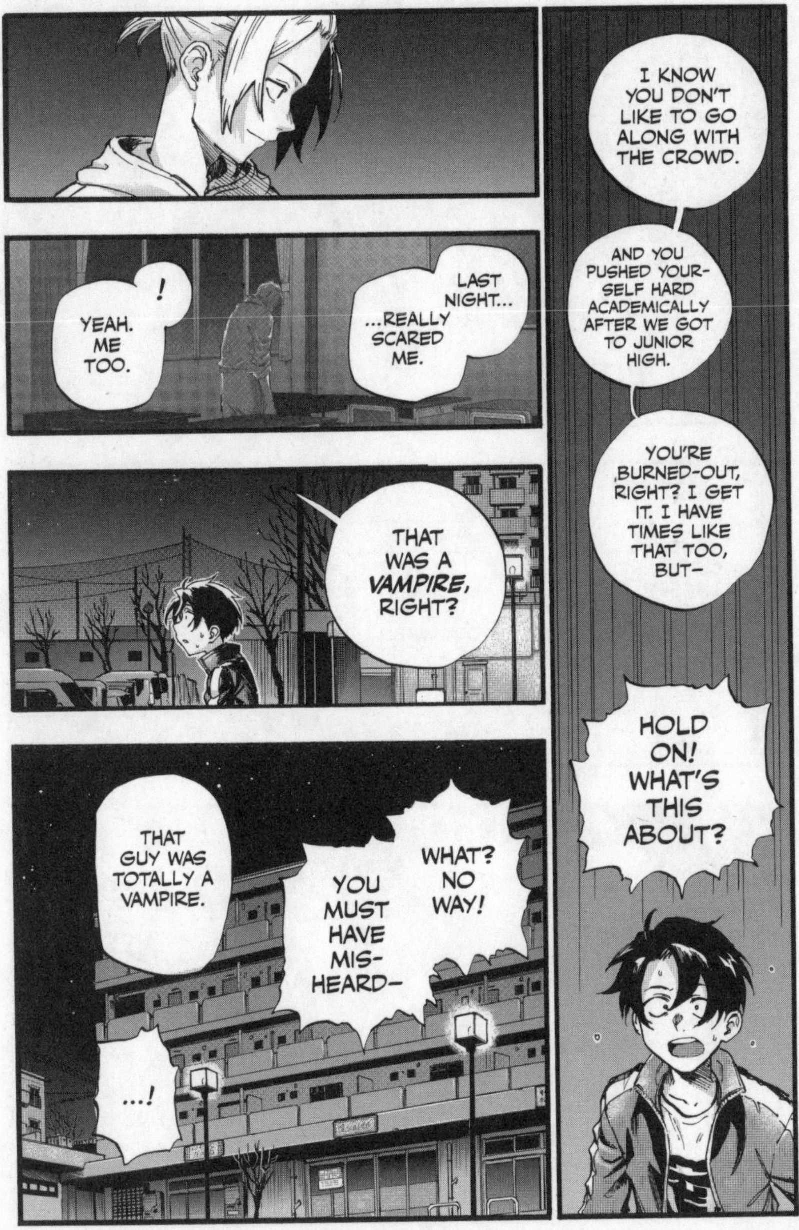
I KNOW YOU DON'T LIKE TO GO ALONG WITH THE CROWD.
AND YOU PUSHED YOURSELF HARD ACADEMICALLY AFTER WE GOT TO JUNIOR HIGH.
YOU'RE BURNED-OUT, RIGHT? I GET IT. I HAVE TIMES LIKE THAT TOO, BUT–
HOLD ON! WHAT'S THIS ABOUT?
LAST NIGHT... ...REALLY SCARED ME.
!
YEAH. ME TOO.
THAT WAS A *VAMPIRE,* RIGHT?
WHAT? NO WAY! YOU MUST HAVE MISHEARD–
THAT GUY WAS TOTALLY A VAMPIRE.
...!

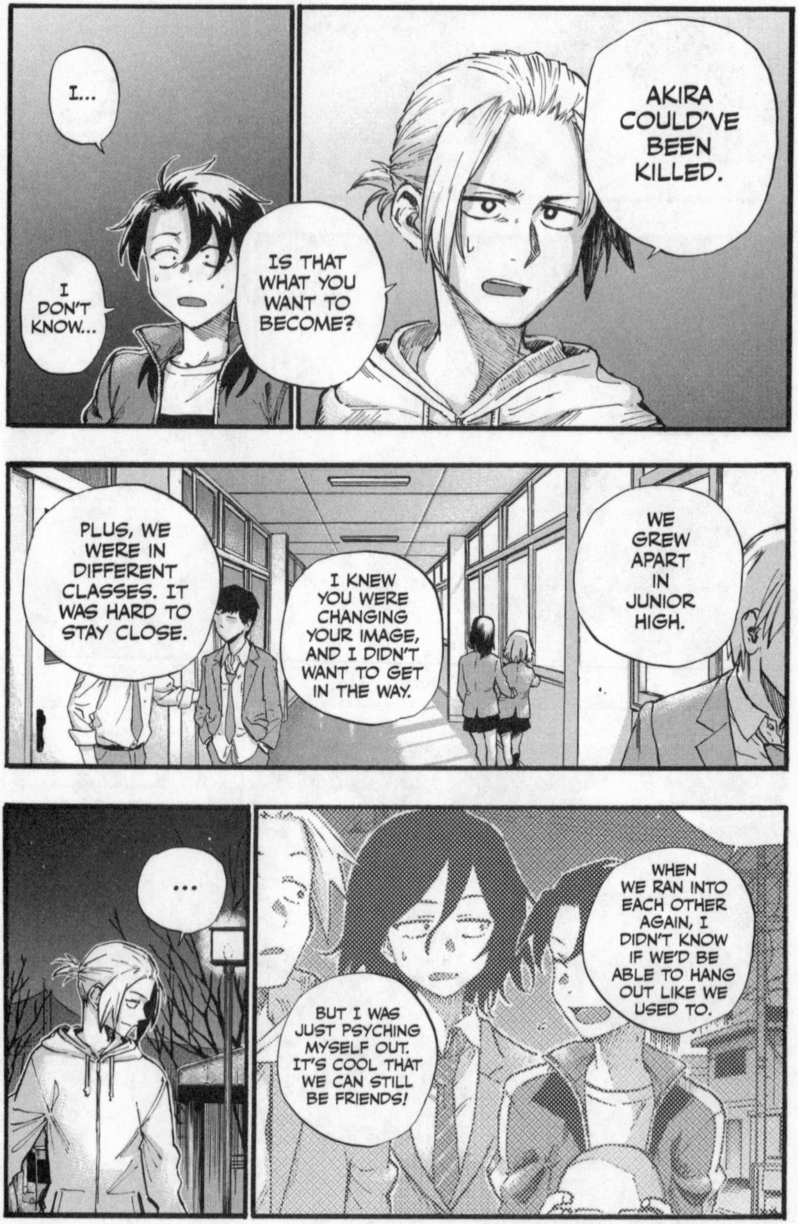
AKIRA COULD'VE BEEN KILLED.
IS THAT WHAT YOU WANT TO BECOME?
I...
I DON'T KNOW...
WE GREW APART IN JUNIOR HIGH.
I KNEW YOU WERE CHANGING YOUR IMAGE, AND I DIDN'T WANT TO GET IN THE WAY.
PLUS, WE WERE IN DIFFERENT CLASSES. IT WAS HARD TO STAY CLOSE.
WHEN WE RAN INTO EACH OTHER AGAIN, I DIDN'T KNOW IF WE'D BE ABLE TO HANG OUT LIKE WE USED TO.
BUT I WAS JUST PSYCHING MYSELF OUT. IT'S COOL THAT WE CAN STILL BE FRIENDS!
...

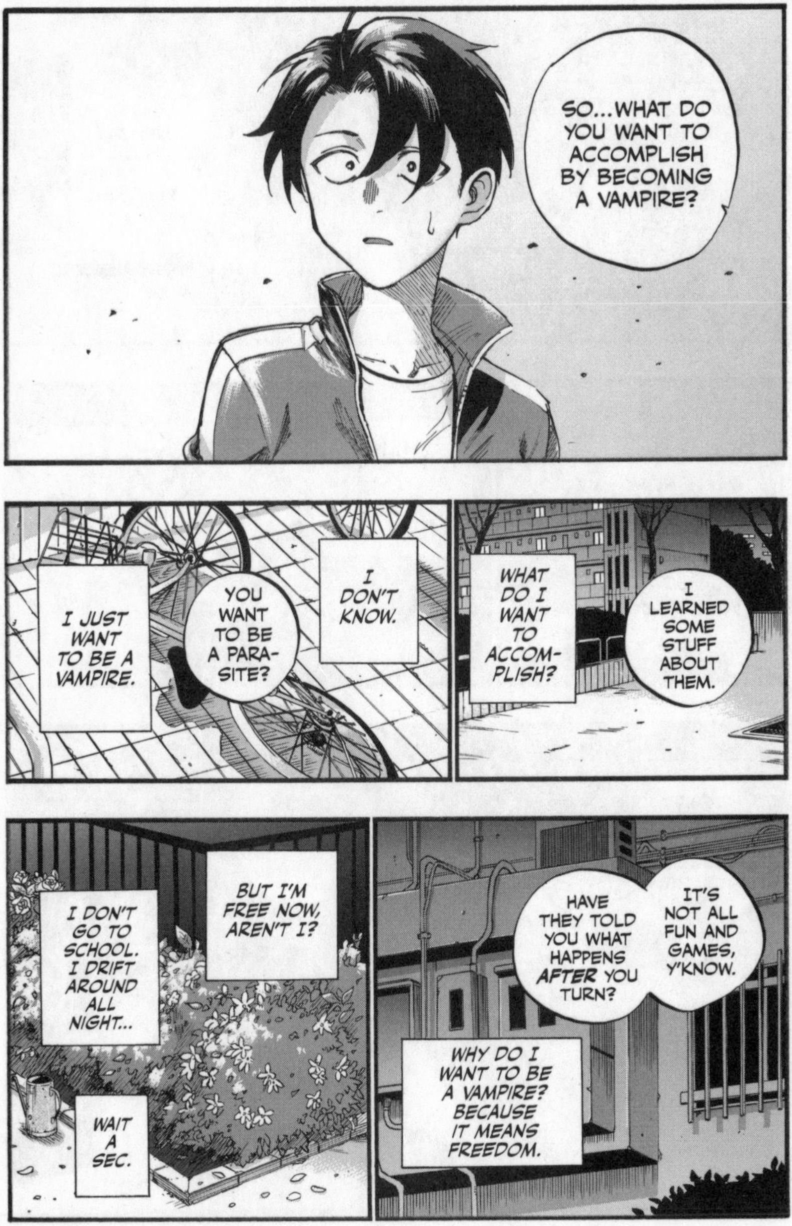
SO...WHAT DO YOU WANT TO ACCOMPLISH BY BECOMING A VAMPIRE?
I LEARNED SOME STUFF ABOUT THEM.
WHAT DO I WANT TO ACCOMPLISH?
I DON'T KNOW.
YOU WANT TO BE A PARASITE?
I JUST WANT TO BE A VAMPIRE.
IT'S NOT ALL FUN AND GAMES, Y'KNOW.
HAVE THEY TOLD YOU WHAT HAPPENS **AFTER** YOU TURN?
WHY DO I WANT TO BE A VAMPIRE? BECAUSE IT MEANS FREEDOM.
BUT I'M FREE NOW, AREN'T I?
I DON'T GO TO SCHOOL. I DRIFT AROUND ALL NIGHT...
WAIT A SEC.

WHY DO I WANT TO BE A VAMPIRE?
TO BE WITH NAZUNA.
NO, THAT'S NOT IT...
I'M WITH NAZUNA BECAUSE I WANT HER TO TURN ME.
SO I NEED TO FALL IN LOVE WITH HER.
THIS IS GOING IN CIRCLES! I WANT TO FALL IN LOVE WITH HER, SO SHE CAN TURN ME INTO A VAMPIRE, SO...
GSHK
!
C'MON, ANSWER ME!
YOU WANNA TRICK HUMANS INTO LETTING YOU SUCK THEM DRY?

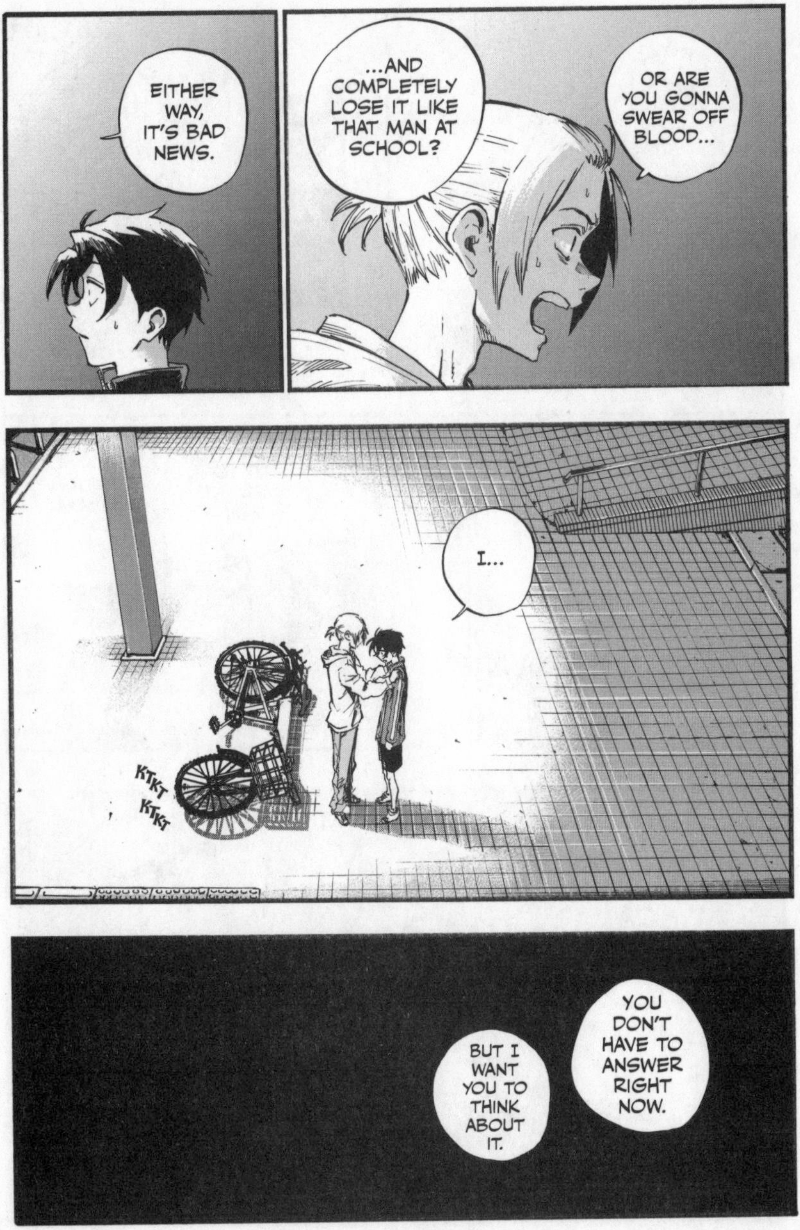
OR ARE YOU GONNA SWEAR OFF BLOOD...
...AND COMPLETELY LOSE IT LIKE THAT MAN AT SCHOOL?
EITHER WAY, IT'S BAD NEWS.
I...
KTKT KTKT
YOU DON'T HAVE TO ANSWER RIGHT NOW.
BUT I WANT YOU TO THINK ABOUT IT.

WHAT IT REALLY MEANS TO BE A VAMPIRE.
SLAM
HEY.
HT!
I DIDN'T THINK YOU WERE COMING OVER TONIGHT.
WHAT DID YOUR FRIEND WANT?
TP TP TP
I WAS HOPING FOR A SECOND PLAYER...
?
HUG
WHOA!

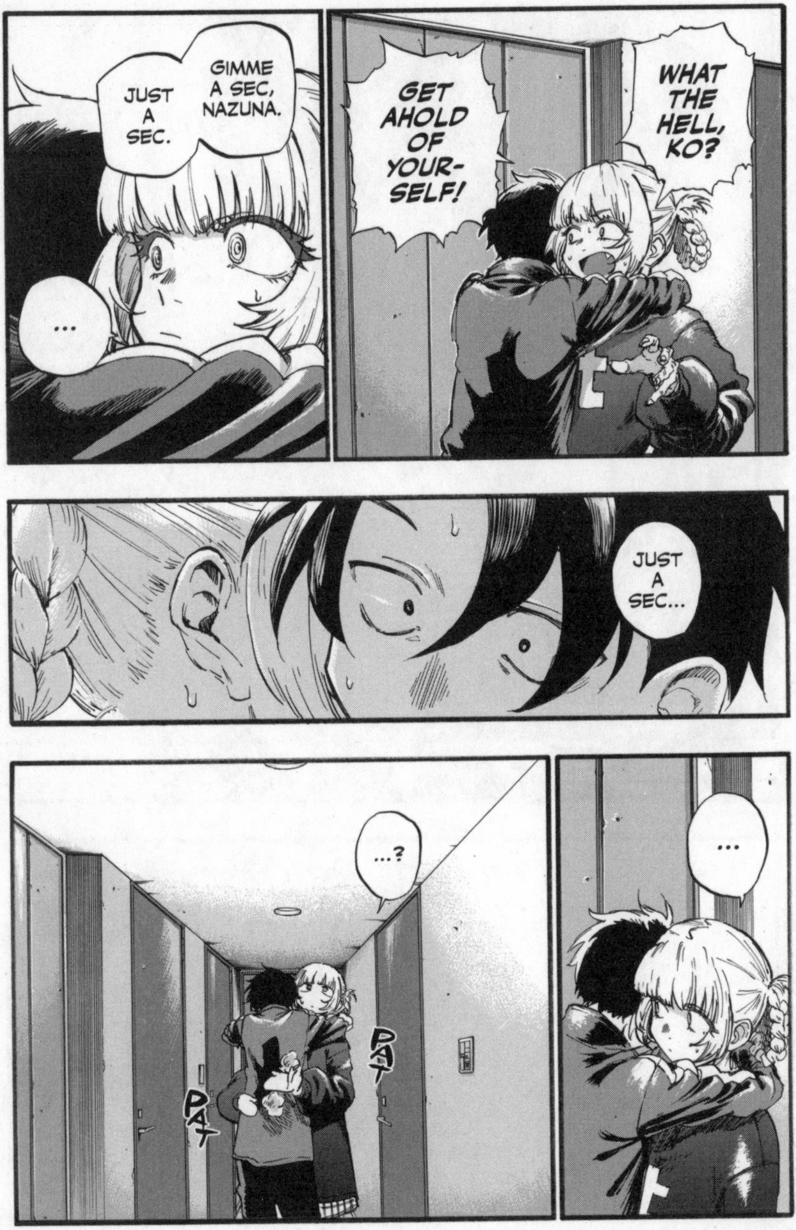
WHAT THE HELL, KO?
GET AHOLD OF YOURSELF!
GIMME A SEC, NAZUNA.
JUST A SEC.
...
JUST A SEC...
...
...?
PAT
PAT

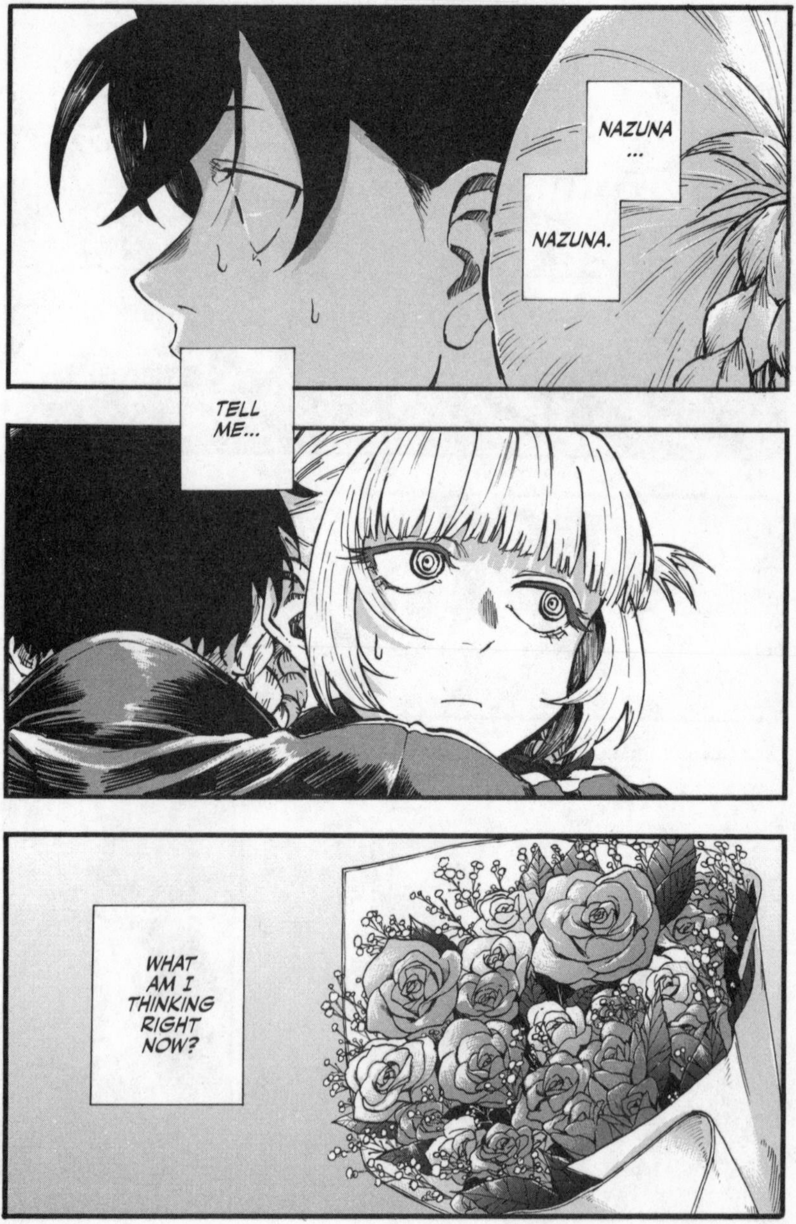
NAZUNA
...
NAZUNA.
TELL ME...
WHAT AM I THINKING RIGHT NOW?

NIGHT 40: MY MOM'S OUT TONIGHT

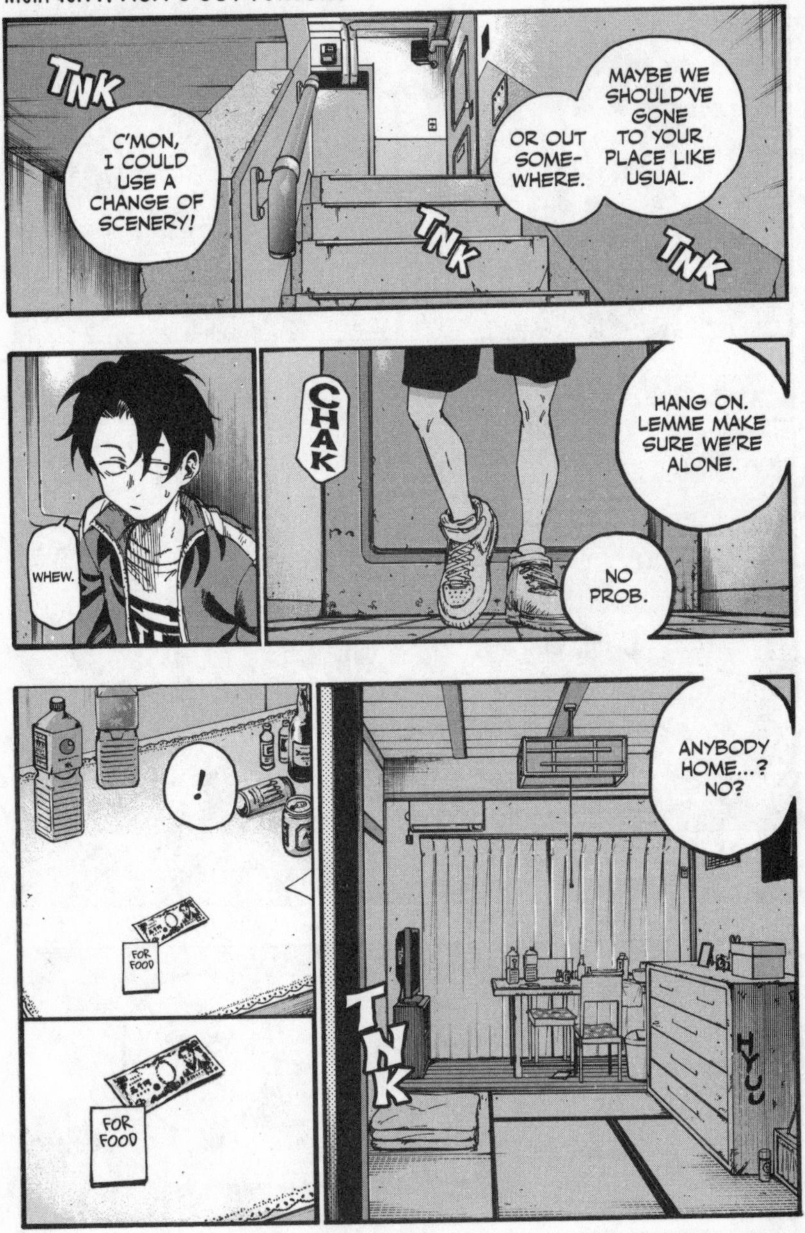
MAYBE WE SHOULD'VE GONE TO YOUR PLACE LIKE USUAL.
OR OUT SOME-WHERE.
TNK
TNK
C'MON, I COULD USE A CHANGE OF SCENERY!
TNK
HANG ON. LEMME MAKE SURE WE'RE ALONE.
NO PROB.
CHAK
WHEW.
ANYBODY HOME...? NO?
TNK
HYUU
!
FOR FOOD
FOR FOOD

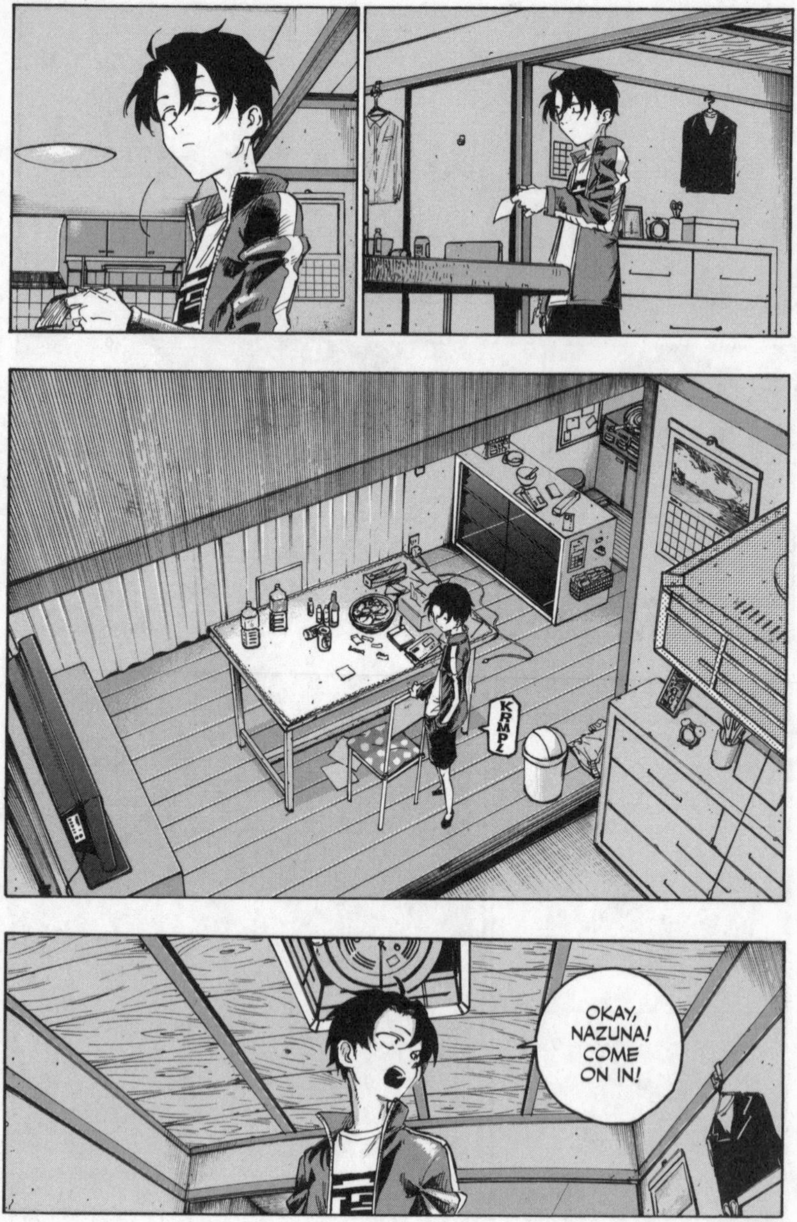
KRMPL
OKAY, NAZUNA! COME ON IN!

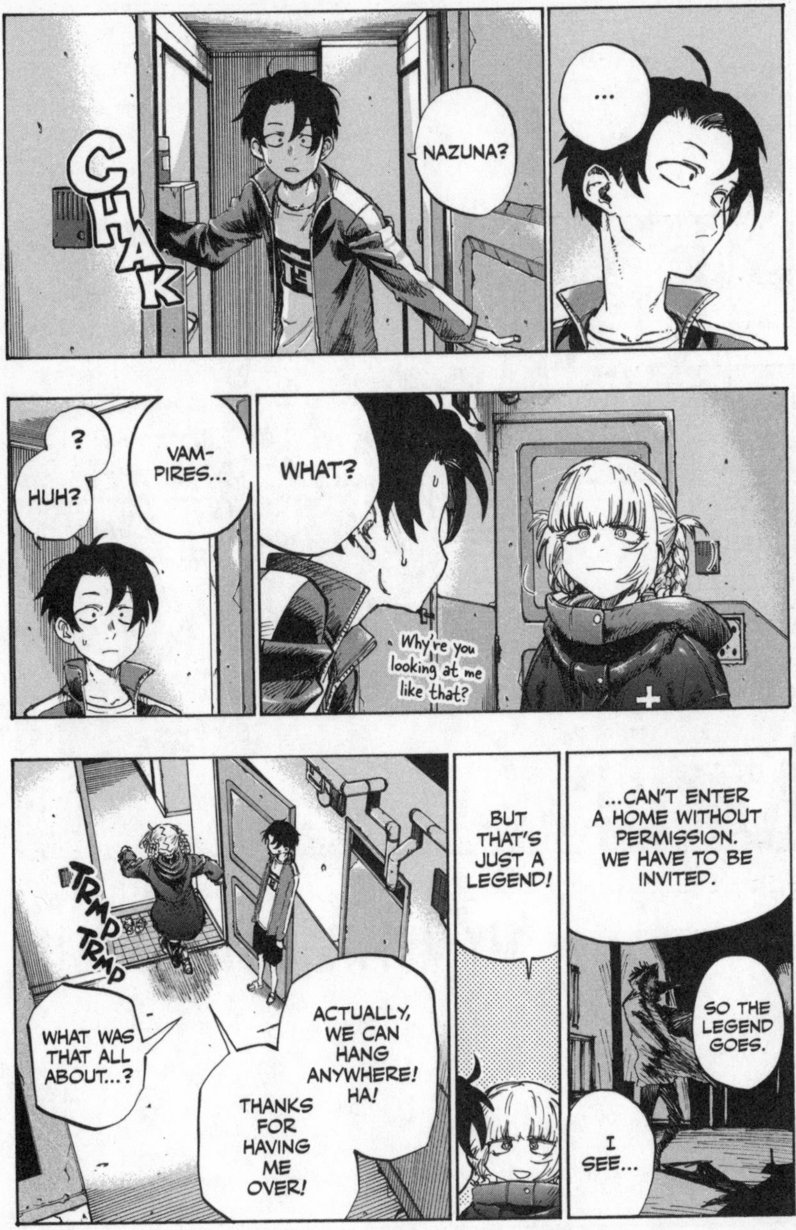
...
NAZUNA?
CHAK
WHAT?
Why're you looking at me like that?
VAM-PIRES...
?
HUH?
...CAN'T ENTER A HOME WITHOUT PERMISSION. WE HAVE TO BE INVITED.
SO THE LEGEND GOES.
I SEE...
BUT THAT'S JUST A LEGEND!
ACTUALLY, WE CAN HANG ANYWHERE! HA!
THANKS FOR HAVING ME OVER!
TRMP TRMP
WHAT WAS THAT ALL ABOUT...?

NIGHT 42:
MY MOM'S OUT TONIGHT

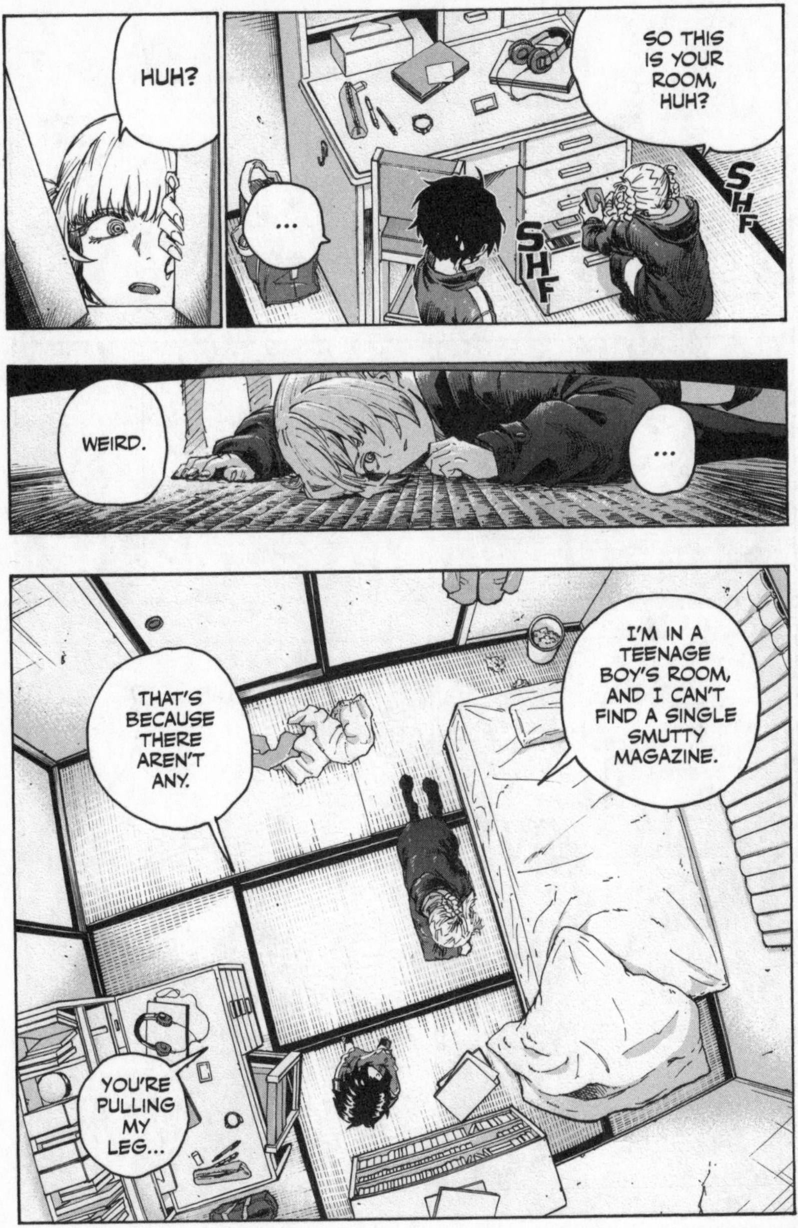
SO THIS IS YOUR ROOM, HUH?
SHF
SHF
...
HUH?
...
WEIRD.
I'M IN A TEENAGE BOY'S ROOM, AND I CAN'T FIND A SINGLE SMUTTY MAGAZINE.
THAT'S BECAUSE THERE AREN'T ANY.
YOU'RE PULLING MY LEG...

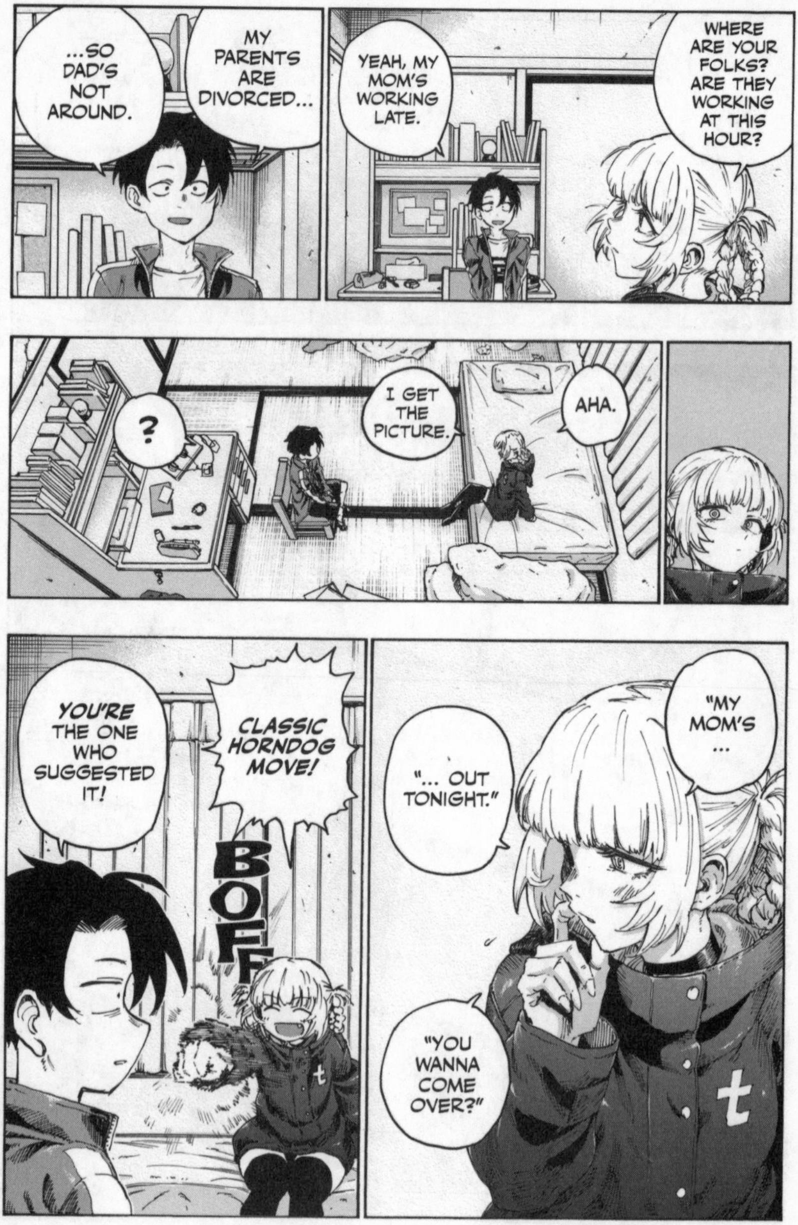
WHERE ARE YOUR FOLKS? ARE THEY WORKING AT THIS HOUR?
YEAH, MY MOM'S WORKING LATE.
MY PARENTS ARE DIVORCED...
...SO DAD'S NOT AROUND.
AHA.
I GET THE PICTURE.
?
"MY MOM'S ...
"... OUT TONIGHT."
"YOU WANNA COME OVER?"
CLASSIC HORNDOG MOVE!
BOFF
YOU'RE THE ONE WHO SUGGESTED IT!

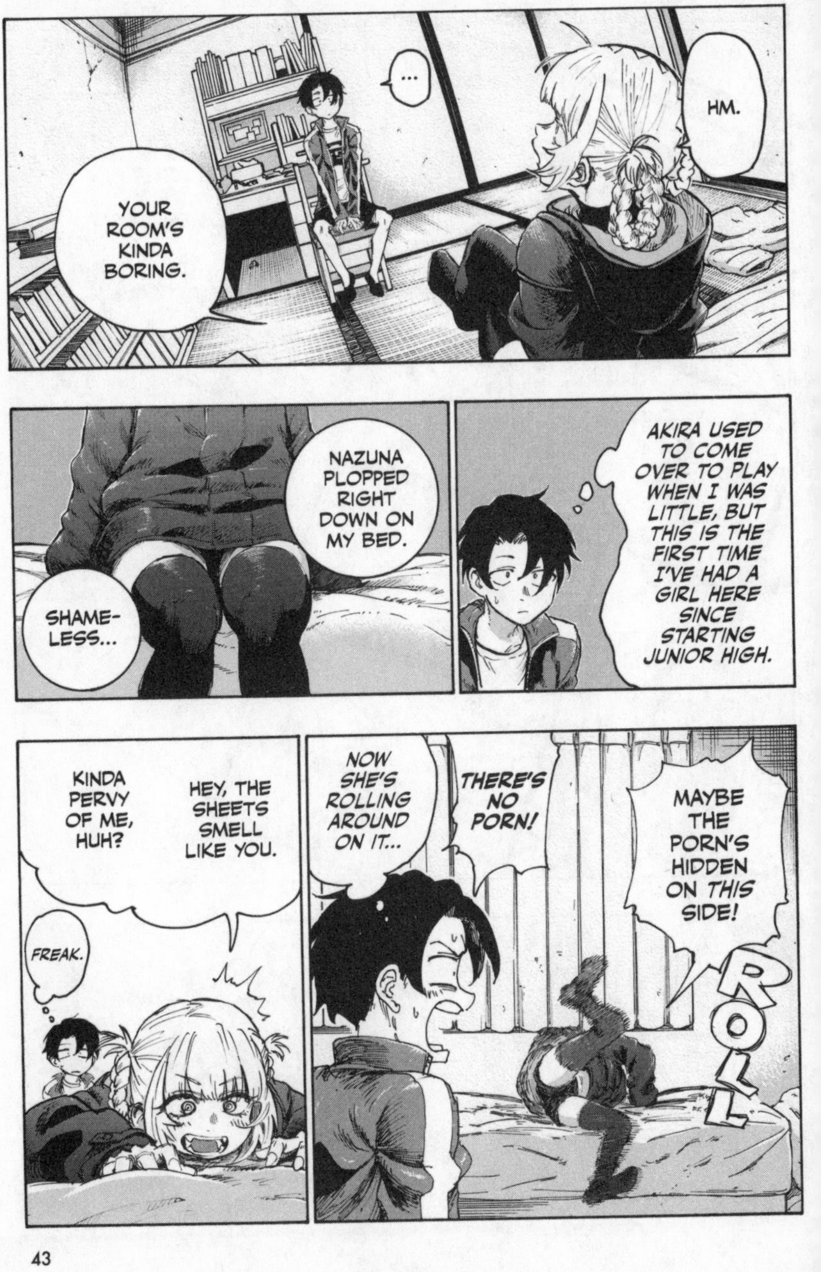
HM.
...
YOUR ROOM'S KINDA BORING.
AKIRA USED TO COME OVER TO PLAY WHEN I WAS LITTLE, BUT THIS IS THE FIRST TIME I'VE HAD A GIRL HERE SINCE STARTING JUNIOR HIGH.
NAZUNA PLOPPED RIGHT DOWN ON MY BED.
SHAME-LESS...
MAYBE THE PORN'S HIDDEN ON *THIS* SIDE!
THERE'S NO PORN!
NOW SHE'S ROLLING AROUND ON IT...
ROLL
HEY, THE SHEETS SMELL LIKE YOU.
KINDA PERVY OF ME, HUH?
FREAK.

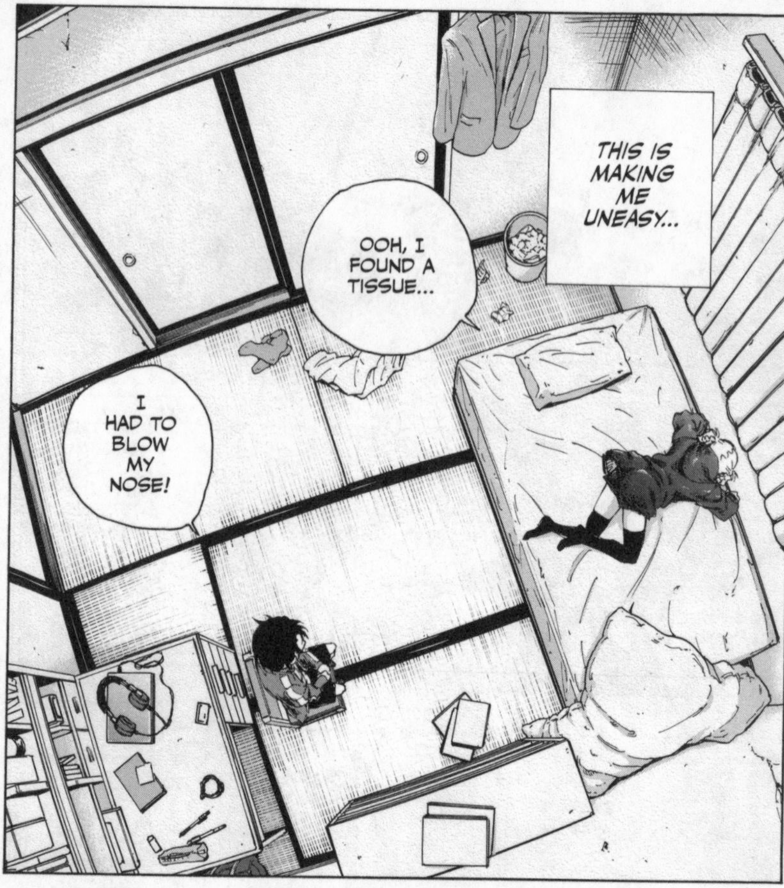
THIS IS MAKING ME UNEASY...
OOH, I FOUND A TISSUE...
I HAD TO BLOW MY NOSE!

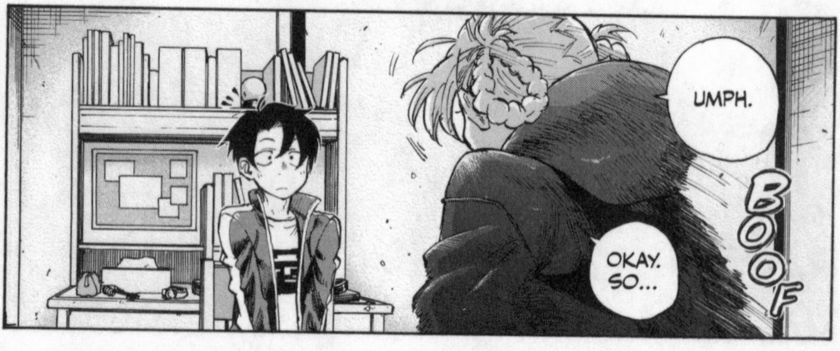
UMPH.
BOOF
OKAY. SO...

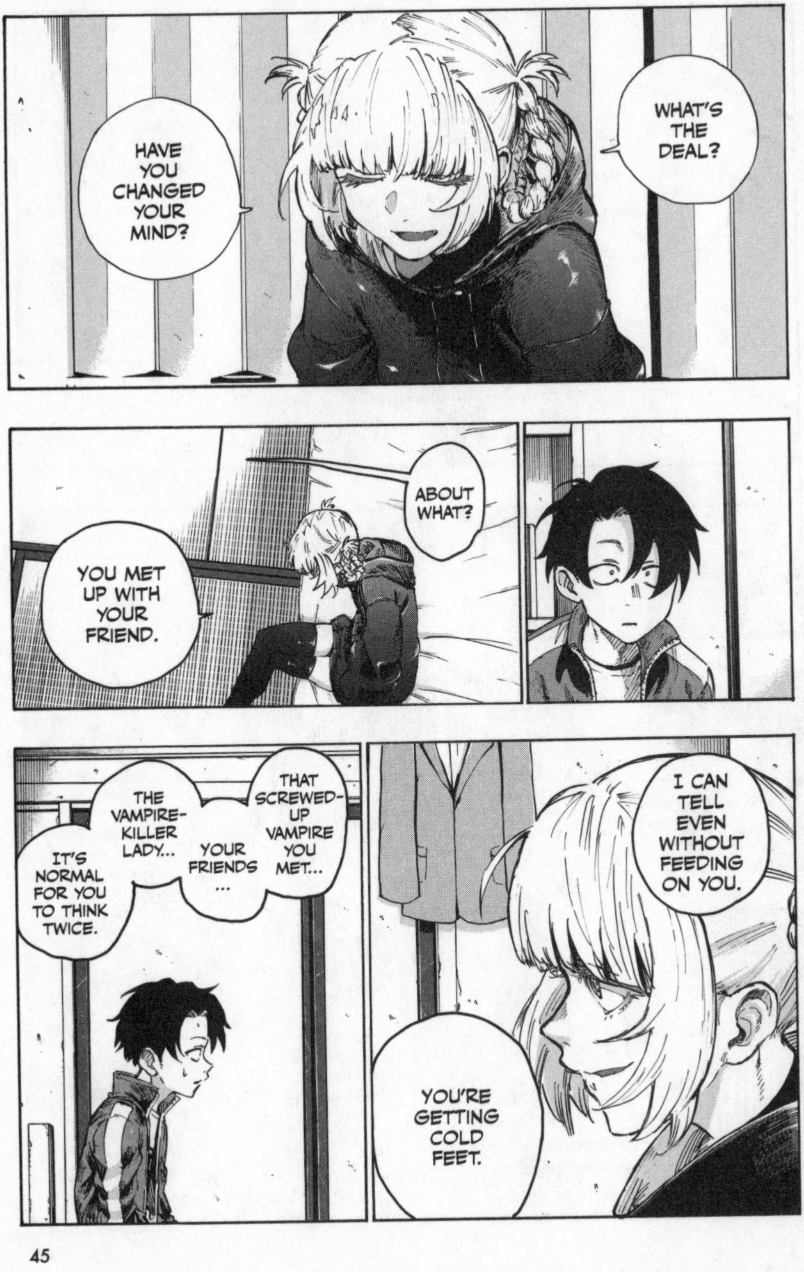
WHAT'S THE DEAL?
HAVE YOU CHANGED YOUR MIND?
ABOUT WHAT?
YOU MET UP WITH YOUR FRIEND.
I CAN TELL EVEN WITHOUT FEEDING ON YOU.
YOU'RE GETTING COLD FEET.
THAT SCREWED-UP VAMPIRE YOU MET...
YOUR FRIENDS ...
THE VAMPIRE-KILLER LADY...
IT'S NORMAL FOR YOU TO THINK TWICE.

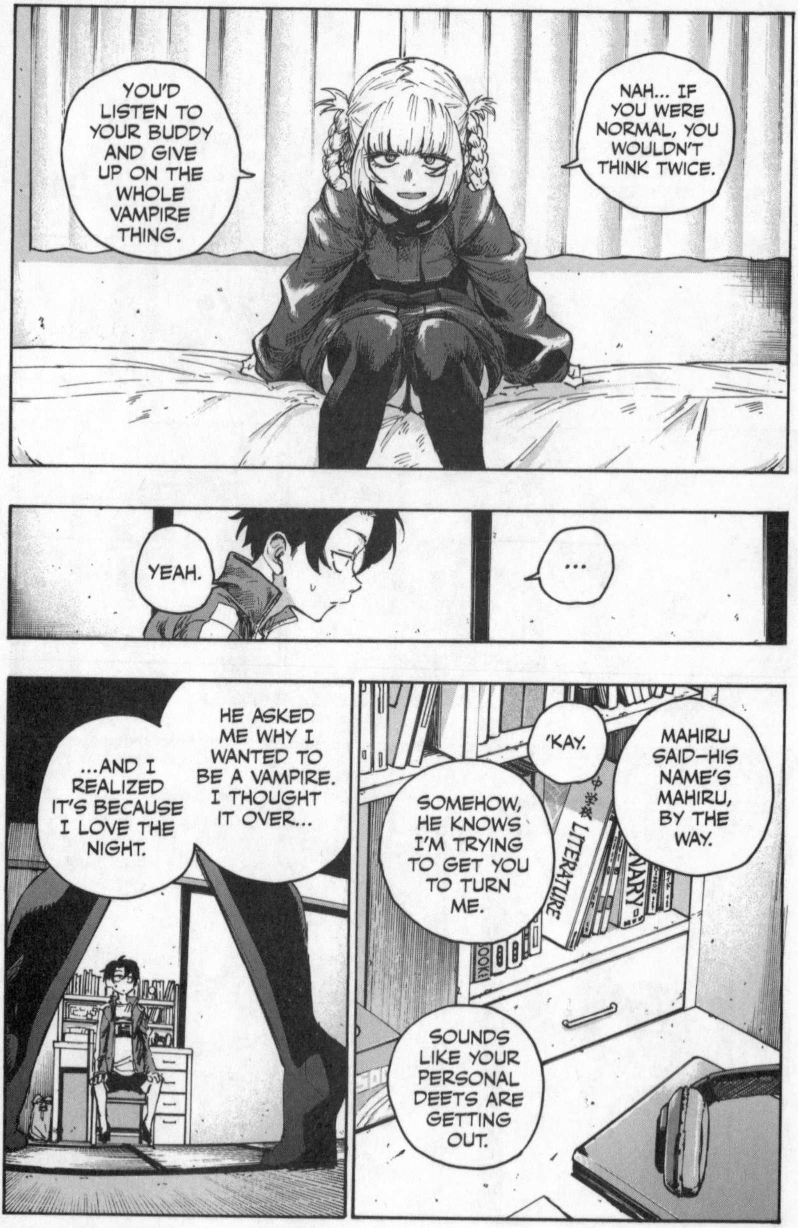
NAH... IF YOU WERE NORMAL, YOU WOULDN'T THINK TWICE.
YOU'D LISTEN TO YOUR BUDDY AND GIVE UP ON THE WHOLE VAMPIRE THING.
...
YEAH.
MAHIRU SAID—HIS NAME'S MAHIRU, BY THE WAY.
'KAY.
SOMEHOW, HE KNOWS I'M TRYING TO GET YOU TO TURN ME.
LITERATURE
SOUNDS LIKE YOUR PERSONAL DEETS ARE GETTING OUT.
HE ASKED ME WHY I WANTED TO BE A VAMPIRE. I THOUGHT IT OVER...
...AND I REALIZED IT'S BECAUSE I LOVE THE NIGHT.

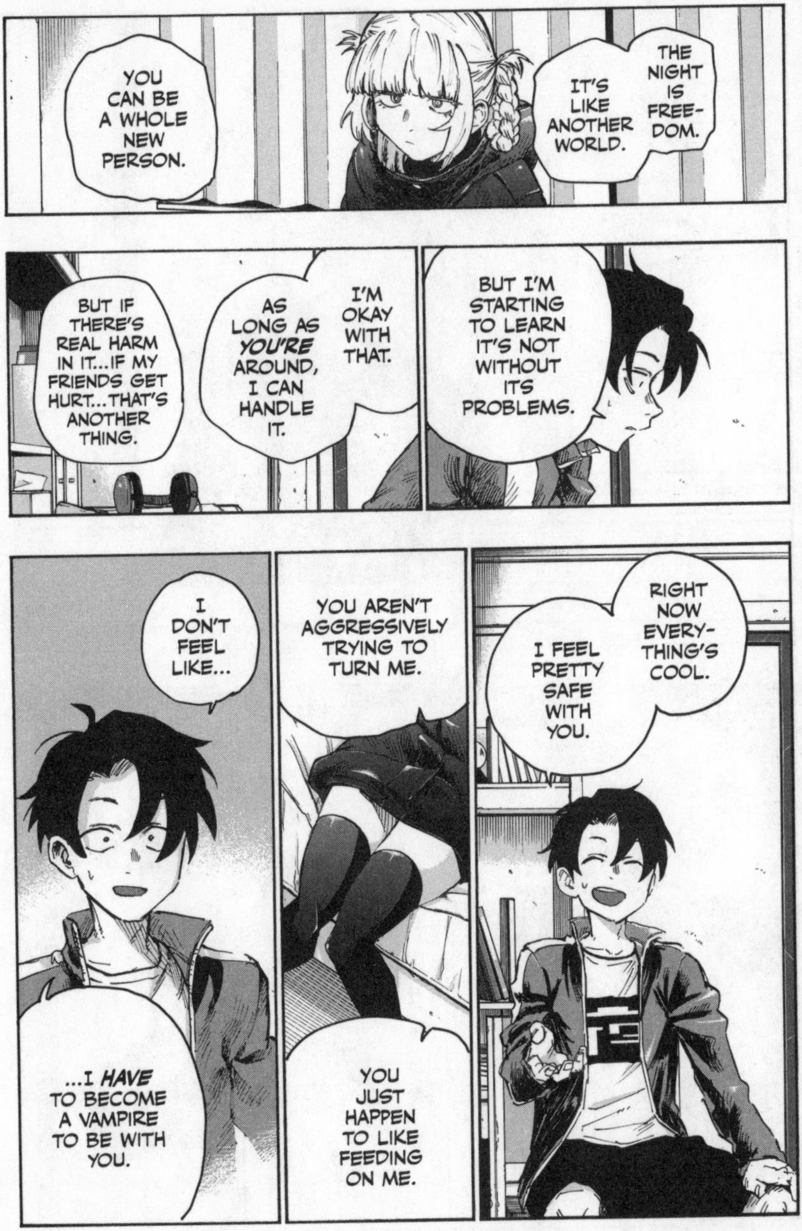
THE NIGHT IS FREE-DOM.
IT'S LIKE ANOTHER WORLD.
YOU CAN BE A WHOLE NEW PERSON.
BUT I'M STARTING TO LEARN IT'S NOT WITHOUT ITS PROBLEMS.
I'M OKAY WITH THAT.
AS LONG AS *YOU'RE* AROUND, I CAN HANDLE IT.
BUT IF THERE'S REAL HARM IN IT...IF MY FRIENDS GET HURT...THAT'S ANOTHER THING.
RIGHT NOW EVERY-THING'S COOL.
I FEEL PRETTY SAFE WITH YOU.
YOU AREN'T AGGRESSIVELY TRYING TO TURN ME.
YOU JUST HAPPEN TO LIKE FEEDING ON ME.
I DON'T FEEL LIKE...
...I *HAVE* TO BECOME A VAMPIRE TO BE WITH YOU.

TRUE.
WHAT'S ...
...WITH THAT LOOK?
IT'S ALMOST LIKE...
PUTTING ALL THAT ON HOLD FOR A SEC... HEAR MY SIDE OUT.
LIKE...

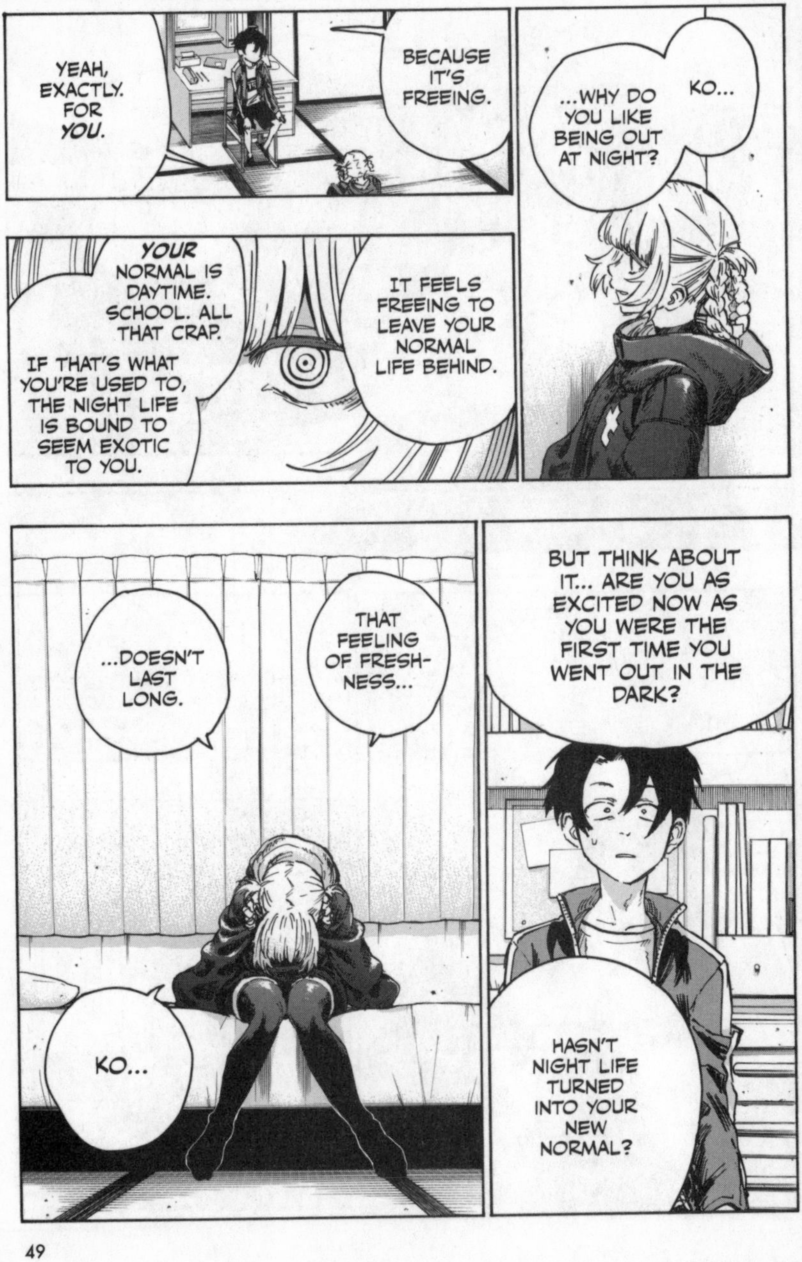
KO...
...WHY DO YOU LIKE BEING OUT AT NIGHT?
BECAUSE IT'S FREEING.
YEAH, EXACTLY. FOR *YOU*.
IT FEELS FREEING TO LEAVE YOUR NORMAL LIFE BEHIND.
YOUR NORMAL IS DAYTIME. SCHOOL. ALL THAT CRAP.
IF THAT'S WHAT YOU'RE USED TO, THE NIGHT LIFE IS BOUND TO SEEM EXOTIC TO YOU.
BUT THINK ABOUT IT... ARE YOU AS EXCITED NOW AS YOU WERE THE FIRST TIME YOU WENT OUT IN THE DARK?
HASN'T NIGHT LIFE TURNED INTO YOUR NEW NORMAL?
THAT FEELING OF FRESH-NESS...
...DOESN'T LAST LONG.
KO...

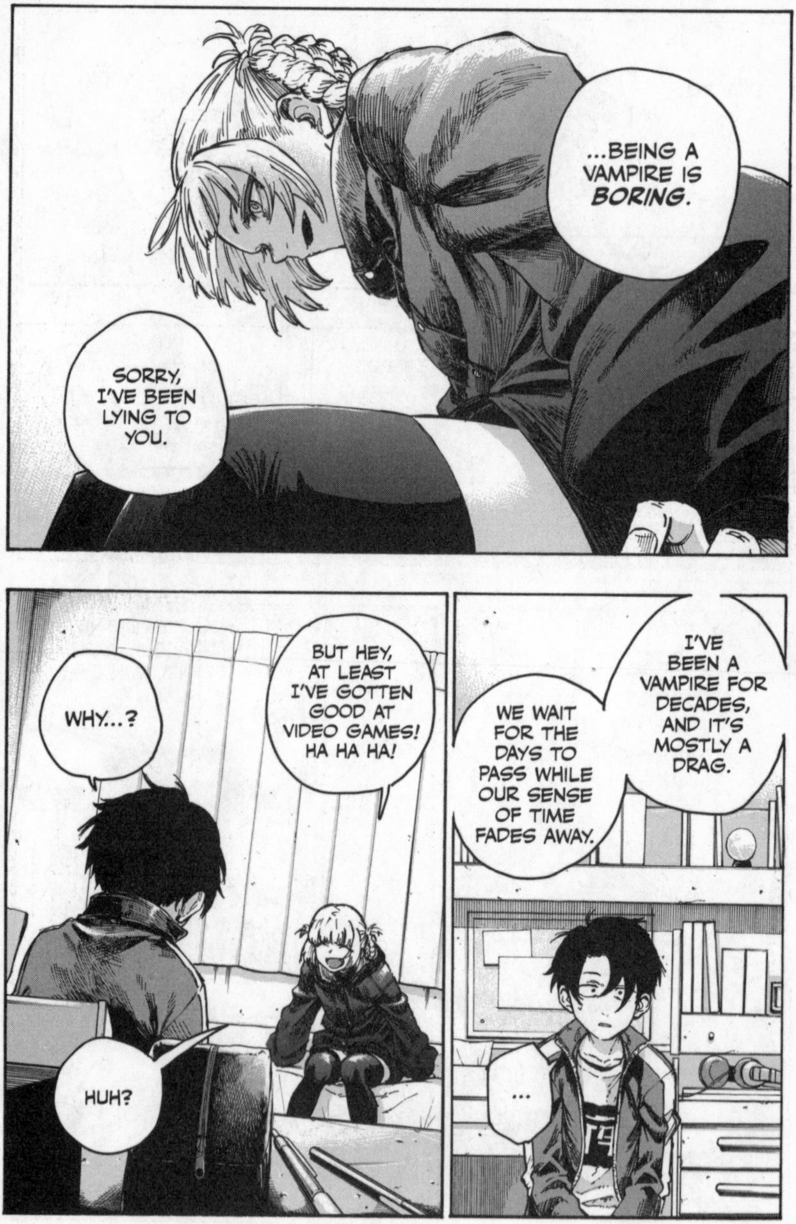
...BEING A VAMPIRE IS *BORING*.
SORRY, I'VE BEEN LYING TO YOU.
I'VE BEEN A VAMPIRE FOR DECADES, AND IT'S MOSTLY A DRAG.
WE WAIT FOR THE DAYS TO PASS WHILE OUR SENSE OF TIME FADES AWAY.
...
BUT HEY, AT LEAST I'VE GOTTEN GOOD AT VIDEO GAMES! HA HA HA!
WHY...?
HUH?

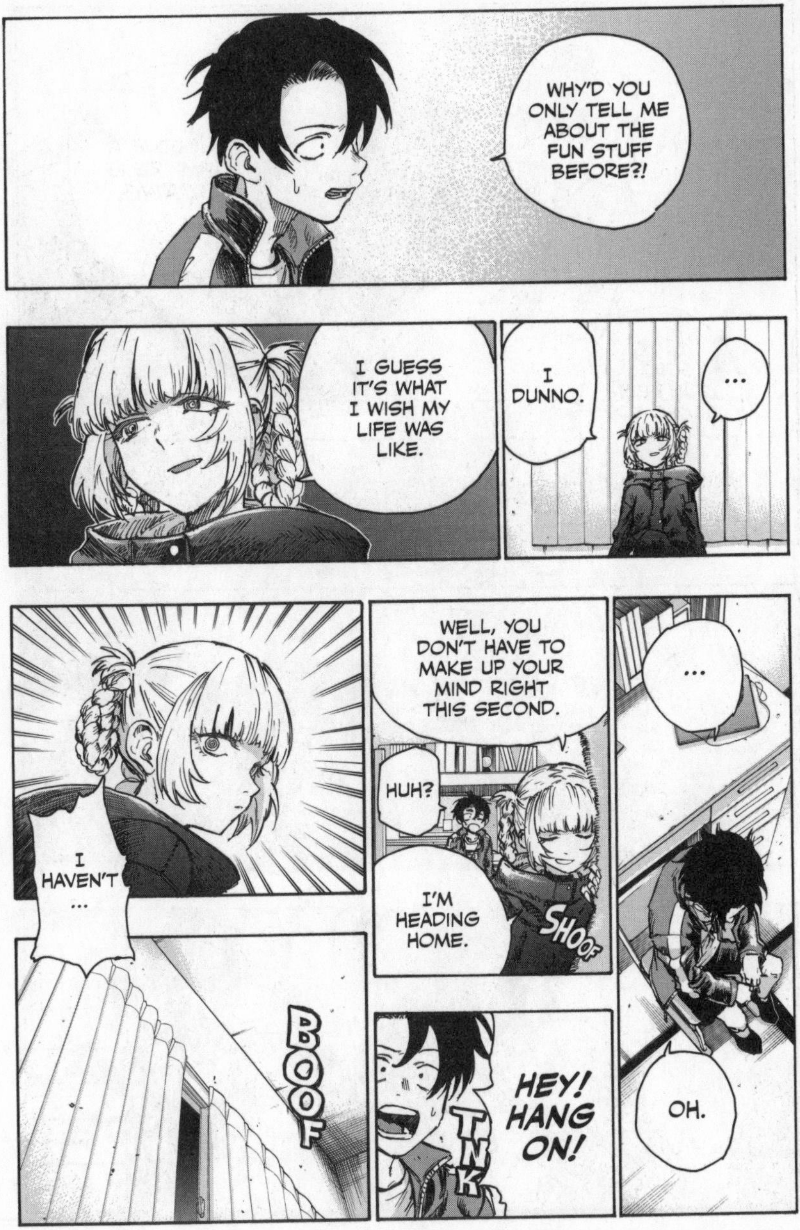
WHY'D YOU ONLY TELL ME ABOUT THE FUN STUFF BEFORE?!
...
I DUNNO.
I GUESS IT'S WHAT I WISH MY LIFE WAS LIKE.
...
OH.
WELL, YOU DON'T HAVE TO MAKE UP YOUR MIND RIGHT THIS SECOND.
HUH?
I'M HEADING HOME.
SHOOF
HEY! HANG ON!
TNK
I HAVEN'T ...
BOOF

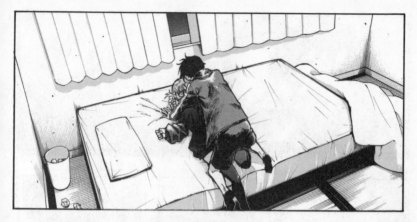

UH...

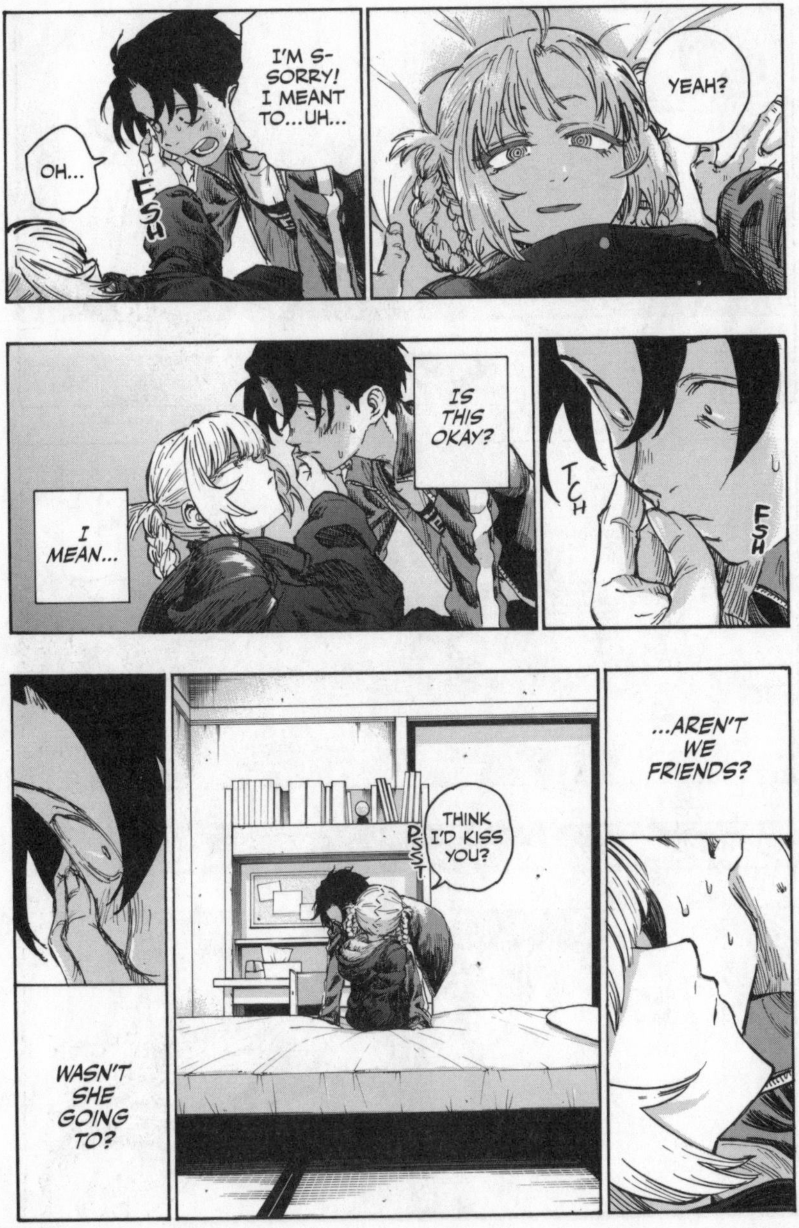
YEAH?
I'M S-SORRY! I MEANT TO...UH...
OH...
FSH
TCH
FSH
IS THIS OKAY?
I MEAN...
...AREN'T WE FRIENDS?
THINK I'D KISS YOU?
PSST
WASN'T SHE GOING TO?

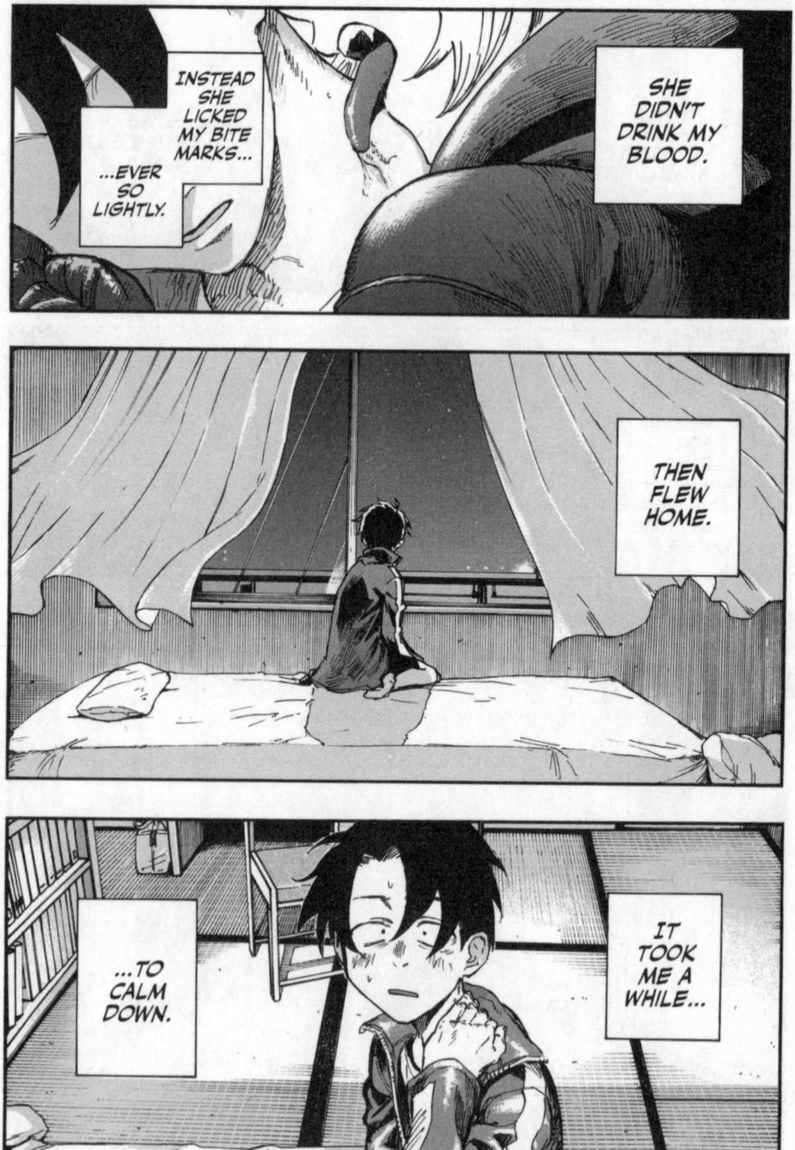
SHE DIDN'T DRINK MY BLOOD.
INSTEAD SHE LICKED MY BITE MARKS...
...EVER SO LIGHTLY.
THEN FLEW HOME.
IT TOOK ME A WHILE...
...TO CALM DOWN.

NIGHT 43: I DON'T SEE IT THAT WAY

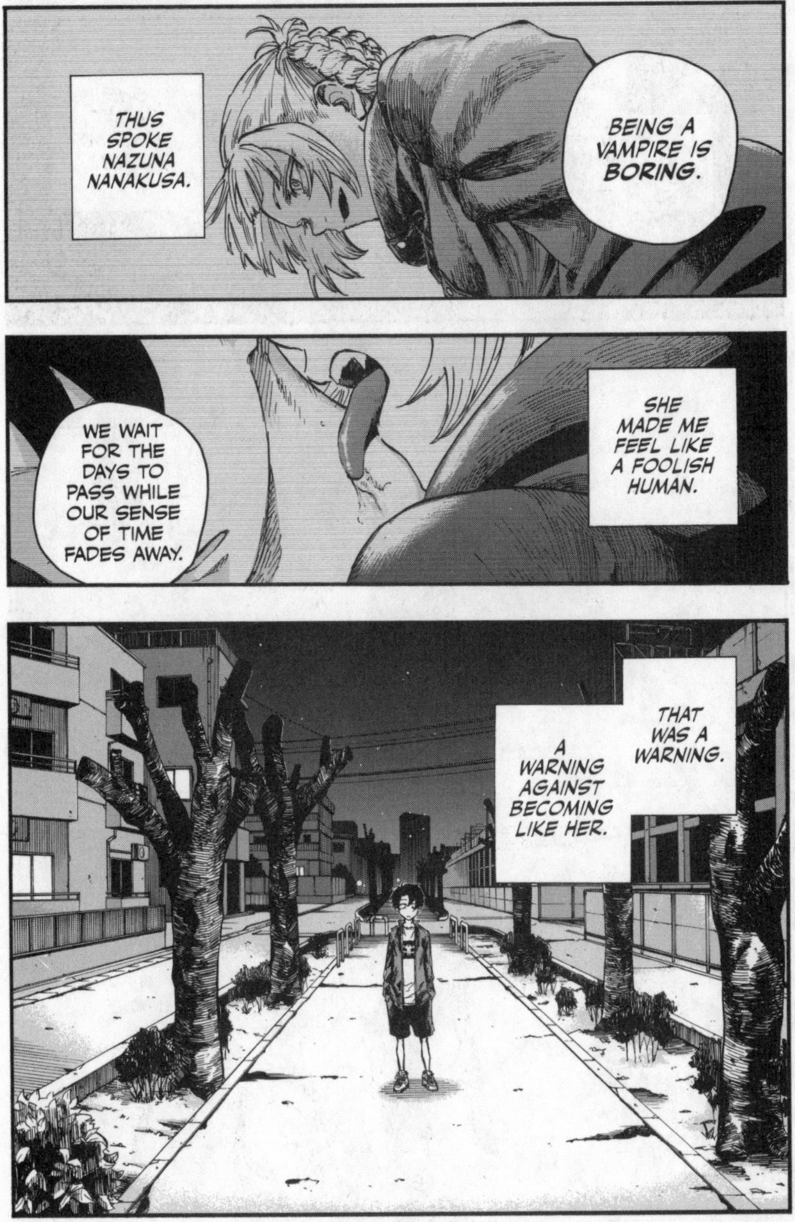
BEING A VAMPIRE IS BORING.
THUS SPOKE NAZUNA NANAKUSA.
SHE MADE ME FEEL LIKE A FOOLISH HUMAN.
WE WAIT FOR THE DAYS TO PASS WHILE OUR SENSE OF TIME FADES AWAY.
THAT WAS A WARNING.
A WARNING AGAINST BECOMING LIKE HER.

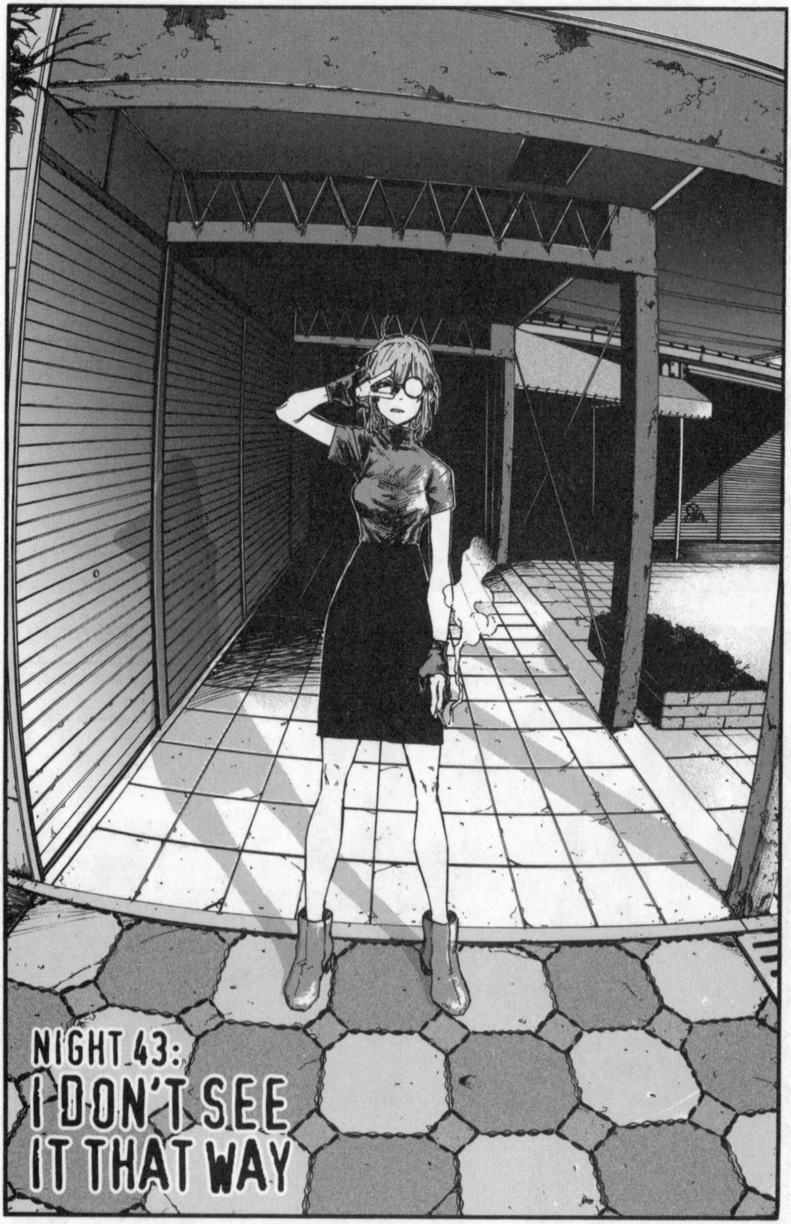
NIGHT 43:
I DON'T SEE IT THAT WAY

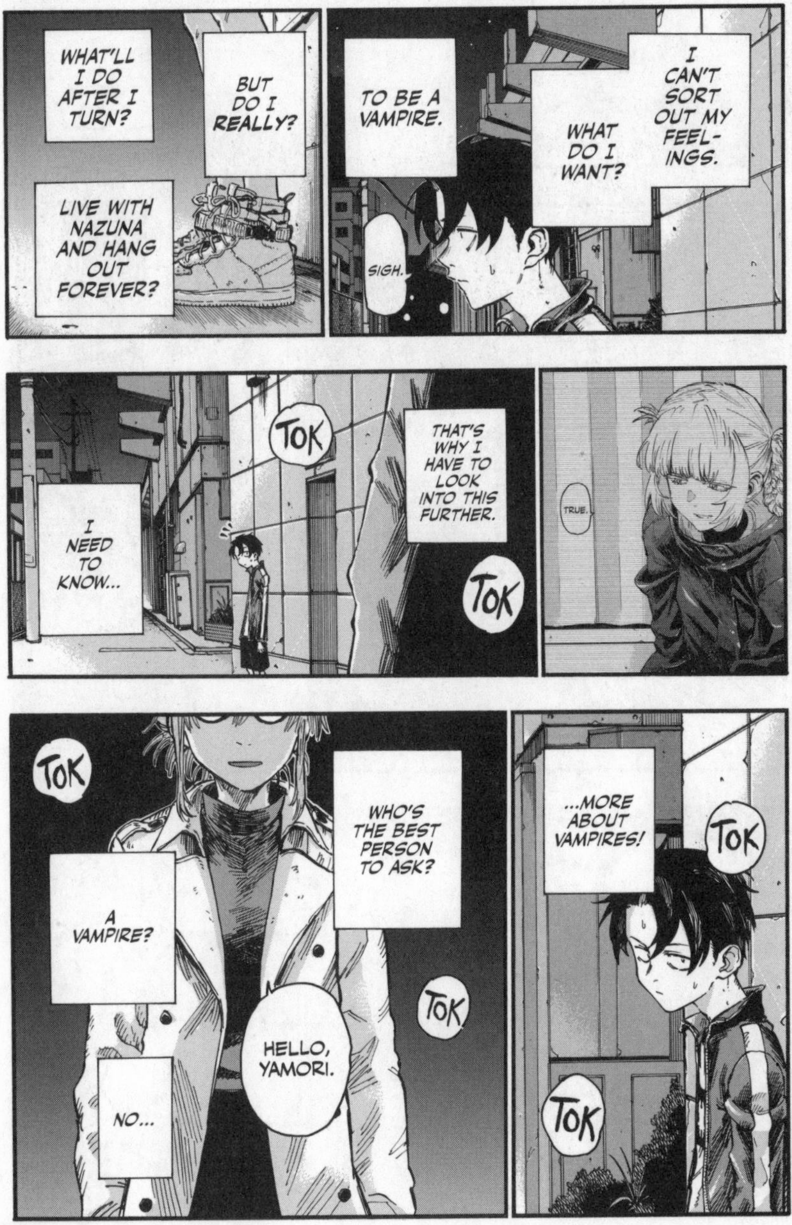
I CAN'T SORT OUT MY FEEL-INGS.
WHAT DO I WANT?
TO BE A VAMPIRE.
SIGH.
BUT DO I REALLY?
WHAT'LL I DO AFTER I TURN?
LIVE WITH NAZUNA AND HANG OUT FOREVER?
TRUE.
TOK
THAT'S WHY I HAVE TO LOOK INTO THIS FURTHER.
TOK
I NEED TO KNOW...
...MORE ABOUT VAMPIRES!
TOK
TOK
WHO'S THE BEST PERSON TO ASK?
TOK
A VAMPIRE?
TOK
HELLO, YAMORI.
NO...

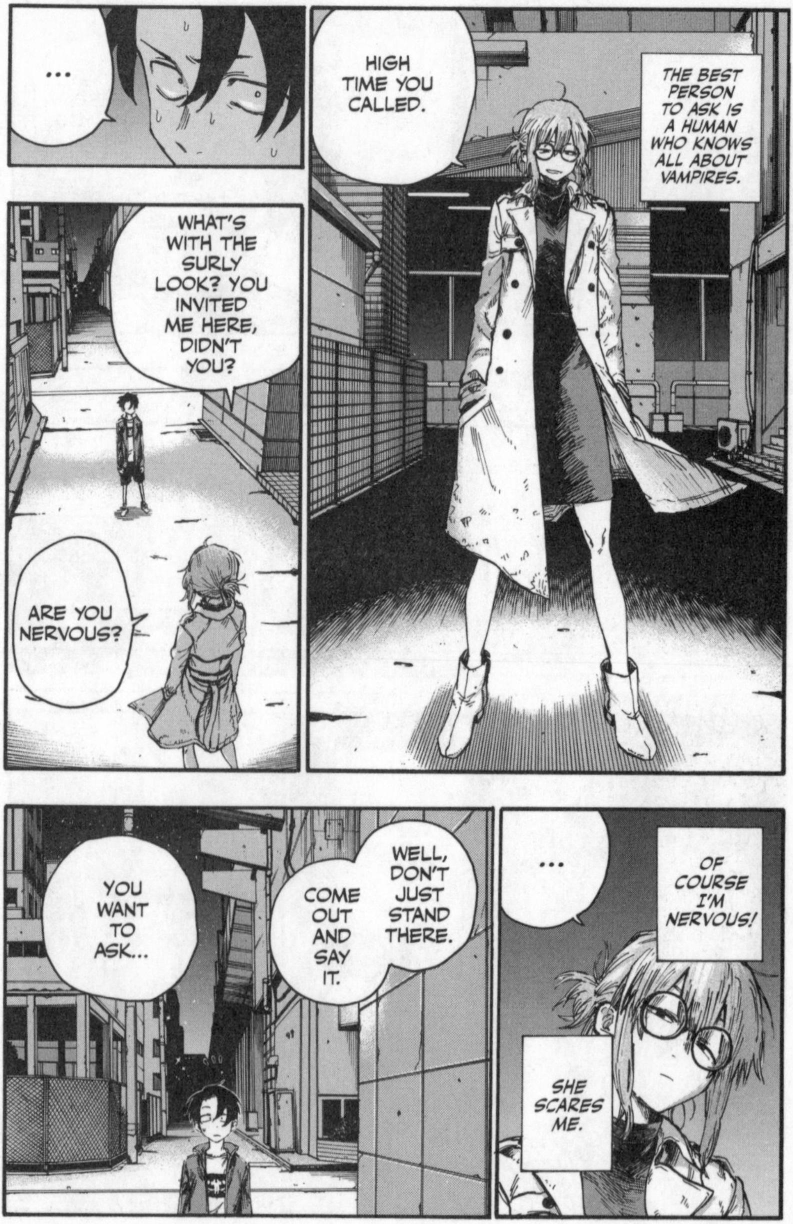
THE BEST PERSON TO ASK IS A HUMAN WHO KNOWS ALL ABOUT VAMPIRES.
HIGH TIME YOU CALLED.
...
WHAT'S WITH THE SURLY LOOK? YOU INVITED ME HERE, DIDN'T YOU?
ARE YOU NERVOUS?
OF COURSE I'M NERVOUS!
...
SHE SCARES ME.
WELL, DON'T JUST STAND THERE.
COME OUT AND SAY IT.
YOU WANT TO ASK...

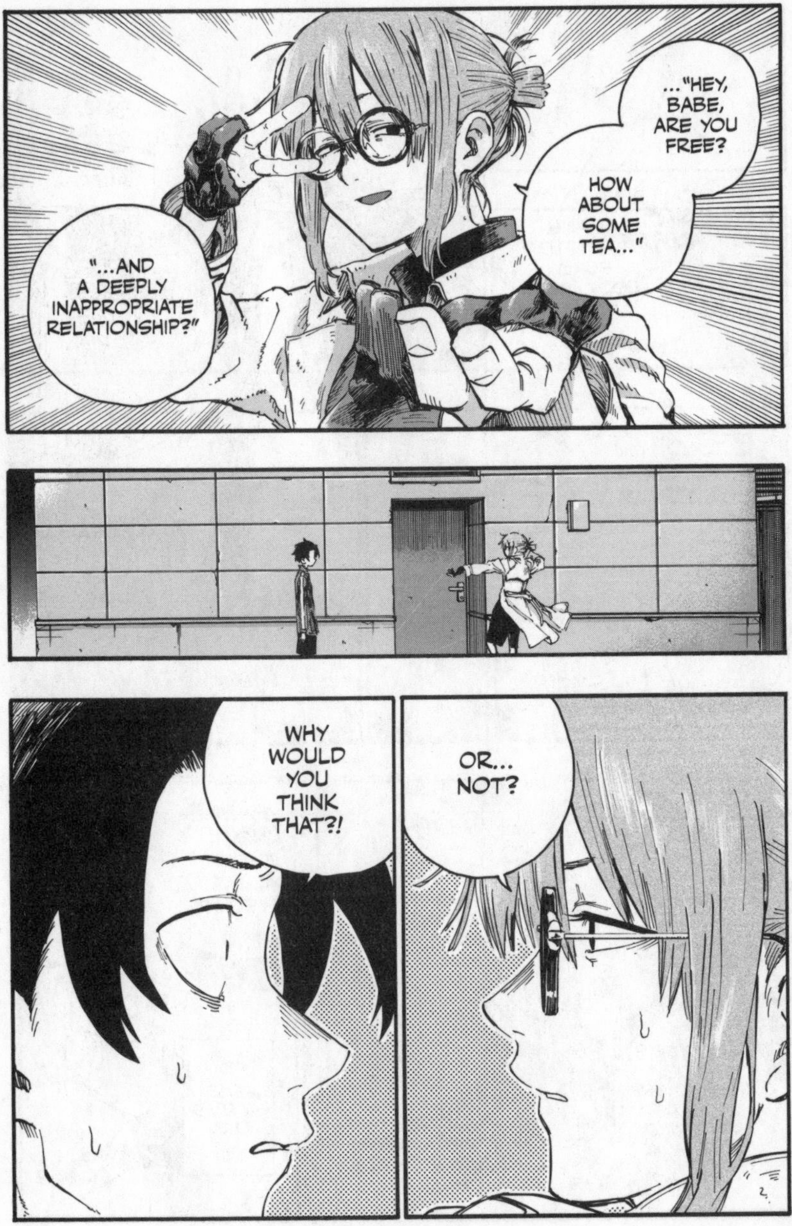
..."HEY, BABE, ARE YOU FREE?
HOW ABOUT SOME TEA..."
"...AND A DEEPLY INAPPROPRIATE RELATIONSHIP?"
OR... NOT?
WHY WOULD YOU THINK THAT?!

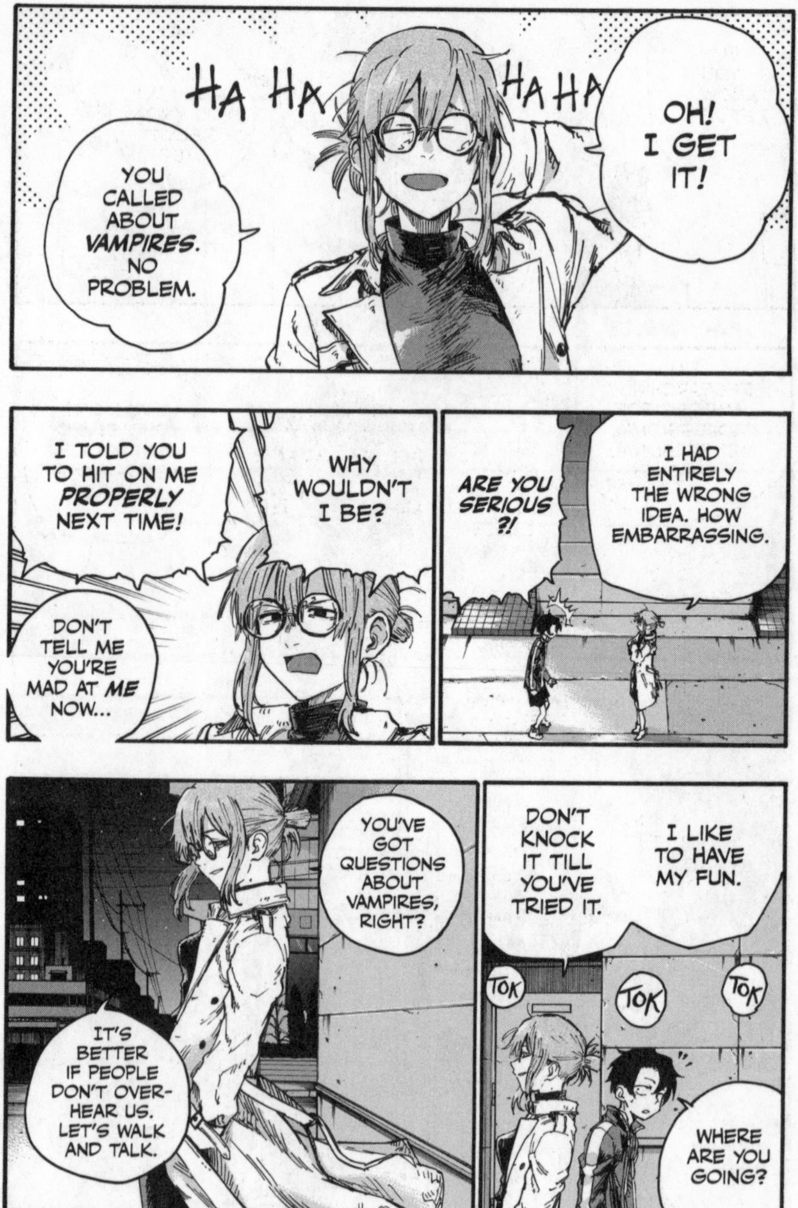
OH! I GET IT!
HA HA
HA HA
YOU CALLED ABOUT VAMPIRES. NO PROBLEM.
I HAD ENTIRELY THE WRONG IDEA. HOW EMBARRASSING.
ARE YOU SERIOUS?!
WHY WOULDN'T I BE?
I TOLD YOU TO HIT ON ME PROPERLY NEXT TIME!
DON'T TELL ME YOU'RE MAD AT ME NOW...
I LIKE TO HAVE MY FUN.
DON'T KNOCK IT TILL YOU'VE TRIED IT.
TOK
TOK
TOK
WHERE ARE YOU GOING?
YOU'VE GOT QUESTIONS ABOUT VAMPIRES, RIGHT?
IT'S BETTER IF PEOPLE DON'T OVER-HEAR US. LET'S WALK AND TALK.

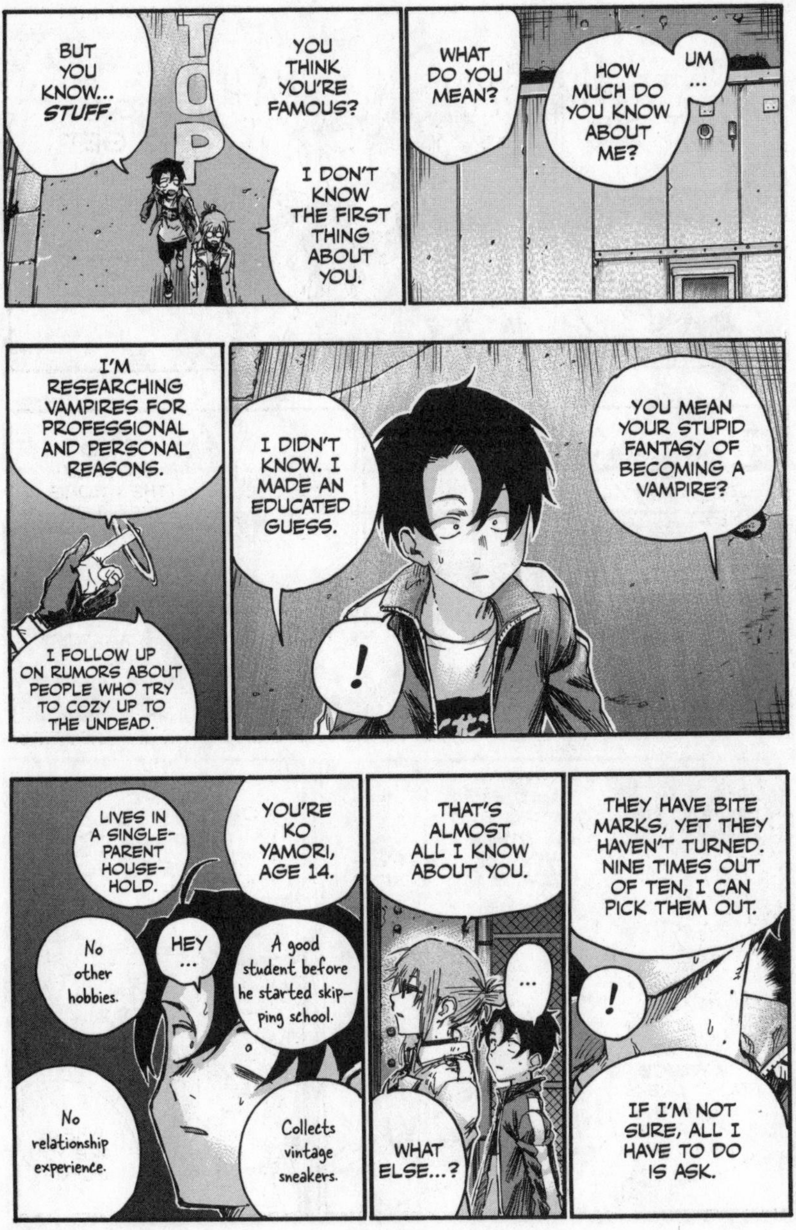
UM ...
HOW MUCH DO YOU KNOW ABOUT ME?
WHAT DO YOU MEAN?
YOU THINK YOU'RE FAMOUS?
I DON'T KNOW THE FIRST THING ABOUT YOU.
TOP
BUT YOU KNOW... *STUFF.*
YOU MEAN YOUR STUPID FANTASY OF BECOMING A VAMPIRE?
I DIDN'T KNOW. I MADE AN EDUCATED GUESS.
!
I'M RESEARCHING VAMPIRES FOR PROFESSIONAL AND PERSONAL REASONS.
I FOLLOW UP ON RUMORS ABOUT PEOPLE WHO TRY TO COZY UP TO THE UNDEAD.
THEY HAVE BITE MARKS, YET THEY HAVEN'T TURNED. NINE TIMES OUT OF TEN, I CAN PICK THEM OUT.
!
IF I'M NOT SURE, ALL I HAVE TO DO IS ASK.
THAT'S ALMOST ALL I KNOW ABOUT YOU.
...
WHAT ELSE...?
YOU'RE KO YAMORI, AGE 14.
LIVES IN A SINGLE-PARENT HOUSE-HOLD.
A good student before he started skip-ping school.
HEY ...
No other hobbies.
Collects vintage sneakers.
No relationship experience.

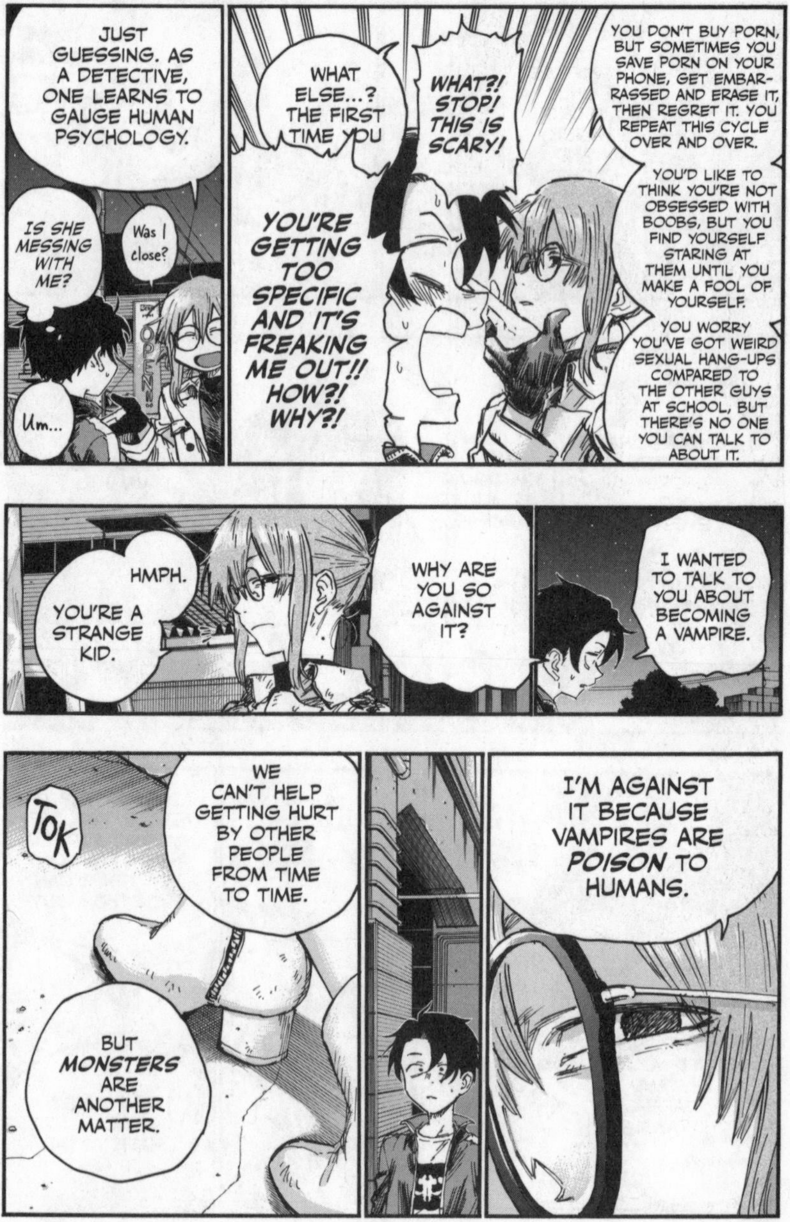
YOU DON'T BUY PORN, BUT SOMETIMES YOU SAVE PORN ON YOUR PHONE, GET EMBARRASSED AND ERASE IT, THEN REGRET IT. YOU REPEAT THIS CYCLE OVER AND OVER.
YOU'D LIKE TO THINK YOU'RE NOT OBSESSED WITH BOOBS, BUT YOU FIND YOURSELF STARING AT THEM UNTIL YOU MAKE A FOOL OF YOURSELF.
YOU WORRY YOU'VE GOT WEIRD SEXUAL HANG-UPS COMPARED TO THE OTHER GUYS AT SCHOOL, BUT THERE'S NO ONE YOU CAN TALK TO ABOUT IT.
WHAT?! STOP! THIS IS SCARY!
WHAT ELSE...? THE FIRST TIME YOU
YOU'RE GETTING TOO SPECIFIC AND IT'S FREAKING ME OUT!! HOW?! WHY?!
JUST GUESSING. AS A DETECTIVE, ONE LEARNS TO GAUGE HUMAN PSYCHOLOGY.
Was I close?
IS SHE MESSING WITH ME?
OPEN
Um...
I WANTED TO TALK TO YOU ABOUT BECOMING A VAMPIRE.
WHY ARE YOU SO AGAINST IT?
HMPH.
YOU'RE A STRANGE KID.
I'M AGAINST IT BECAUSE VAMPIRES ARE POISON TO HUMANS.
WE CAN'T HELP GETTING HURT BY OTHER PEOPLE FROM TIME TO TIME.
TOK
BUT MONSTERS ARE ANOTHER MATTER.

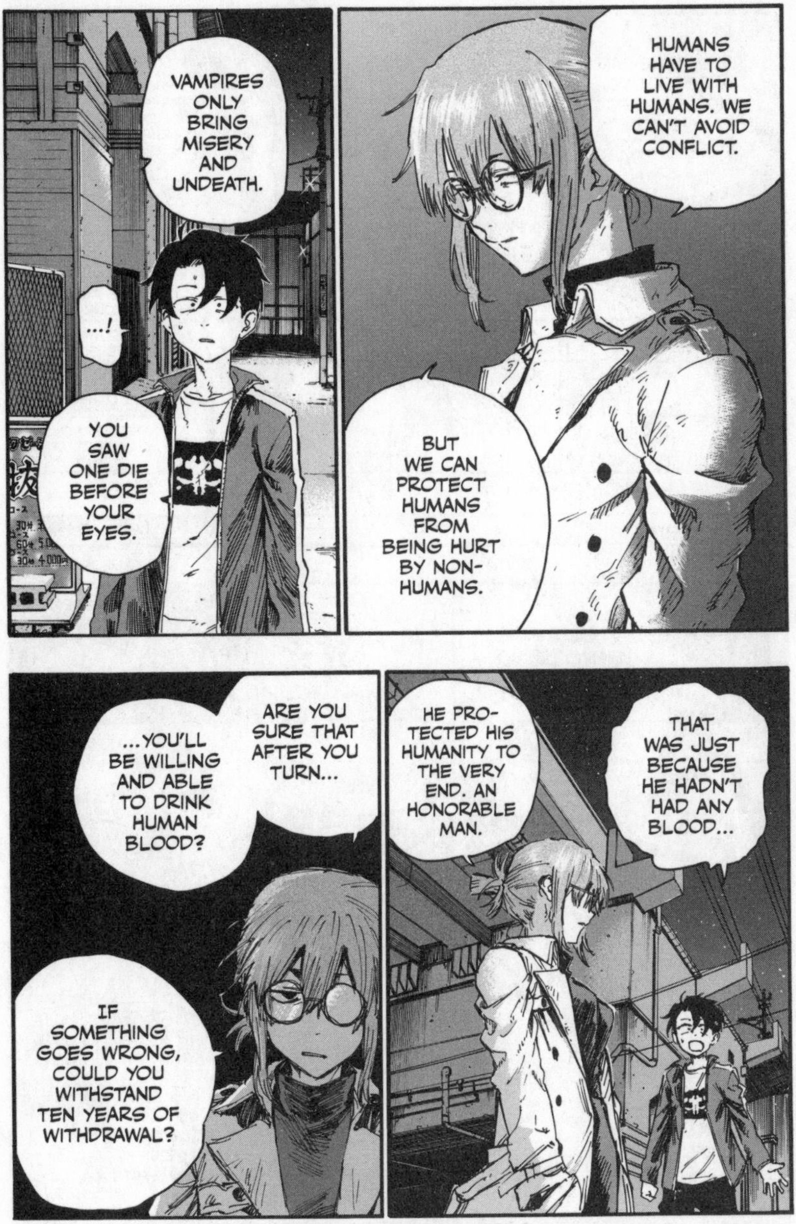
HUMANS HAVE TO LIVE WITH HUMANS. WE CAN'T AVOID CONFLICT.
BUT WE CAN PROTECT HUMANS FROM BEING HURT BY NON-HUMANS.
VAMPIRES ONLY BRING MISERY AND UNDEATH.
...!
YOU SAW ONE DIE BEFORE YOUR EYES.
THAT WAS JUST BECAUSE HE HADN'T HAD ANY BLOOD...
HE PROTECTED HIS HUMANITY TO THE VERY END. AN HONORABLE MAN.
ARE YOU SURE THAT AFTER YOU TURN...
...YOU'LL BE WILLING AND ABLE TO DRINK HUMAN BLOOD?
IF SOMETHING GOES WRONG, COULD YOU WITHSTAND TEN YEARS OF WITHDRAWAL?

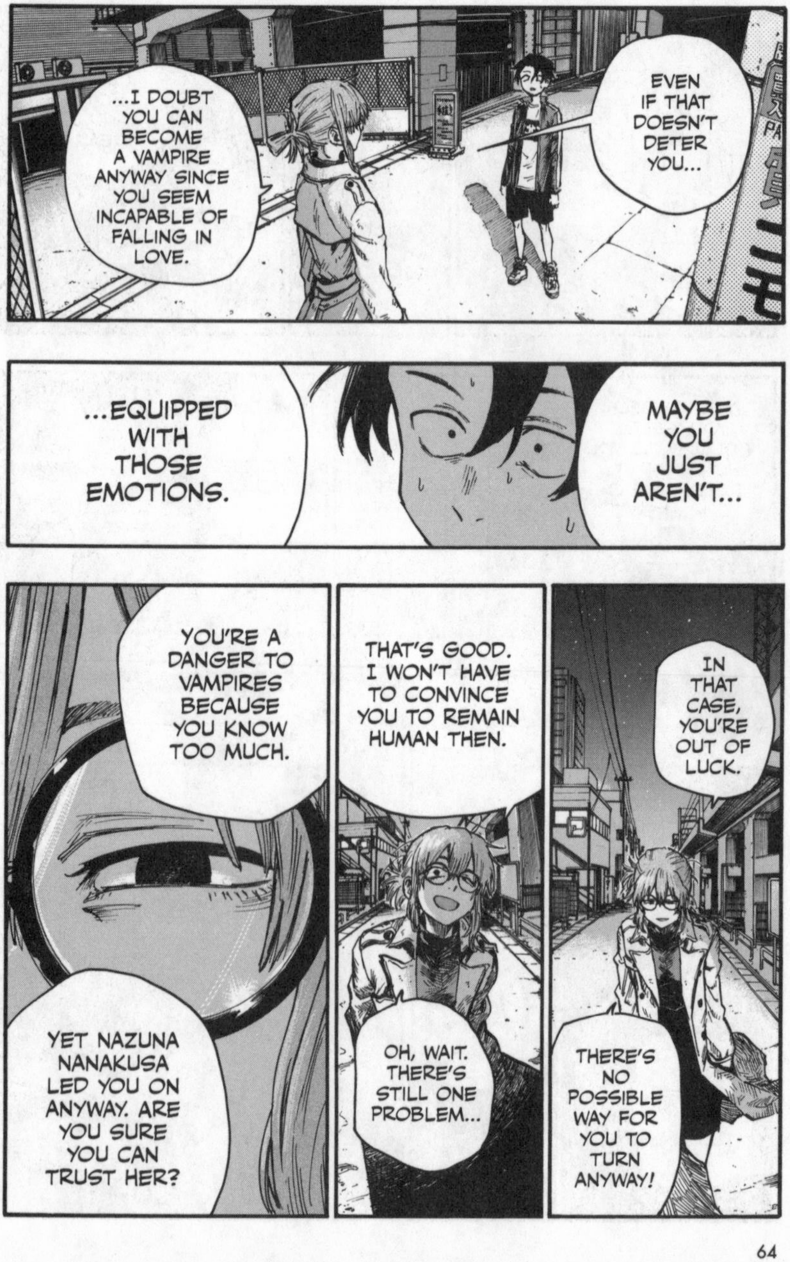
EVEN IF THAT DOESN'T DETER YOU...
...I DOUBT YOU CAN BECOME A VAMPIRE ANYWAY SINCE YOU SEEM INCAPABLE OF FALLING IN LOVE.
MAYBE YOU JUST AREN'T...
...EQUIPPED WITH THOSE EMOTIONS.
IN THAT CASE, YOU'RE OUT OF LUCK.
THERE'S NO POSSIBLE WAY FOR YOU TO TURN ANYWAY!
THAT'S GOOD. I WON'T HAVE TO CONVINCE YOU TO REMAIN HUMAN THEN.
OH, WAIT. THERE'S STILL ONE PROBLEM...
YOU'RE A DANGER TO VAMPIRES BECAUSE YOU KNOW TOO MUCH.
YET NAZUNA NANAKUSA LED YOU ON ANYWAY. ARE YOU SURE YOU CAN TRUST HER?

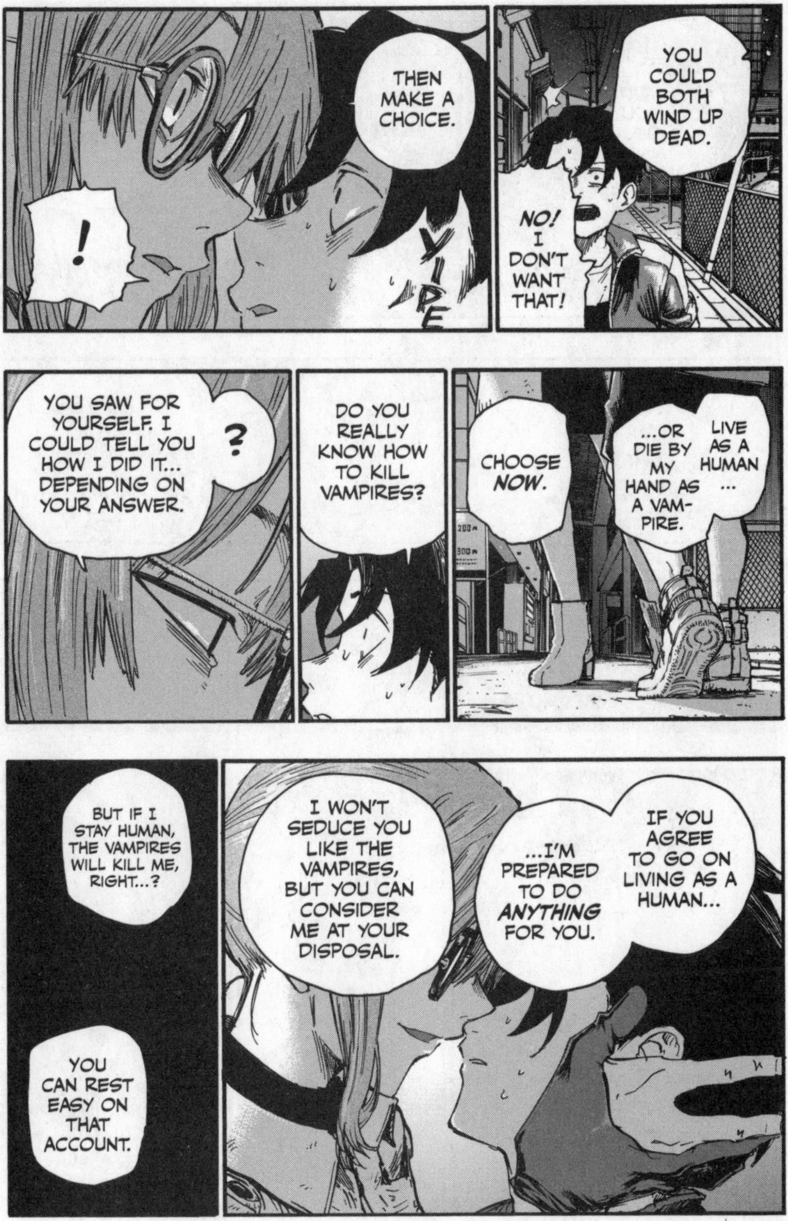
YOU COULD BOTH WIND UP DEAD.
NO! I DON'T WANT THAT!
THEN MAKE A CHOICE.
YIPE
!
LIVE AS A HUMAN ...
...OR DIE BY MY HAND AS A VAMPIRE.
CHOOSE NOW.
DO YOU REALLY KNOW HOW TO KILL VAMPIRES?
?
YOU SAW FOR YOURSELF. I COULD TELL YOU HOW I DID IT... DEPENDING ON YOUR ANSWER.
IF YOU AGREE TO GO ON LIVING AS A HUMAN...
...I'M PREPARED TO DO ANYTHING FOR YOU.
I WON'T SEDUCE YOU LIKE THE VAMPIRES, BUT YOU CAN CONSIDER ME AT YOUR DISPOSAL.
BUT IF I STAY HUMAN, THE VAMPIRES WILL KILL ME, RIGHT...?
YOU CAN REST EASY ON THAT ACCOUNT.

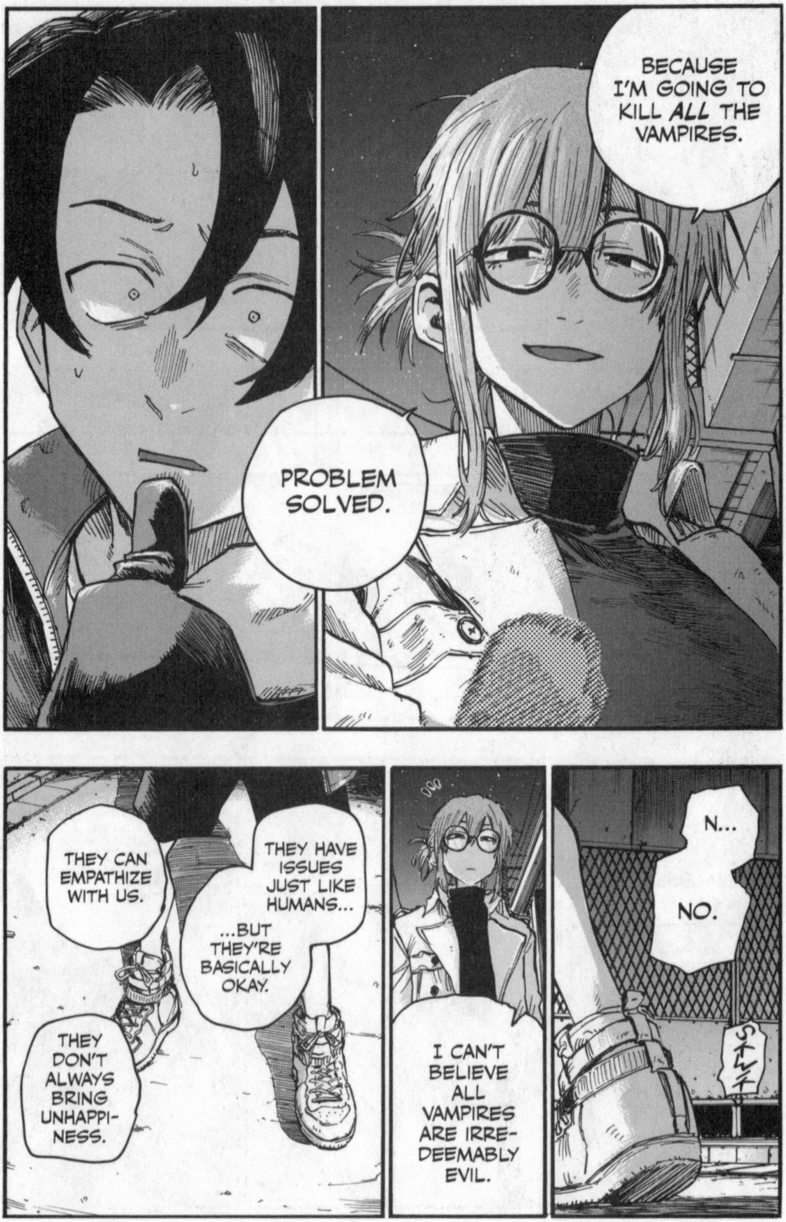
BECAUSE I'M GOING TO KILL ***ALL*** THE VAMPIRES.
PROBLEM SOLVED.
N...
NO.
I CAN'T BELIEVE ALL VAMPIRES ARE IRRE-DEEMABLY EVIL.
THEY HAVE ISSUES JUST LIKE HUMANS...
...BUT THEY'RE BASICALLY OKAY.
THEY CAN EMPATHIZE WITH US.
THEY DON'T ALWAYS BRING UNHAPPI-NESS.

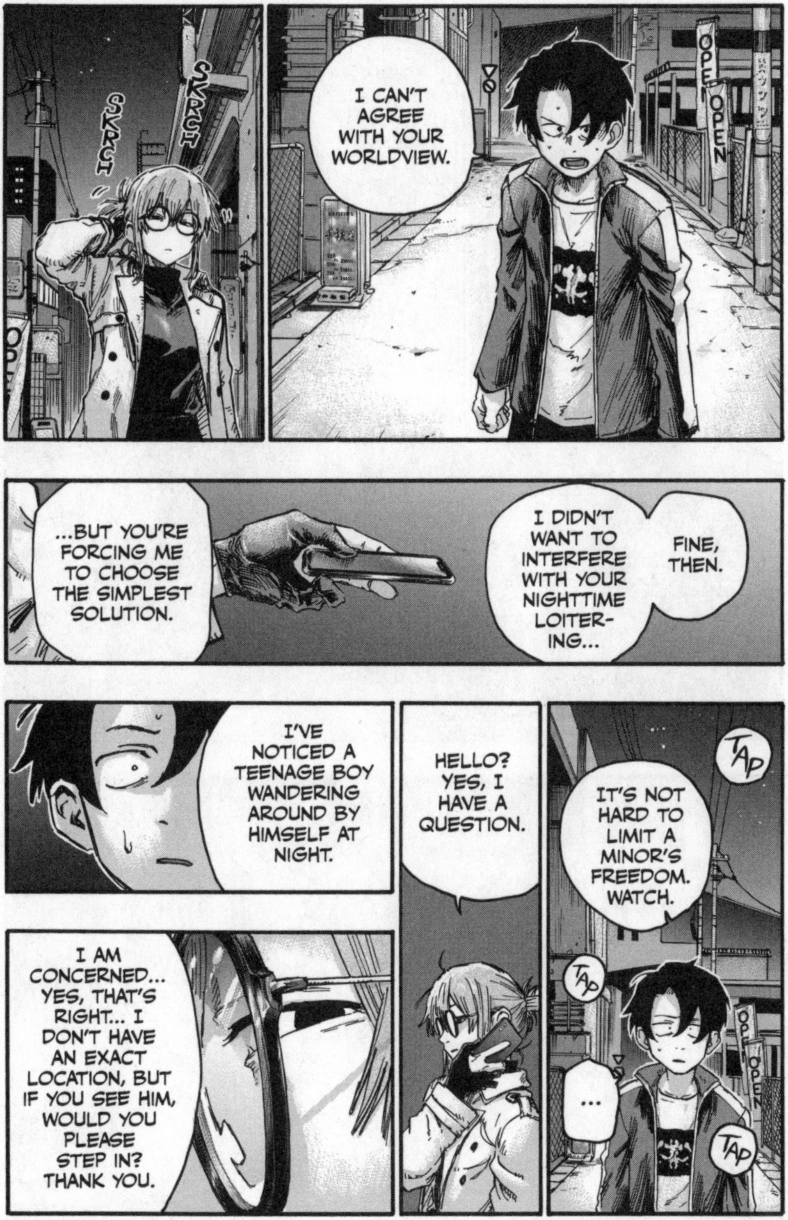
I CAN'T AGREE WITH YOUR WORLDVIEW.
SKRCH
SKRCH
FINE, THEN.
I DIDN'T WANT TO INTERFERE WITH YOUR NIGHTTIME LOITER-ING...
...BUT YOU'RE FORCING ME TO CHOOSE THE SIMPLEST SOLUTION.
TAP
IT'S NOT HARD TO LIMIT A MINOR'S FREEDOM. WATCH.
TAP
...
TAP
HELLO? YES, I HAVE A QUESTION.
I'VE NOTICED A TEENAGE BOY WANDERING AROUND BY HIMSELF AT NIGHT.
I AM CONCERNED... YES, THAT'S RIGHT... I DON'T HAVE AN EXACT LOCATION, BUT IF YOU SEE HIM, WOULD YOU PLEASE STEP IN? THANK YOU.

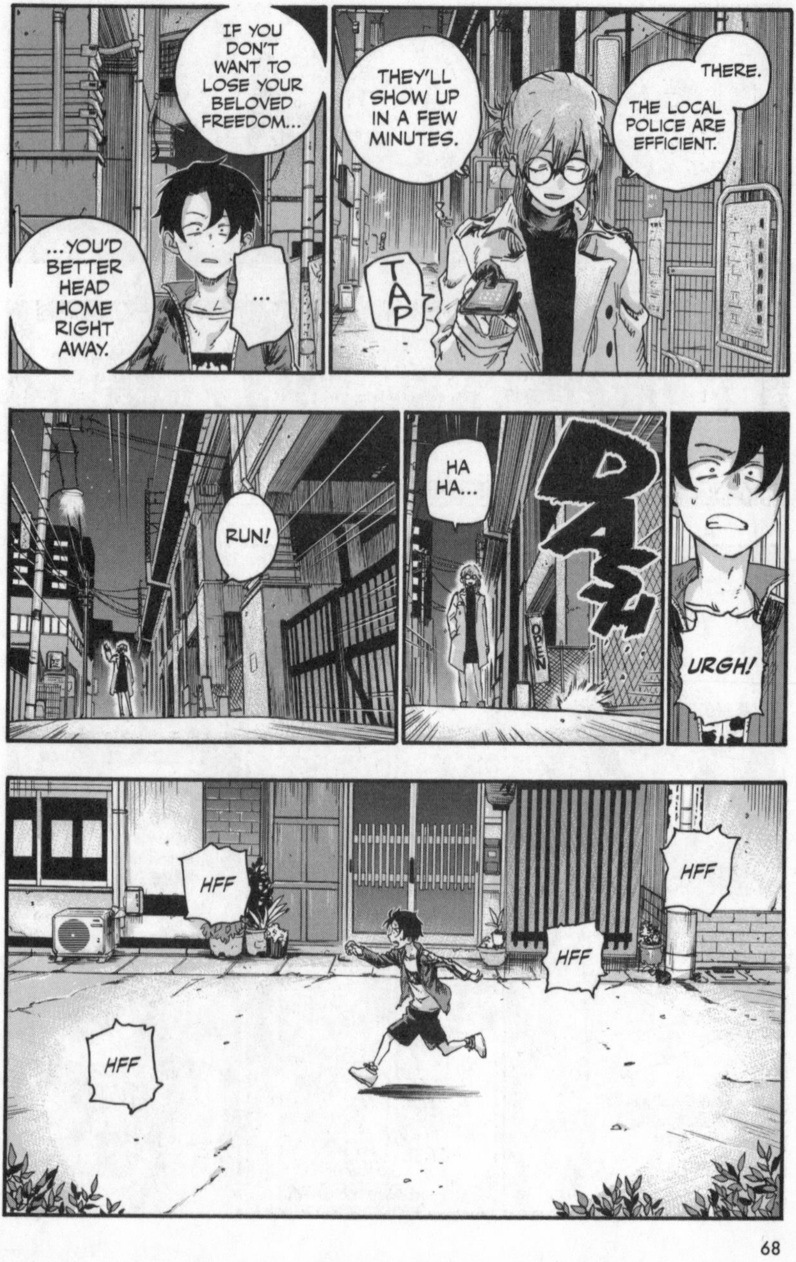
THERE.
THE LOCAL POLICE ARE EFFICIENT.
THEY'LL SHOW UP IN A FEW MINUTES.
TAP
IF YOU DON'T WANT TO LOSE YOUR BELOVED FREEDOM...
...
...YOU'D BETTER HEAD HOME RIGHT AWAY.
URGH!
HA HA...
DASH
OPEN
RUN!
HFF
HFF
HFF
HFF

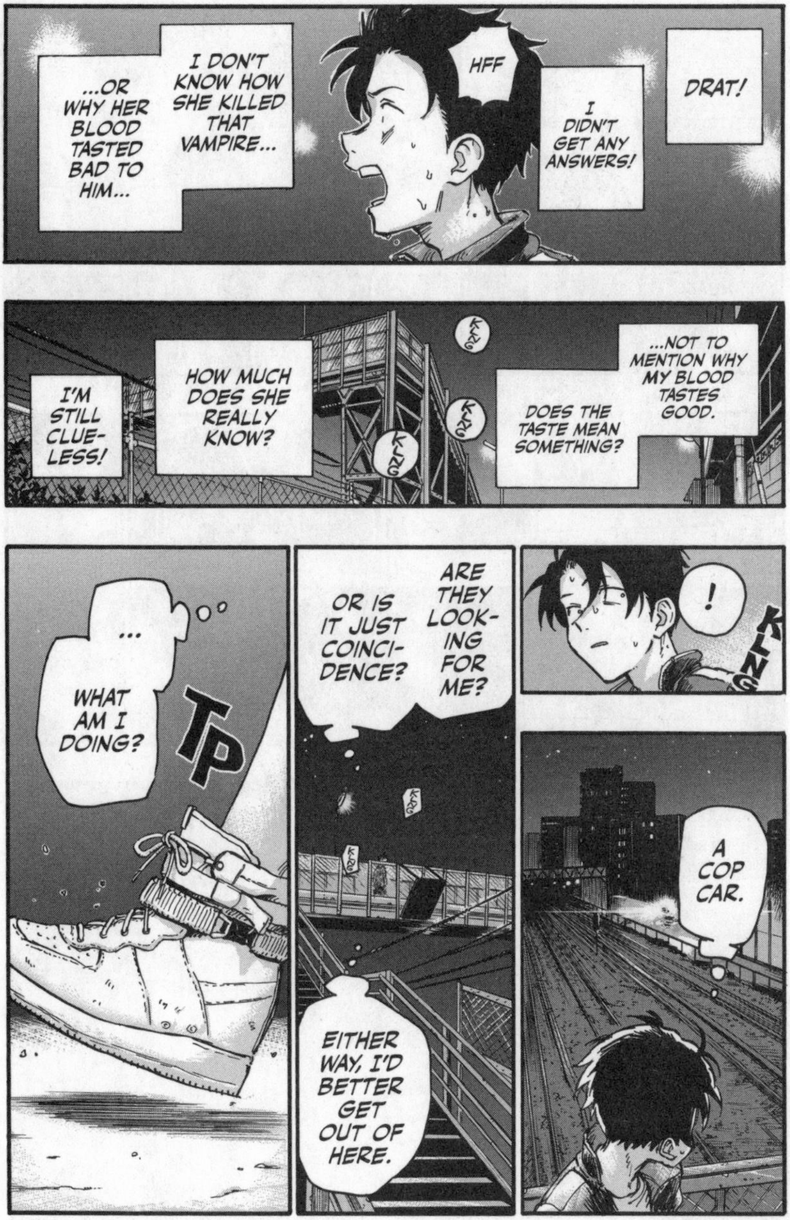
DRAT!
I DIDN'T GET ANY ANSWERS!
HFF
I DON'T KNOW HOW SHE KILLED THAT VAMPIRE...
...OR WHY HER BLOOD TASTED BAD TO HIM...
...NOT TO MENTION WHY MY BLOOD TASTES GOOD.
DOES THE TASTE MEAN SOMETHING?
KLNG
KLNG
KLNG
HOW MUCH DOES SHE REALLY KNOW?
I'M STILL CLUE-LESS!
!
KLNG
A COP CAR.
ARE THEY LOOK-ING FOR ME?
OR IS IT JUST COINCI-DENCE?
EITHER WAY, I'D BETTER GET OUT OF HERE.
...
WHAT AM I DOING?
TP

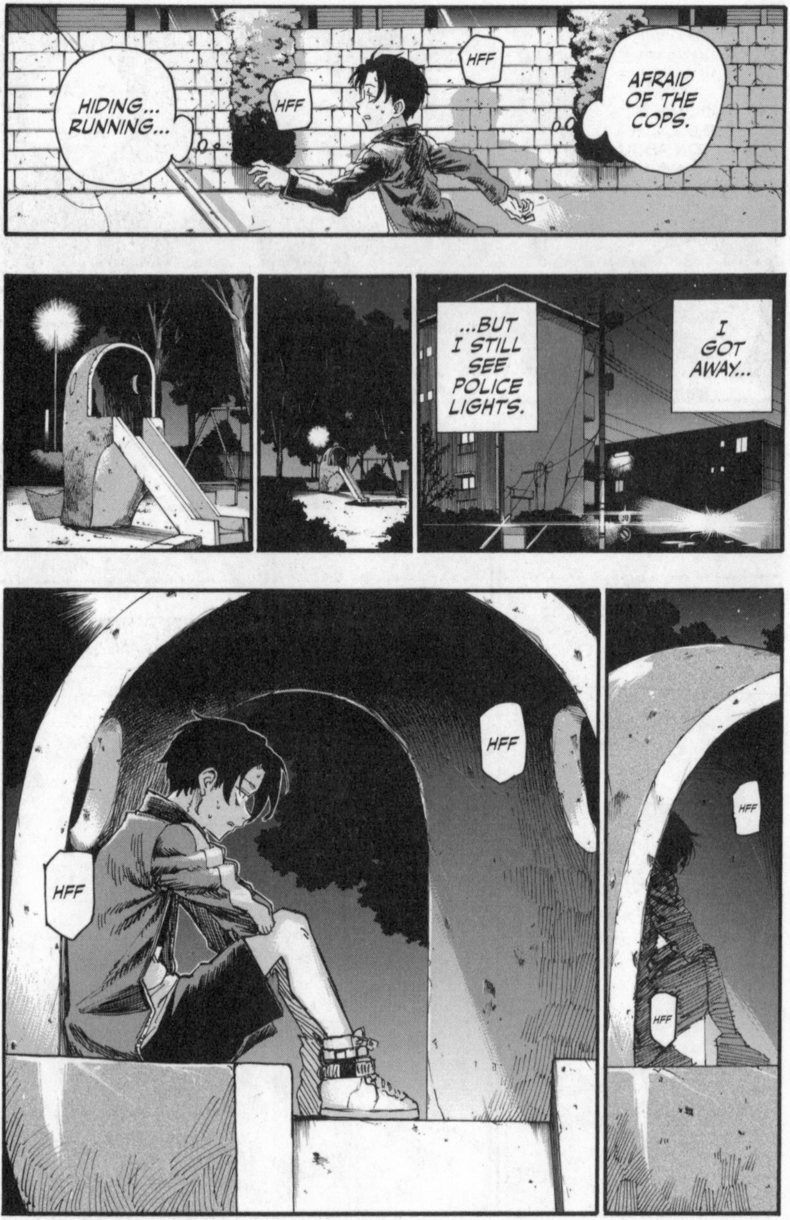
AFRAID OF THE COPS.
HFF
HFF
HIDING... RUNNING...
I GOT AWAY...
...BUT I STILL SEE POLICE LIGHTS.
HFF
HFF
HFF
HFF

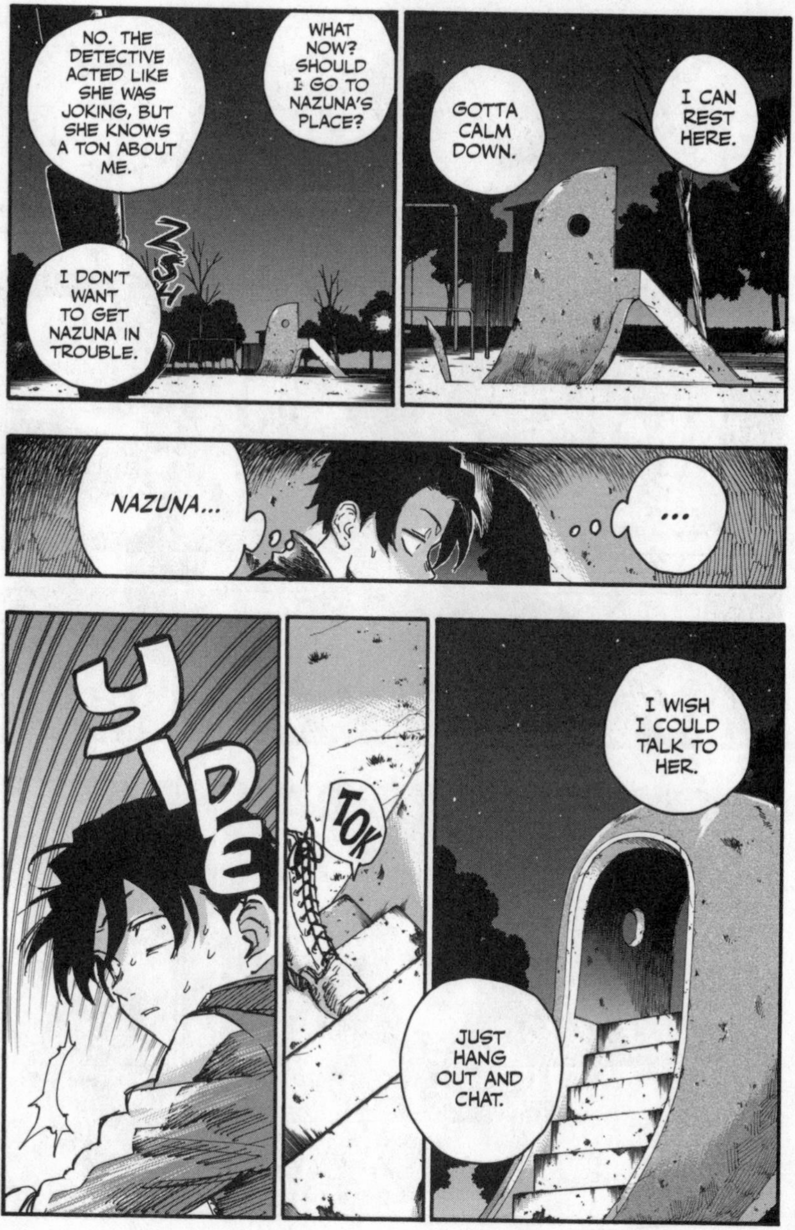
I CAN REST HERE.
GOTTA CALM DOWN.
WHAT NOW? SHOULD I GO TO NAZUNA'S PLACE?
NO. THE DETECTIVE ACTED LIKE SHE WAS JOKING, BUT SHE KNOWS A TON ABOUT ME.
ZSH
I DON'T WANT TO GET NAZUNA IN TROUBLE.
...
NAZUNA...
I WISH I COULD TALK TO HER.
JUST HANG OUT AND CHAT.
TOK
YIPE

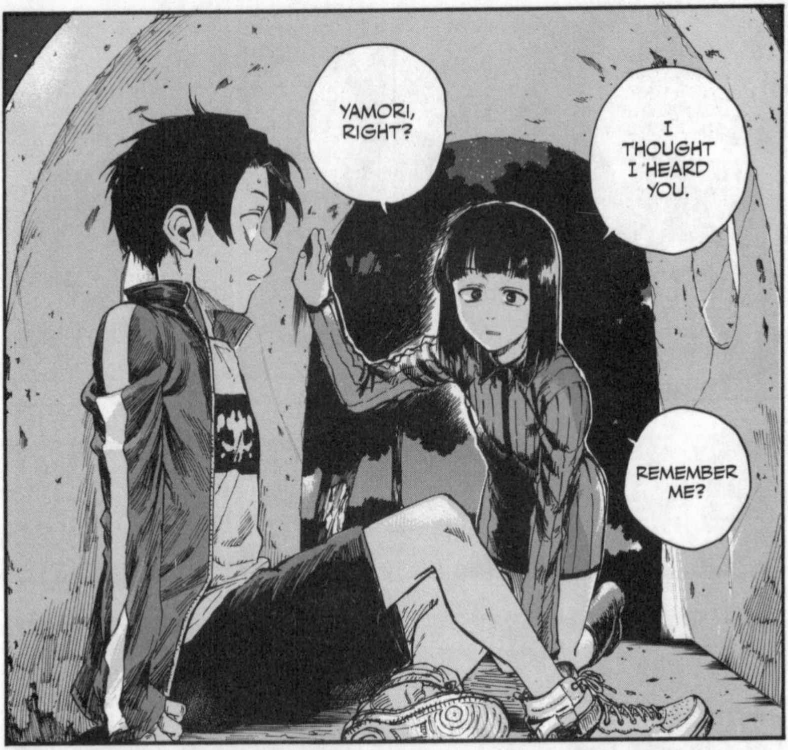
I THOUGHT I HEARD YOU.
YAMORI, RIGHT?
REMEMBER ME?

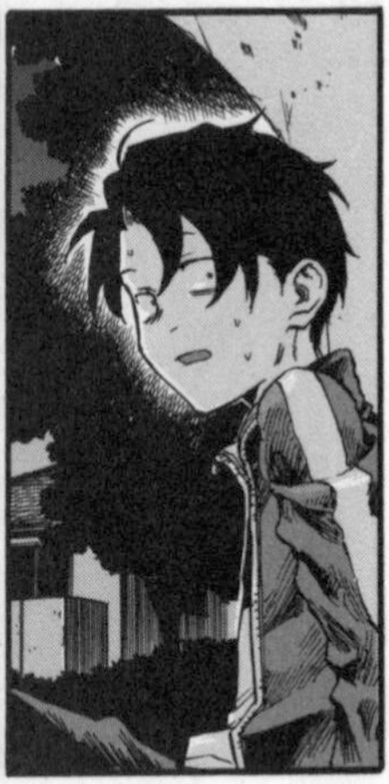

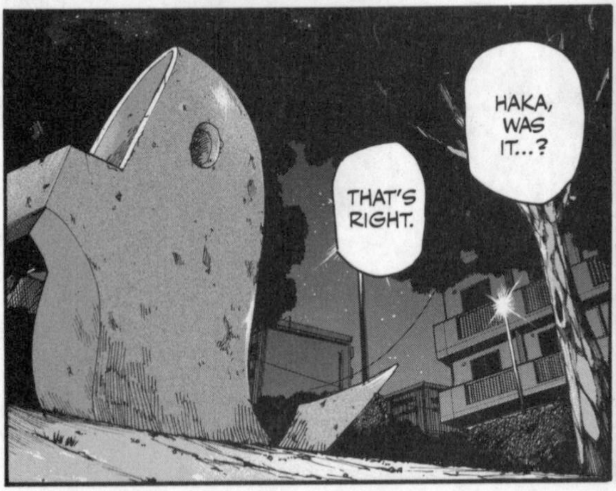
HAKA, WAS IT...?
THAT'S RIGHT.

NIGHT 44: WHAT'S THERE, IS THERE

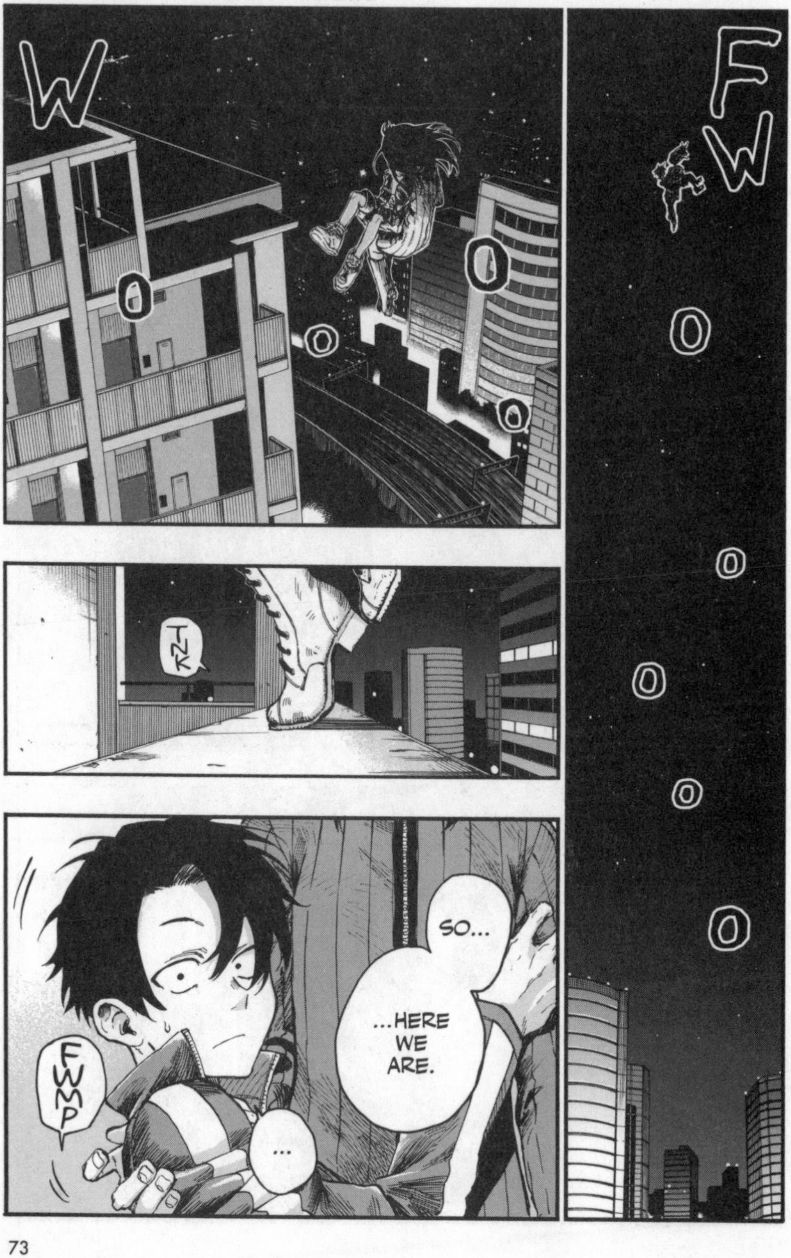
FWOOOOO
WOOOO
TNK
SO...
...HERE WE ARE.
...
FWMP

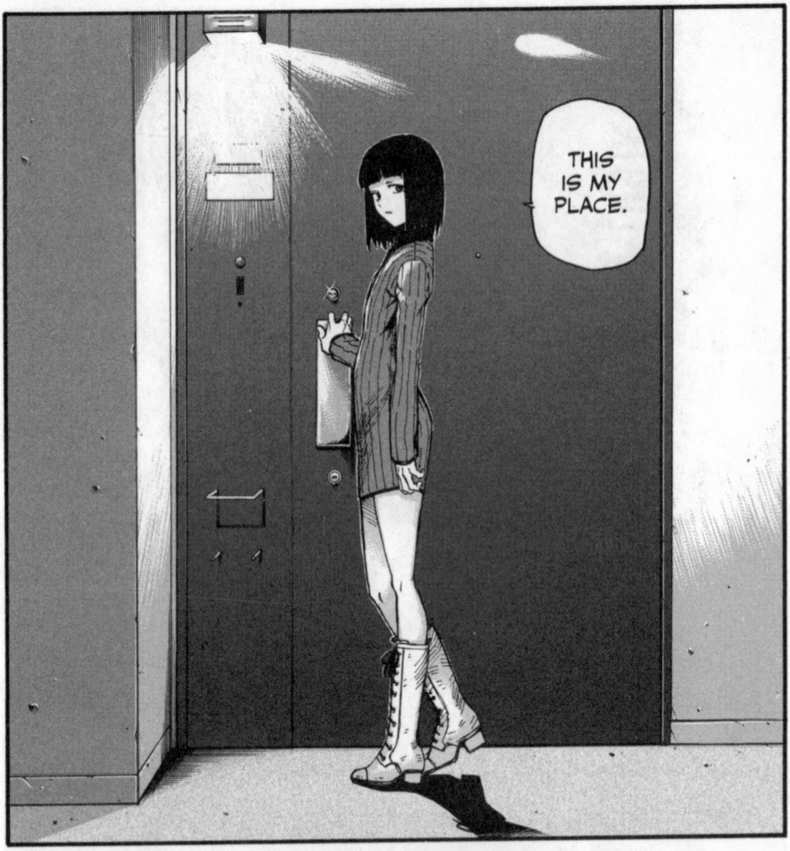
THIS IS MY PLACE.
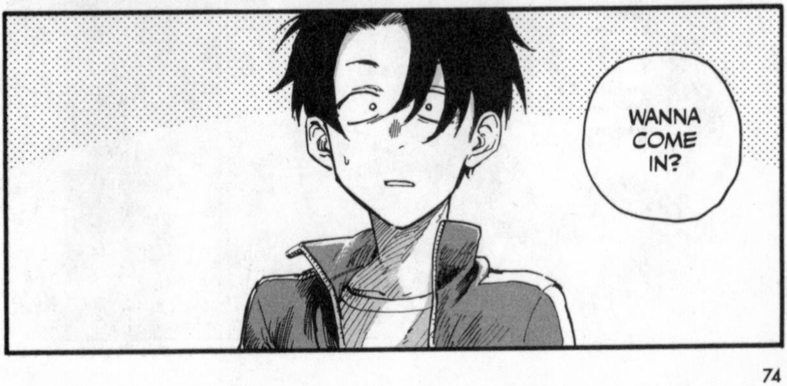
WANNA COME IN?

NIGHT 44: WHAT'S THERE, IS THERE

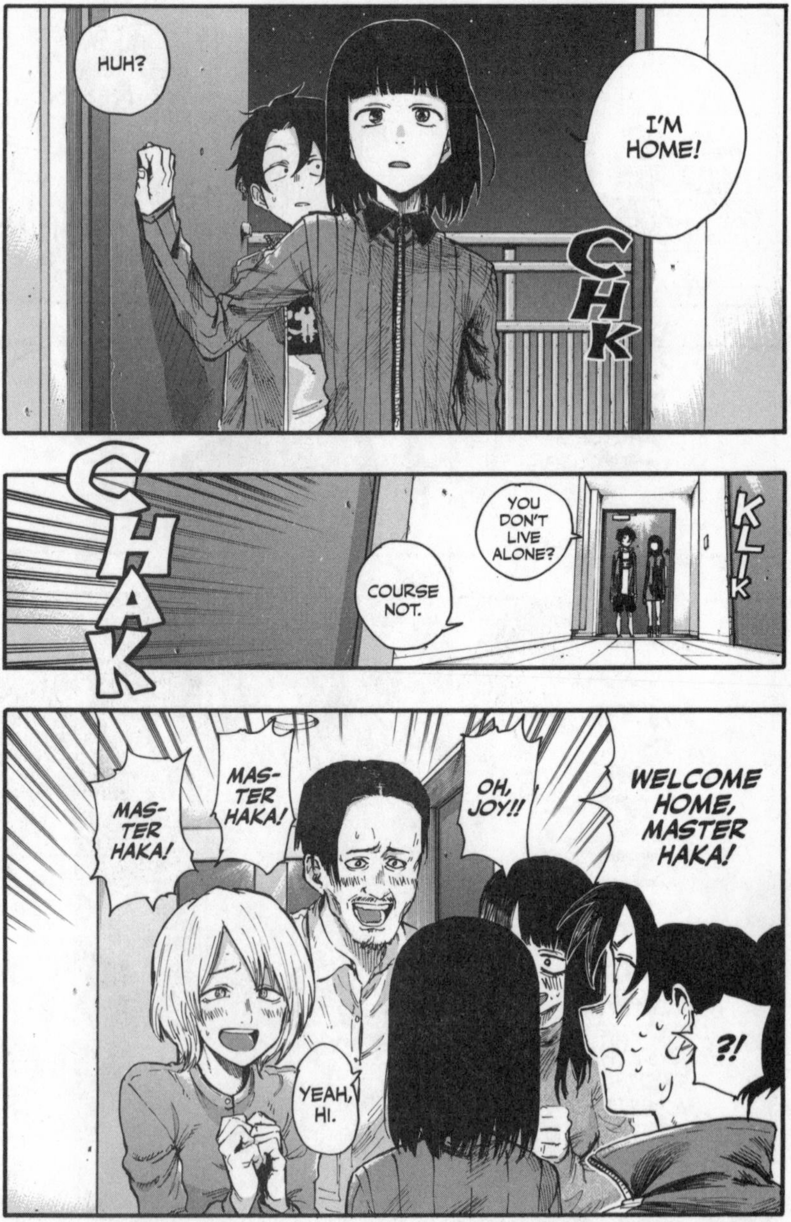
I'M HOME!
CHK
HUH?
KLIK
YOU DON'T LIVE ALONE?
COURSE NOT.
CHAK
WELCOME HOME, MASTER HAKA!
?!
OH, JOY!!
MAS-TER HAKA!
MAS-TER HAKA!
YEAH, HI.

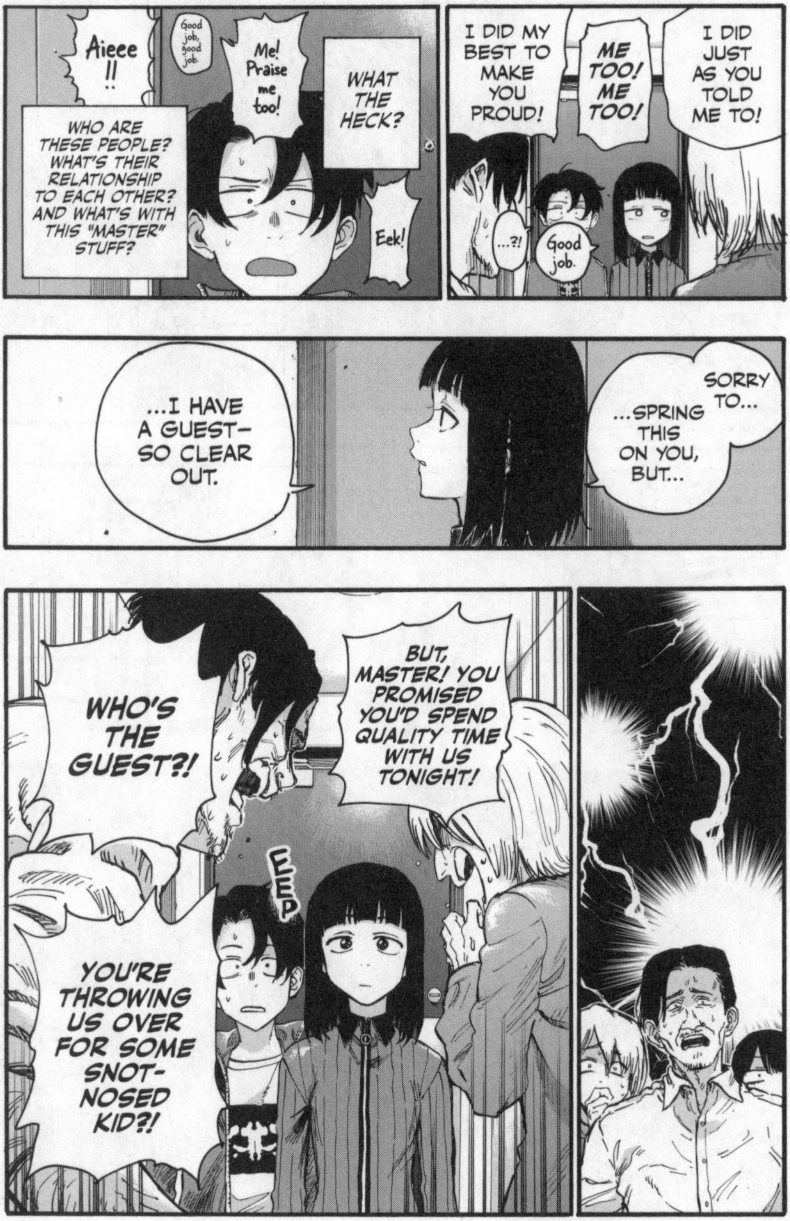
I DID JUST AS YOU TOLD ME TO!
ME TOO! ME TOO!
I DID MY BEST TO MAKE YOU PROUD!
...?!
Good job.
WHAT THE HECK?
Me! Praise me too!
Good job, good job.
Aieee!!
Eek!
WHO ARE THESE PEOPLE? WHAT'S THEIR RELATIONSHIP TO EACH OTHER? AND WHAT'S WITH THIS "MASTER" STUFF?
SORRY TO...
...SPRING THIS ON YOU, BUT...
...I HAVE A GUEST—SO CLEAR OUT.
BUT, MASTER! YOU PROMISED YOU'D SPEND QUALITY TIME WITH US TONIGHT!
WHO'S THE GUEST?!
EEP
YOU'RE THROWING US OVER FOR SOME SNOT-NOSED KID?!

DID YOU HEAR ME?
I TOLD YOU, HE'S MY GUEST.
YIPE
DON'T PUT HIM DOWN.
I DON'T APPROVE OF SUCH BEHAVIOR.
...
HEH
YOU'LL BE GOOD AND DO AS I SAY, WON'T YOU?

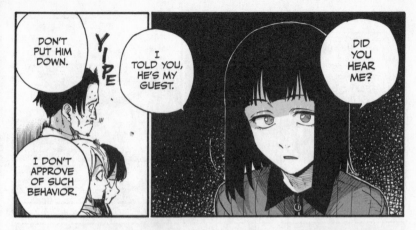

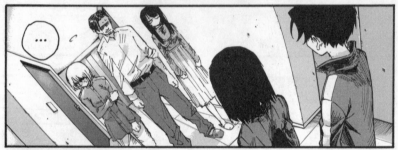

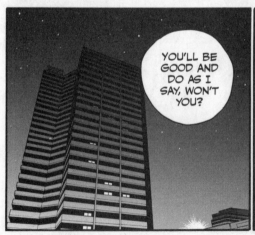

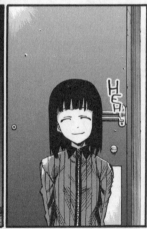

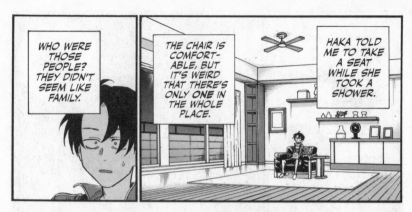

HAKA TOLD ME TO TAKE A SEAT WHILE SHE TOOK A SHOWER.
THE CHAIR IS COMFORTABLE, BUT IT'S WEIRD THAT THERE'S ONLY ONE IN THE WHOLE PLACE.
WHO WERE THOSE PEOPLE? THEY DIDN'T SEEM LIKE FAMILY.
THEY MUST BE HUMANS WHO WANT TO GET TURNED.
BUT THEY WERE BOTH MEN AND WOMEN...
I GUESS THAT'S HOW IT GOES.
WHAT'S HAKA'S DEAL?
SHE SEEMS DIFFERENT FROM THE OTHER VAMPIRES I'VE MET. OR MAYBE SHE'S NORMAL AND THE OTHERS ARE WEIRD?
...
I DON'T KNOW MUCH ABOUT VAMPIRES.
INSTEAD OF EXPLAINING THINGS...
...THE DETECTIVE LADY REPORTED ME TO THE COPS!
SHE'S RUINING MY NIGHT LIFE!
WHAT SHOULD I DO?
I'M GETTING OUT OF MY DEPTH...
HEY, YAMORI! COULD YOU COME HERE FOR A SEC?

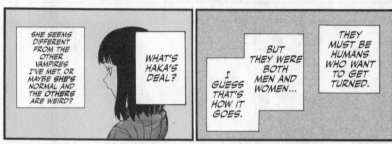

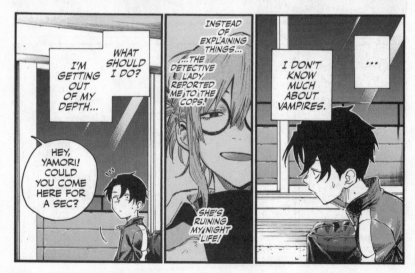

I FORGOT MY TOWEL.
MIND GRABBING ME ONE?
I TOTALLY FORGOT.
I NEVER HAVE TO FETCH IT MYSELF.
I CAN'T BELIEVE HAKA JUST OPENED THE DOOR!
I CAN'T HELP IT, BUT MY EYES ARE MOVING DOWN...
MY BRAIN HAS STOPPED WORKING.
IT'S TAKING MY BRAIN A SECOND TO ACCEPT THAT WHAT'S THERE, IS THERE.
♂

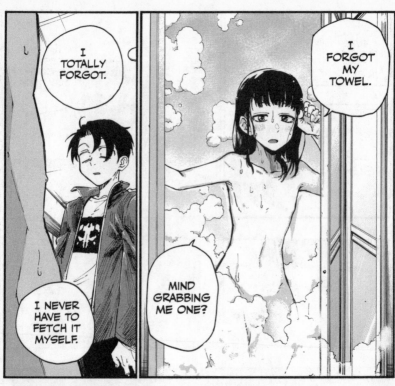

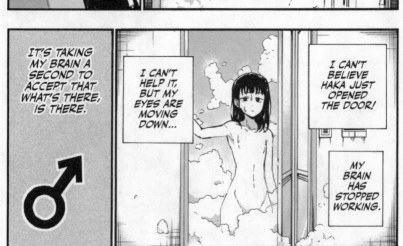

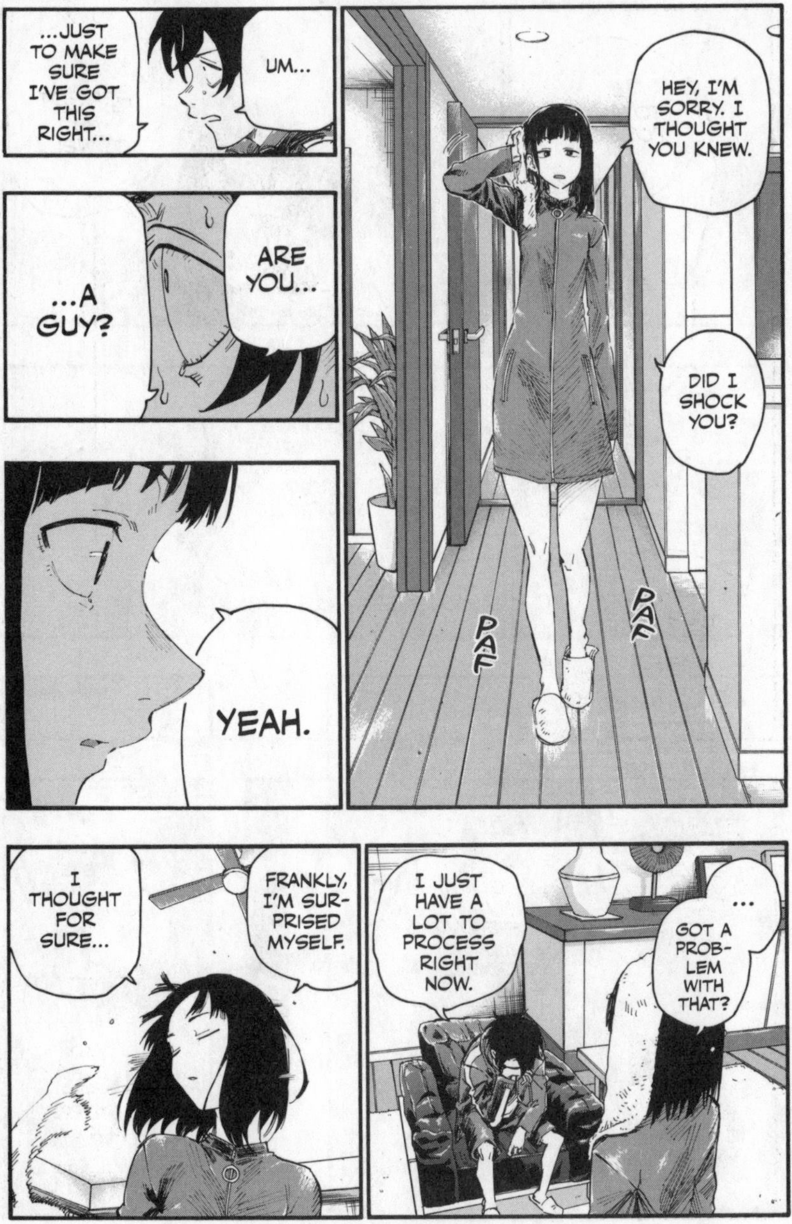
HEY, I'M SORRY. I THOUGHT YOU KNEW.
DID I SHOCK YOU?
PAF
PAF
UM...
...JUST TO MAKE SURE I'VE GOT THIS RIGHT...
ARE YOU...
...A GUY?
YEAH.
... GOT A PROB-LEM WITH THAT?
I JUST HAVE A LOT TO PROCESS RIGHT NOW.
FRANKLY, I'M SUR-PRISED MYSELF.
I THOUGHT FOR SURE...

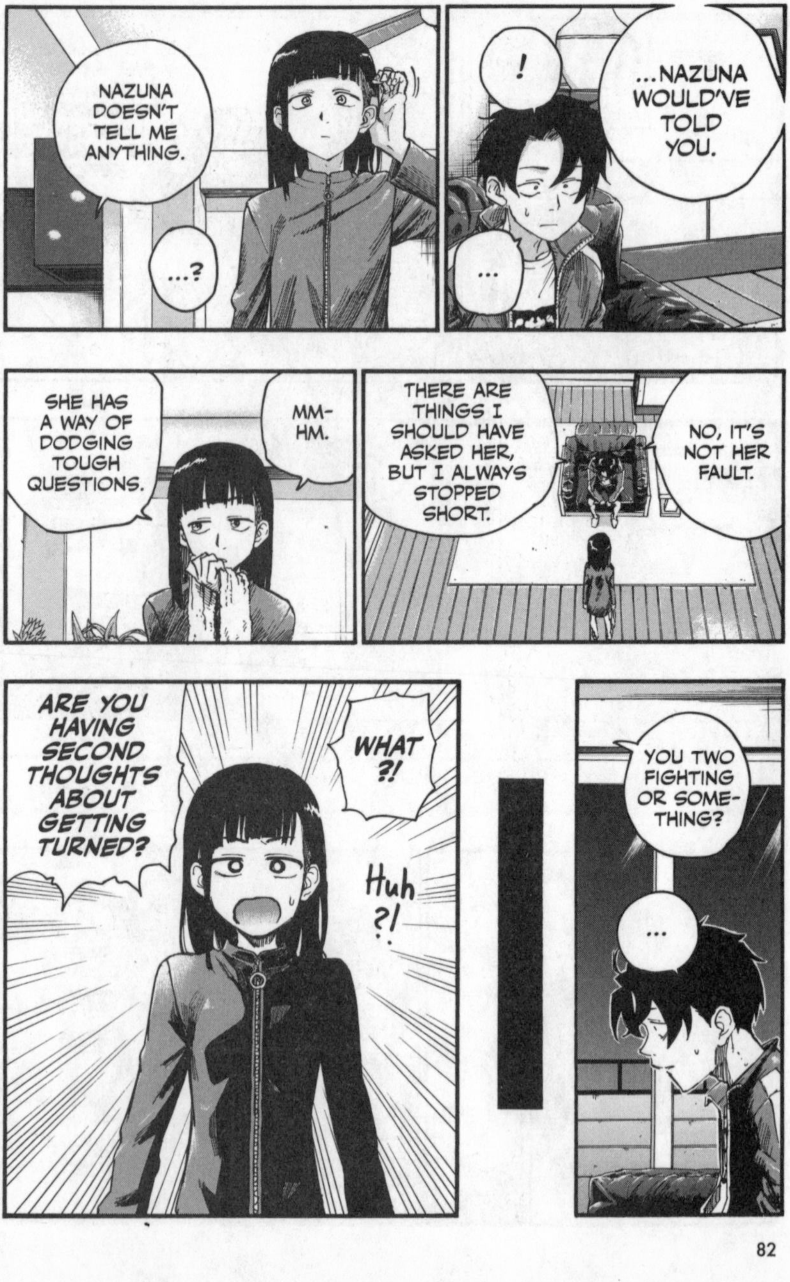
...NAZUNA WOULD'VE TOLD YOU.
!
...
NAZUNA DOESN'T TELL ME ANYTHING.
...?
NO, IT'S NOT HER FAULT.
THERE ARE THINGS I SHOULD HAVE ASKED HER, BUT I ALWAYS STOPPED SHORT.
MM-HM.
SHE HAS A WAY OF DODGING TOUGH QUESTIONS.
YOU TWO FIGHTING OR SOME-THING?
...
WHAT?!
ARE YOU HAVING SECOND THOUGHTS ABOUT GETTING TURNED?
Huh?!

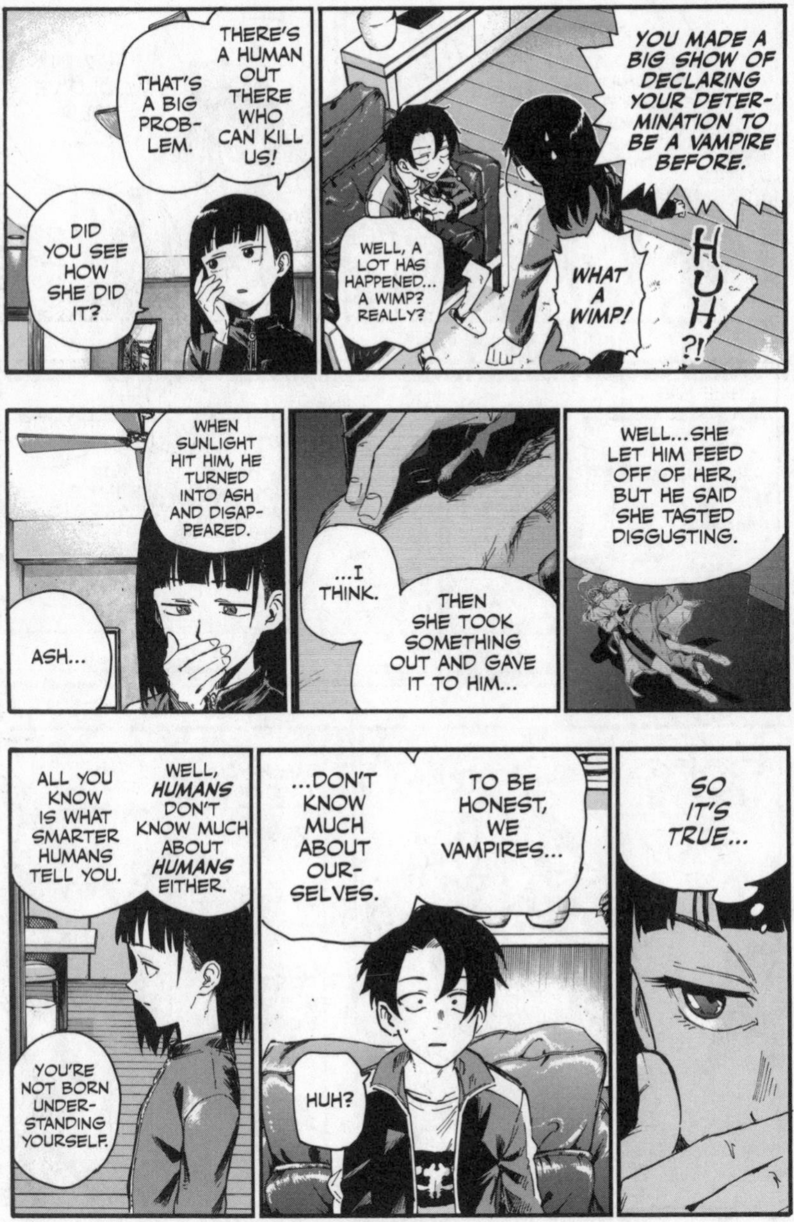

YOU MADE A BIG SHOW OF DECLARING YOUR DETERMINATION TO BE A VAMPIRE BEFORE.
HUH?!
WHAT A WIMP!
WELL, A LOT HAS HAPPENED... A WIMP? REALLY?
THERE'S A HUMAN OUT THERE WHO CAN KILL US!
THAT'S A BIG PROBLEM.
DID YOU SEE HOW SHE DID IT?
WELL...SHE LET HIM FEED OFF OF HER, BUT HE SAID SHE TASTED DISGUSTING.
THEN SHE TOOK SOMETHING OUT AND GAVE IT TO HIM...
...I THINK.
WHEN SUNLIGHT HIT HIM, HE TURNED INTO ASH AND DISAPPEARED.
ASH...
SO IT'S TRUE...
TO BE HONEST, WE VAMPIRES...
...DON'T KNOW MUCH ABOUT OURSELVES.
HUH?
WELL, HUMANS DON'T KNOW MUCH ABOUT HUMANS EITHER.
ALL YOU KNOW IS WHAT SMARTER HUMANS TELL YOU.
YOU'RE NOT BORN UNDERSTANDING YOURSELF.

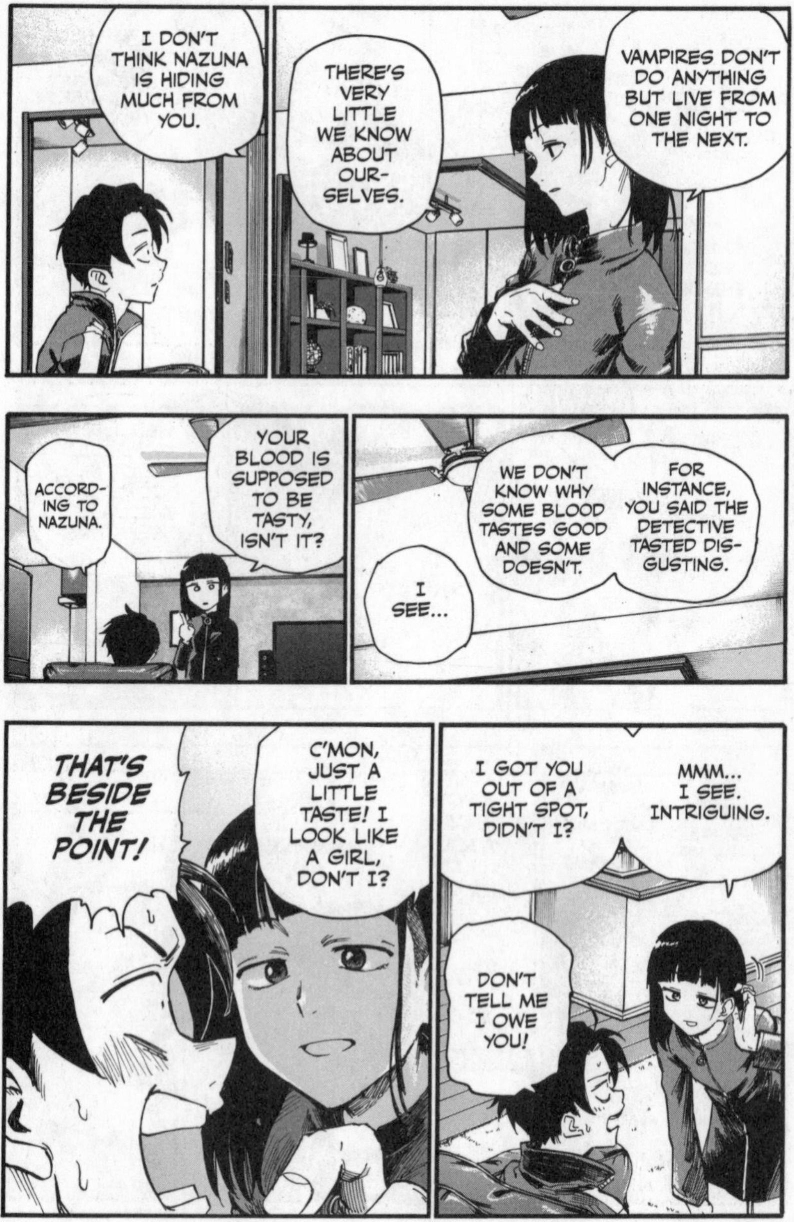
VAMPIRES DON'T DO ANYTHING BUT LIVE FROM ONE NIGHT TO THE NEXT.
THERE'S VERY LITTLE WE KNOW ABOUT OUR-SELVES.
I DON'T THINK NAZUNA IS HIDING MUCH FROM YOU.
FOR INSTANCE, YOU SAID THE DETECTIVE TASTED DIS-GUSTING.
WE DON'T KNOW WHY SOME BLOOD TASTES GOOD AND SOME DOESN'T.
I SEE...
YOUR BLOOD IS SUPPOSED TO BE TASTY, ISN'T IT?
ACCORD-ING TO NAZUNA.
MMM... I SEE. INTRIGUING.
I GOT YOU OUT OF A TIGHT SPOT, DIDN'T I?
DON'T TELL ME I OWE YOU!
C'MON, JUST A LITTLE TASTE! I LOOK LIKE A GIRL, DON'T I?
THAT'S BESIDE THE POINT!

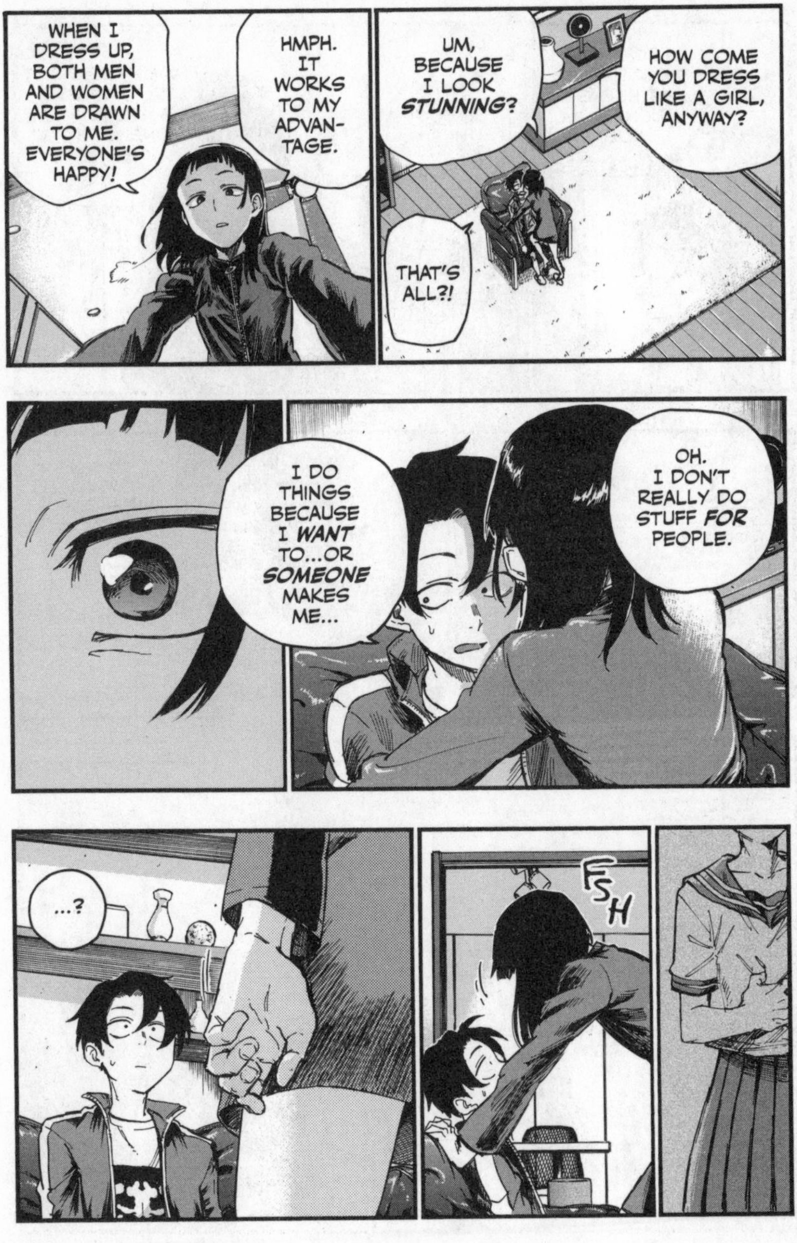
HOW COME YOU DRESS LIKE A GIRL, ANYWAY?
UM, BECAUSE I LOOK *STUNNING*?
THAT'S ALL?!
HMPH. IT WORKS TO MY ADVANTAGE.
WHEN I DRESS UP, BOTH MEN AND WOMEN ARE DRAWN TO ME. EVERYONE'S HAPPY!
OH. I DON'T REALLY DO STUFF ***FOR*** PEOPLE.
I DO THINGS BECAUSE I ***WANT*** TO...OR ***SOMEONE*** MAKES ME...
FSH
...?

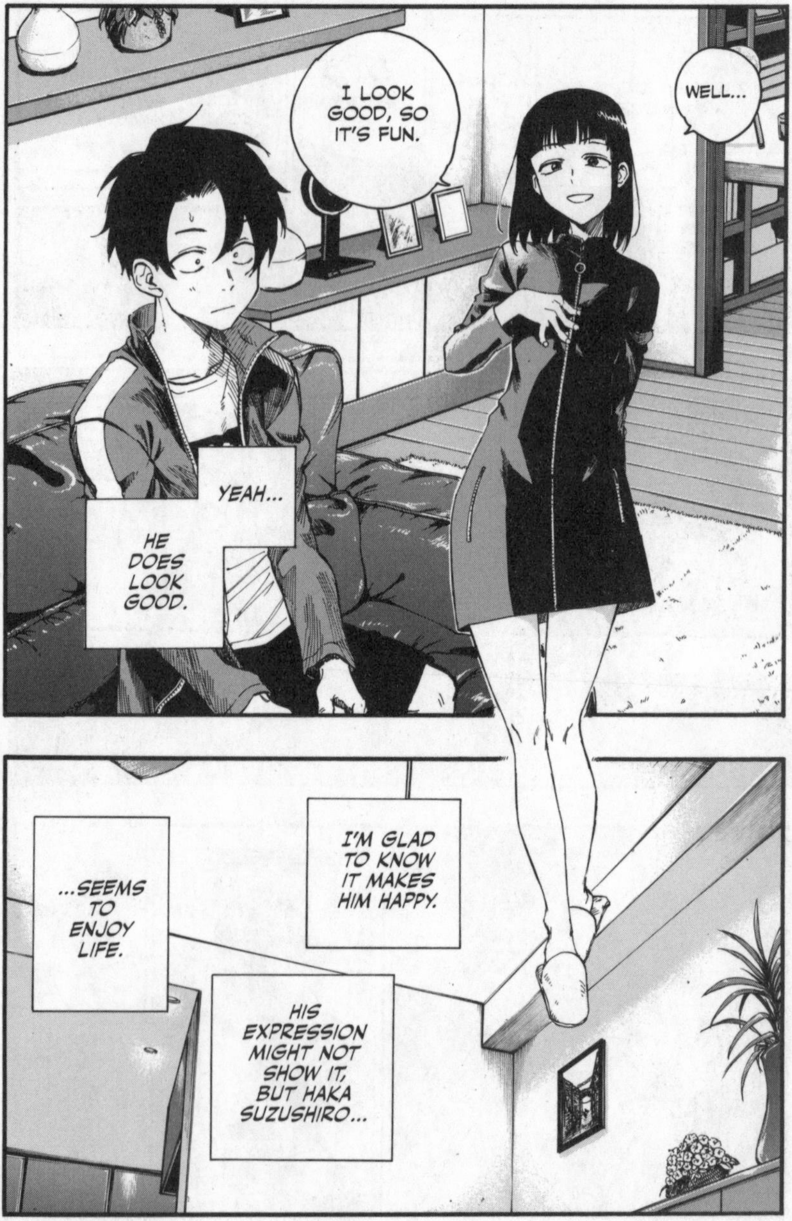
WELL...
I LOOK GOOD, SO IT'S FUN.
YEAH...
HE DOES LOOK GOOD.
HIS EXPRESSION MIGHT NOT SHOW IT, BUT HAKA SUZUSHIRO...
...SEEMS TO ENJOY LIFE.
I'M GLAD TO KNOW IT MAKES HIM HAPPY.

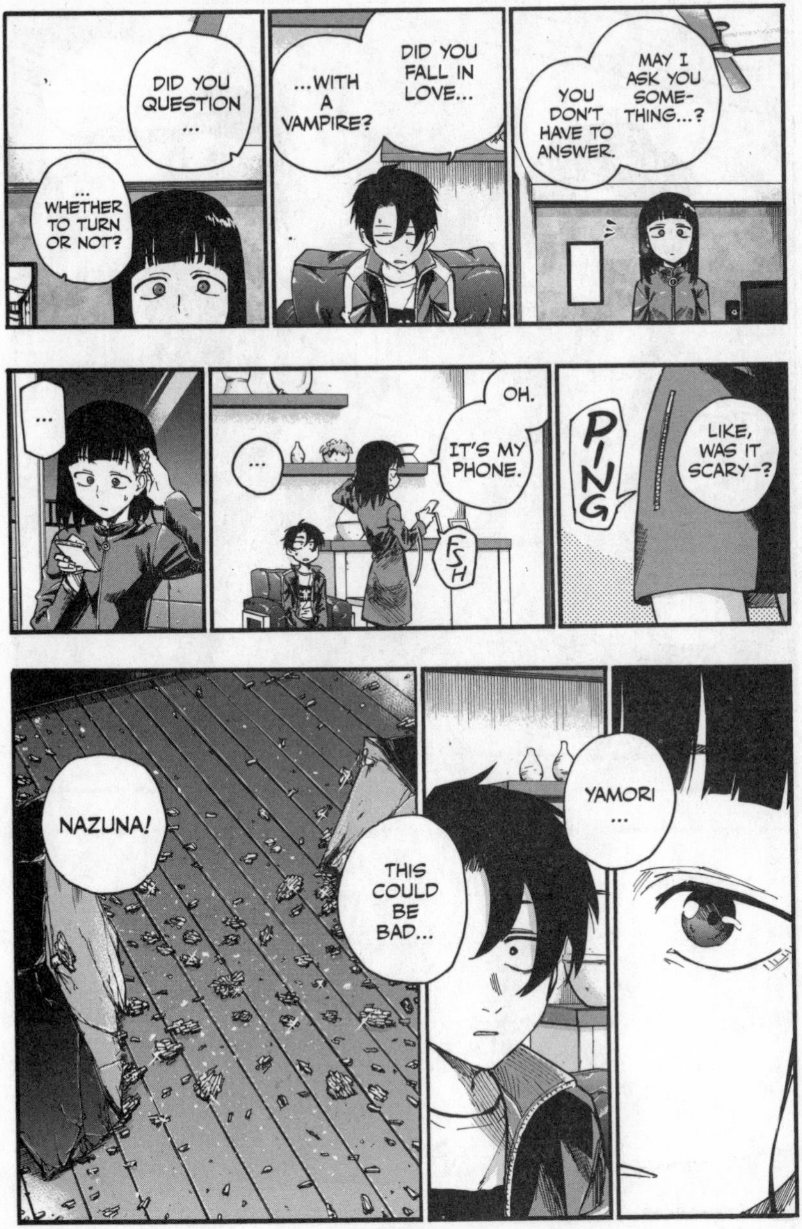
MAY I ASK YOU SOME-THING...?
YOU DON'T HAVE TO ANSWER.
DID YOU FALL IN LOVE...
...WITH A VAMPIRE?
DID YOU QUESTION ...
... WHETHER TO TURN OR NOT?
LIKE, WAS IT SCARY—?
PING
OH.
IT'S MY PHONE.
FSH
...
...
YAMORI ...
THIS COULD BE BAD...
NAZUNA!

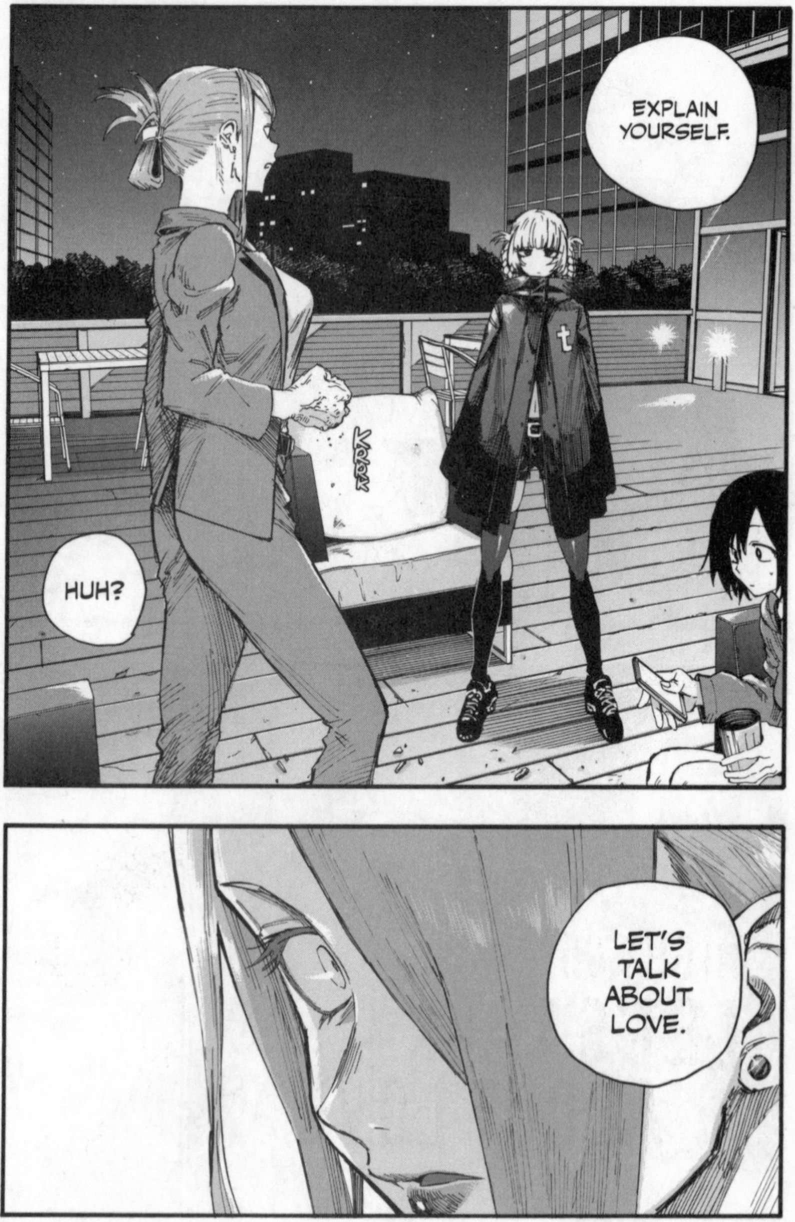
EXPLAIN YOURSELF.
KRRRK
HUH?
LET'S TALK ABOUT LOVE.

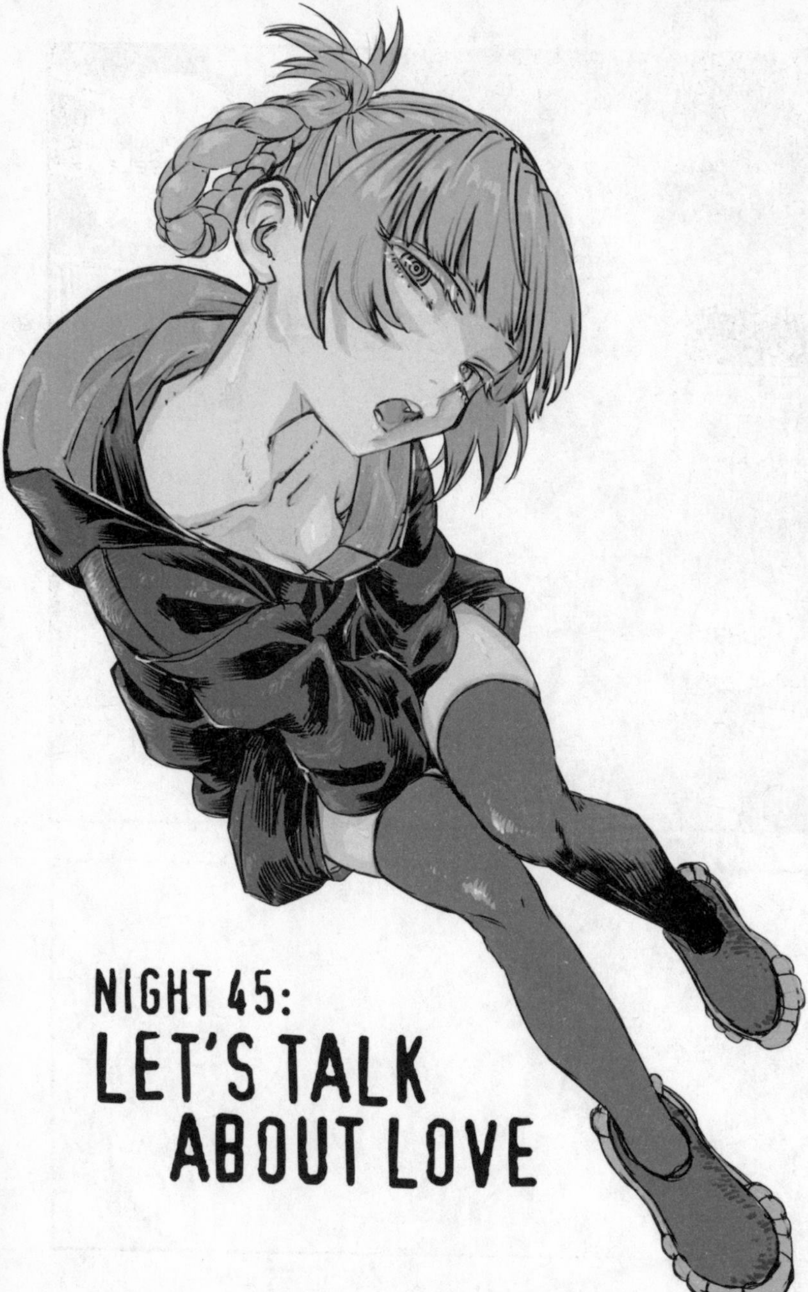

NIGHT 45: LET'S TALK ABOUT LOVE

Call of the Night

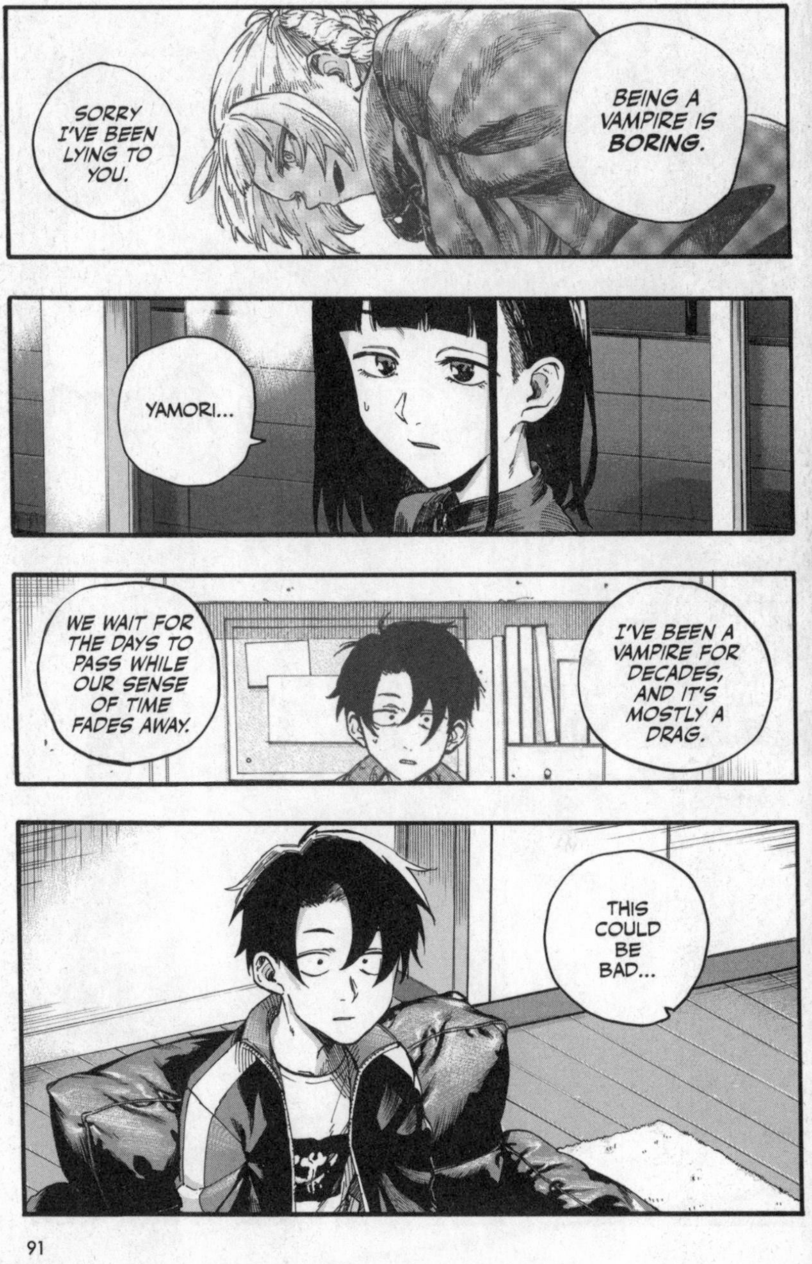
BEING A VAMPIRE IS BORING.
SORRY I'VE BEEN LYING TO YOU.
YAMORI...
I'VE BEEN A VAMPIRE FOR DECADES, AND IT'S MOSTLY A DRAG.
WE WAIT FOR THE DAYS TO PASS WHILE OUR SENSE OF TIME FADES AWAY.
THIS COULD BE BAD...

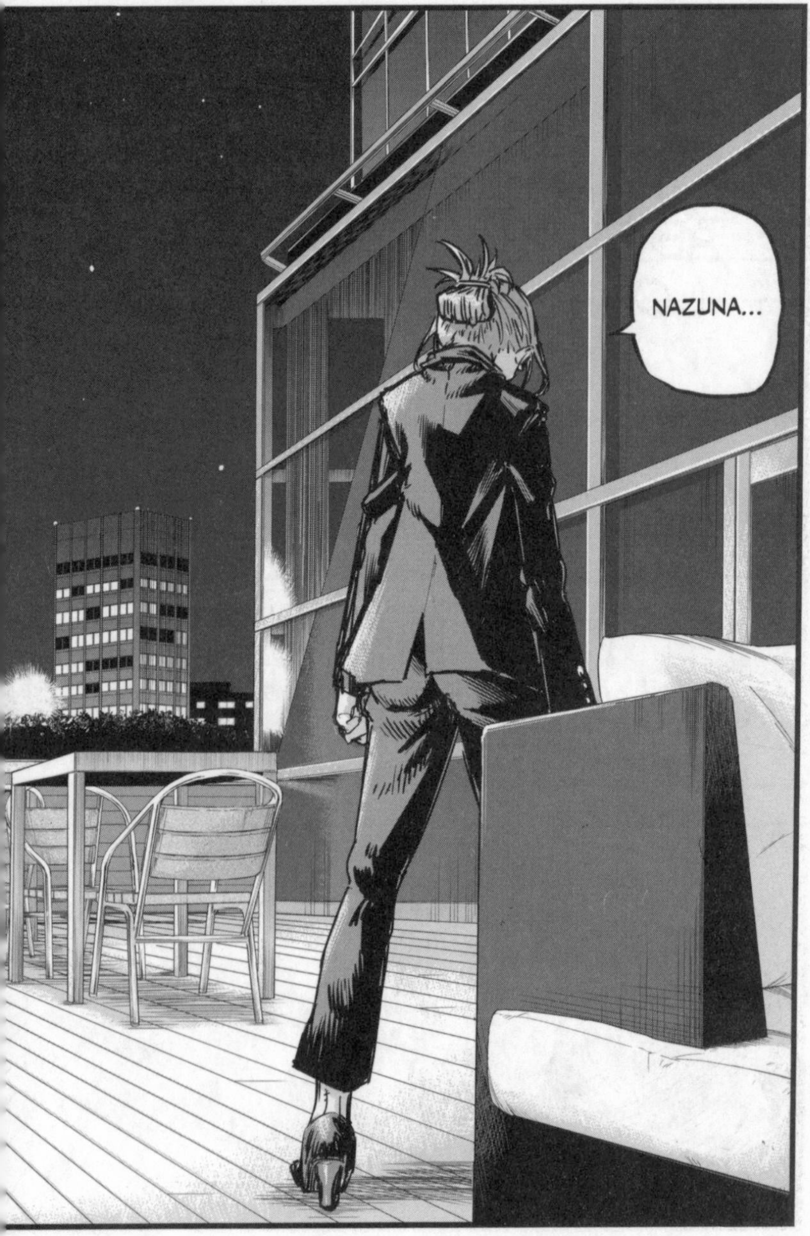
NAZUNA...

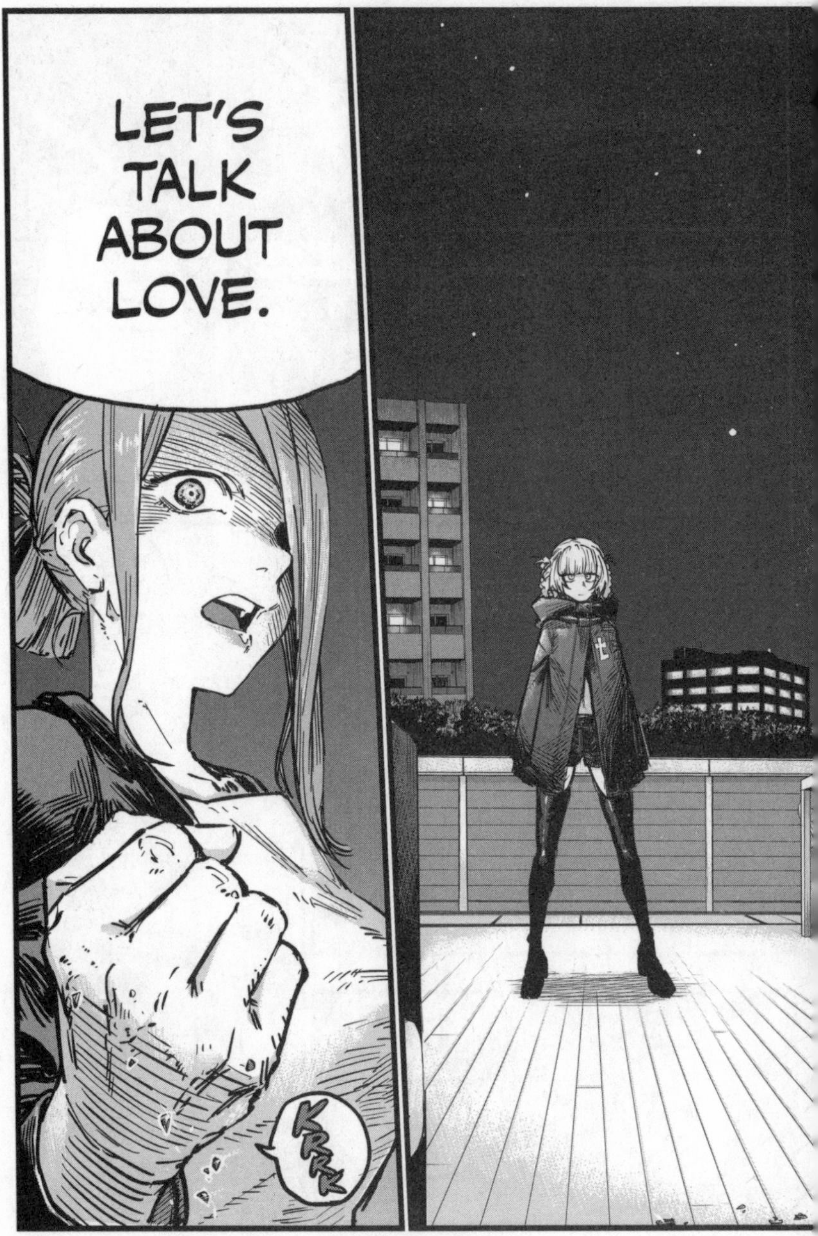
LET'S TALK ABOUT LOVE.
KRRK

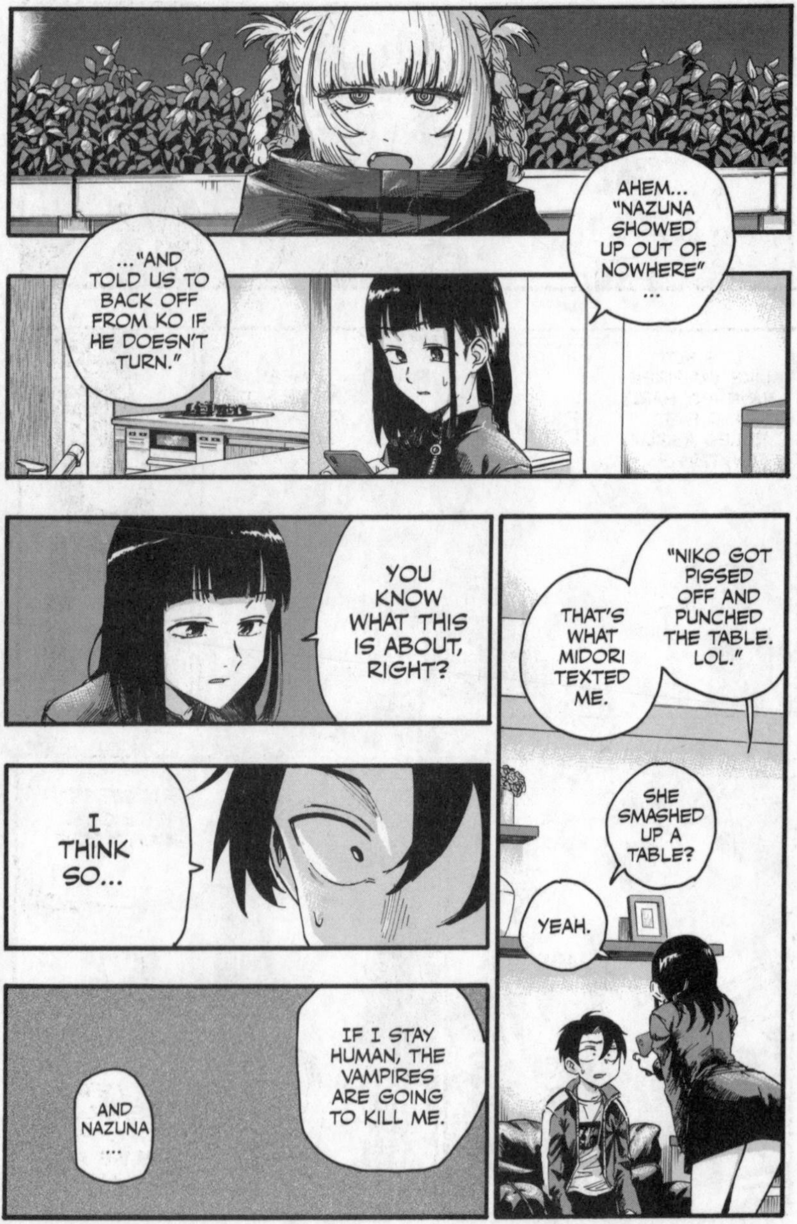
AHEM... "NAZUNA SHOWED UP OUT OF NOWHERE" ...
..."AND TOLD US TO BACK OFF FROM KO IF HE DOESN'T TURN."
"NIKO GOT PISSED OFF AND PUNCHED THE TABLE. LOL."
THAT'S WHAT MIDORI TEXTED ME.
SHE SMASHED UP A TABLE?
YEAH.
YOU KNOW WHAT THIS IS ABOUT, RIGHT?
I THINK SO...
IF I STAY HUMAN, THE VAMPIRES ARE GOING TO KILL ME.
AND NAZUNA ...

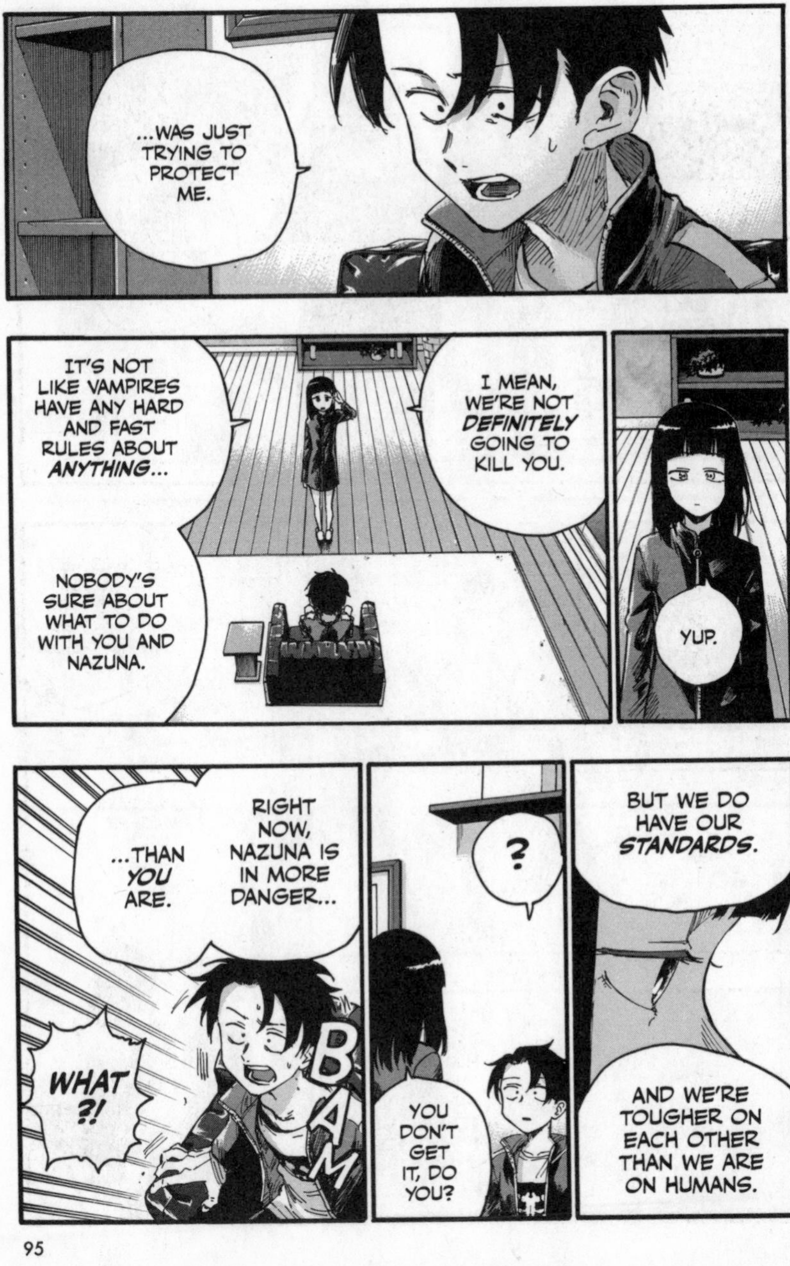
...WAS JUST TRYING TO PROTECT ME.
YUP.
I MEAN, WE'RE NOT *DEFINITELY* GOING TO KILL YOU.
IT'S NOT LIKE VAMPIRES HAVE ANY HARD AND FAST RULES ABOUT *ANYTHING*...
NOBODY'S SURE ABOUT WHAT TO DO WITH YOU AND NAZUNA.
BUT WE DO HAVE OUR *STANDARDS*.
AND WE'RE TOUGHER ON EACH OTHER THAN WE ARE ON HUMANS.
?
YOU DON'T GET IT, DO YOU?
RIGHT NOW, NAZUNA IS IN MORE DANGER...
...THAN *YOU* ARE.
BAM
WHAT ?!

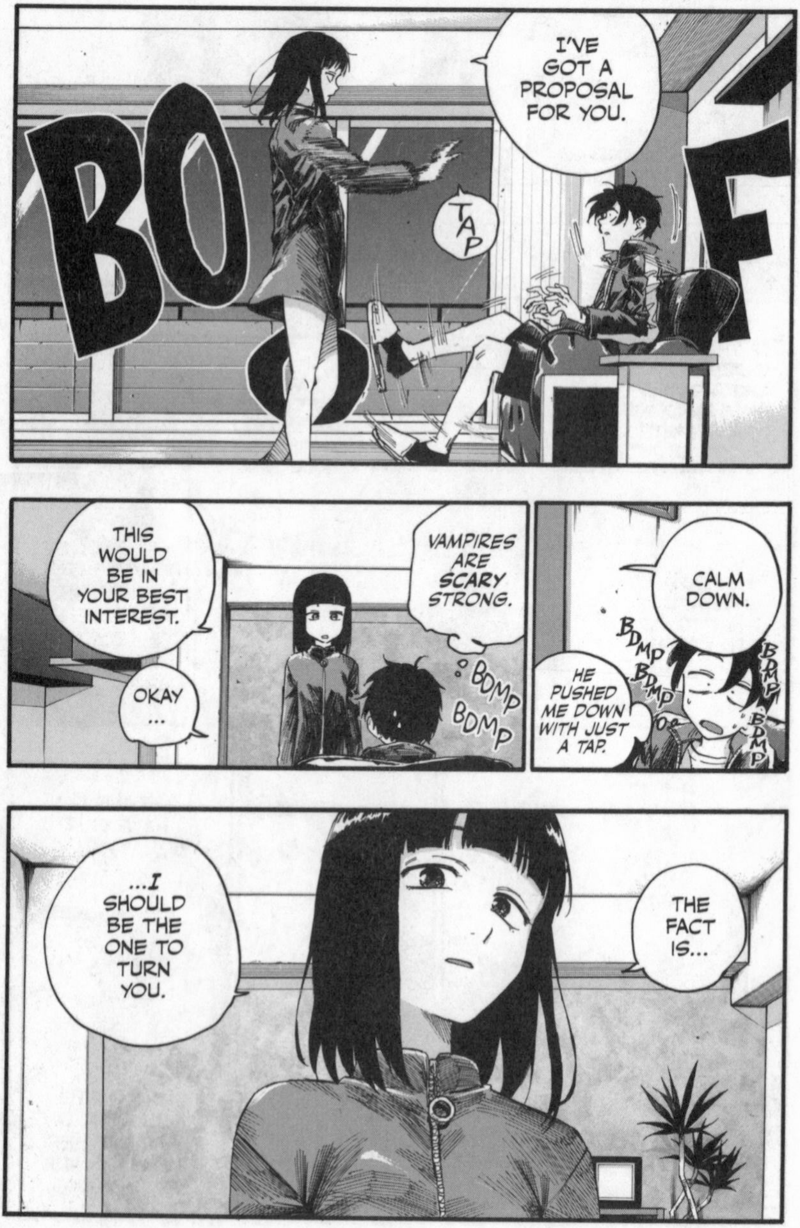
I'VE GOT A PROPOSAL FOR YOU.
TAP
BOF
CALM DOWN.
BDMP BDMP
HE PUSHED ME DOWN WITH JUST A TAP.
BDMP BDMP
VAMPIRES ARE SCARY STRONG.
BDMP BDMP
THIS WOULD BE IN YOUR BEST INTEREST.
OKAY ...
THE FACT IS...
...I SHOULD BE THE ONE TO TURN YOU.

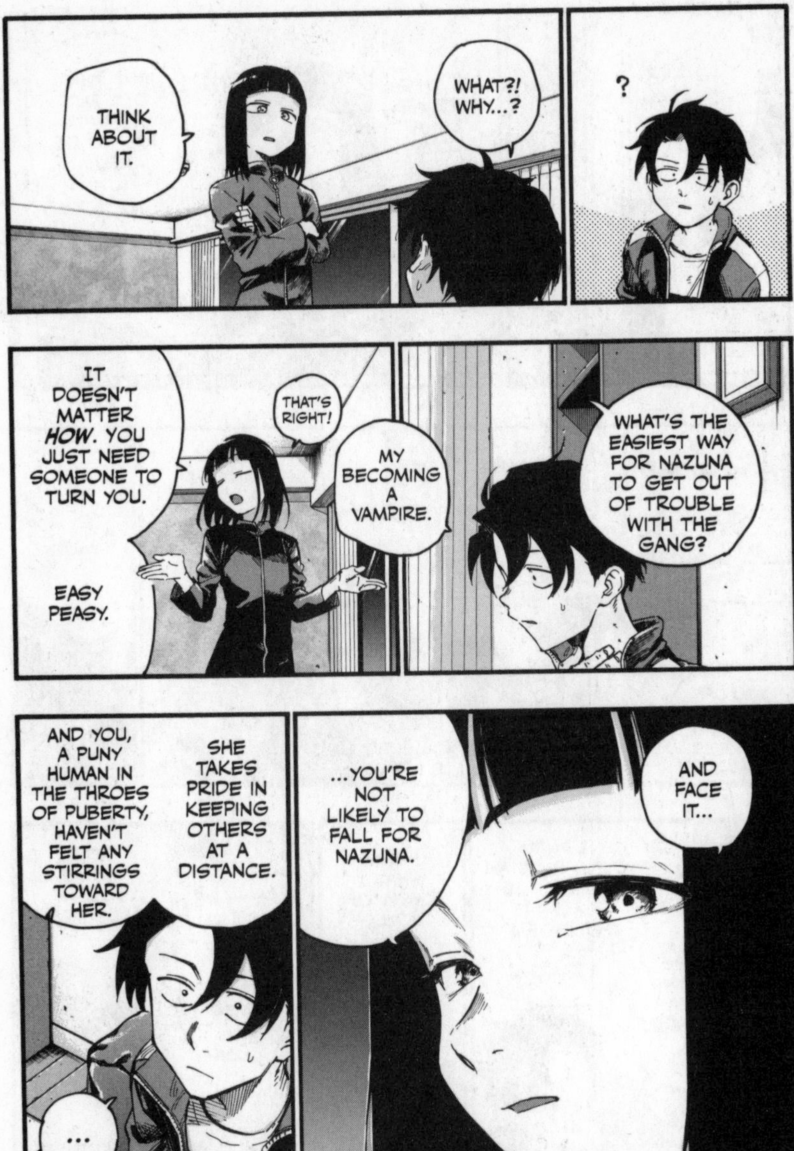
?
WHAT?! WHY...?
THINK ABOUT IT.
WHAT'S THE EASIEST WAY FOR NAZUNA TO GET OUT OF TROUBLE WITH THE GANG?
MY BECOMING A VAMPIRE.
THAT'S RIGHT!
IT DOESN'T MATTER *HOW*. YOU JUST NEED SOMEONE TO TURN YOU.
EASY PEASY.
AND FACE IT...
...YOU'RE NOT LIKELY TO FALL FOR NAZUNA.
SHE TAKES PRIDE IN KEEPING OTHERS AT A DISTANCE.
AND YOU, A PUNY HUMAN IN THE THROES OF PUBERTY, HAVEN'T FELT ANY STIRRINGS TOWARD HER.
...

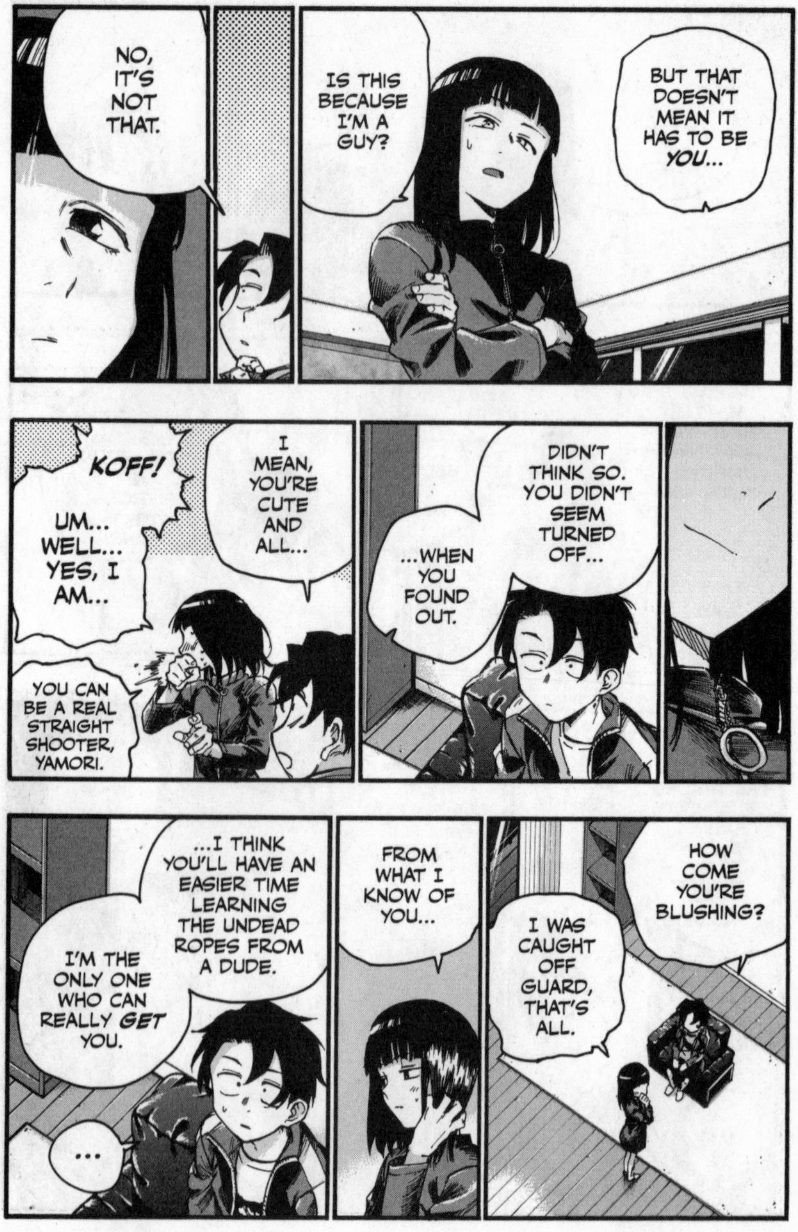
BUT THAT DOESN'T MEAN IT HAS TO BE *YOU*...
IS THIS BECAUSE I'M A GUY?
NO, IT'S NOT THAT.
DIDN'T THINK SO. YOU DIDN'T SEEM TURNED OFF...
...WHEN YOU FOUND OUT.
I MEAN, YOU'RE CUTE AND ALL...
KOFF!
UM... WELL... YES, I AM...
YOU CAN BE A REAL STRAIGHT SHOOTER, YAMORI.
HOW COME YOU'RE BLUSHING?
I WAS CAUGHT OFF GUARD, THAT'S ALL.
FROM WHAT I KNOW OF YOU...
...I THINK YOU'LL HAVE AN EASIER TIME LEARNING THE UNDEAD ROPES FROM A DUDE.
I'M THE ONLY ONE WHO CAN REALLY *GET* YOU.
...

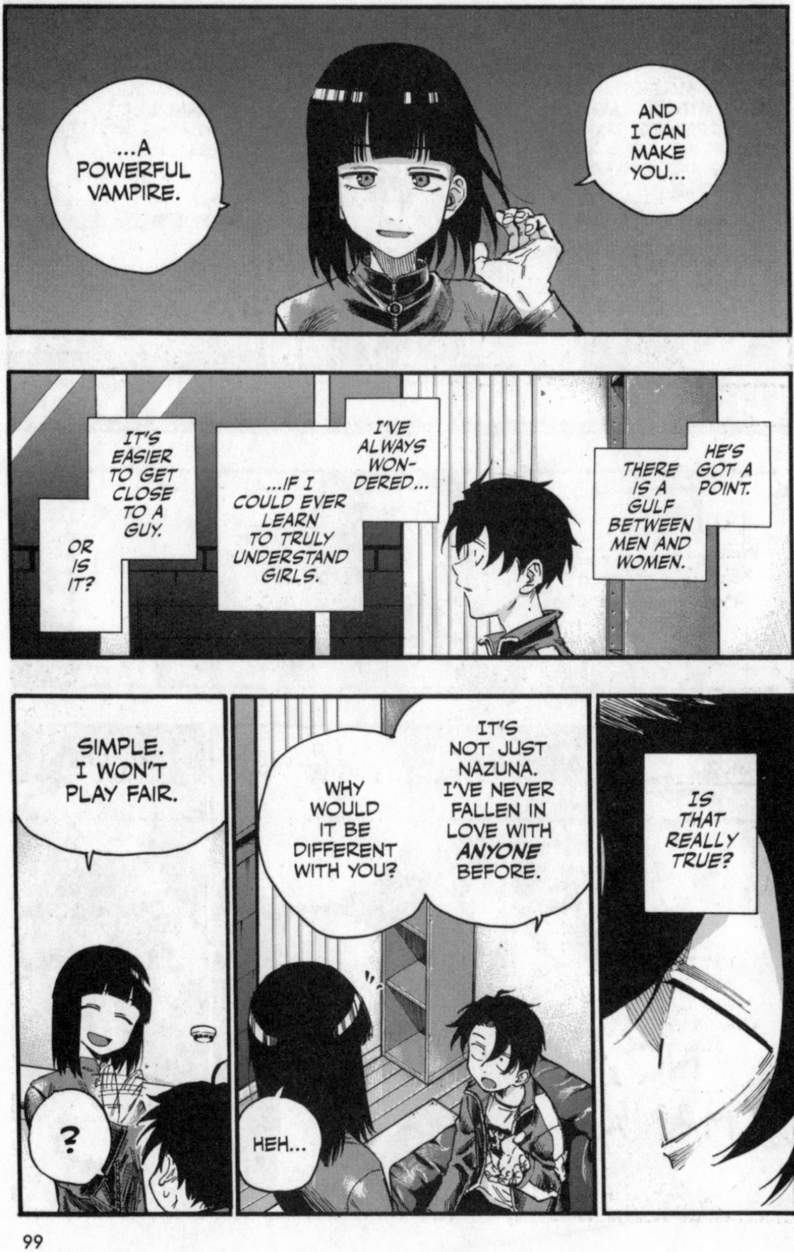
AND I CAN MAKE YOU...
...A POWERFUL VAMPIRE.
HE'S GOT A POINT.
THERE IS A GULF BETWEEN MEN AND WOMEN.
I'VE ALWAYS WONDERED...
...IF I COULD EVER LEARN TO TRULY UNDERSTAND GIRLS.
IT'S EASIER TO GET CLOSE TO A GUY.
OR IS IT?
IS THAT REALLY TRUE?
IT'S NOT JUST NAZUNA. I'VE NEVER FALLEN IN LOVE WITH *ANYONE* BEFORE.
WHY WOULD IT BE DIFFERENT WITH YOU?
HEH...
SIMPLE. I WON'T PLAY FAIR.
?

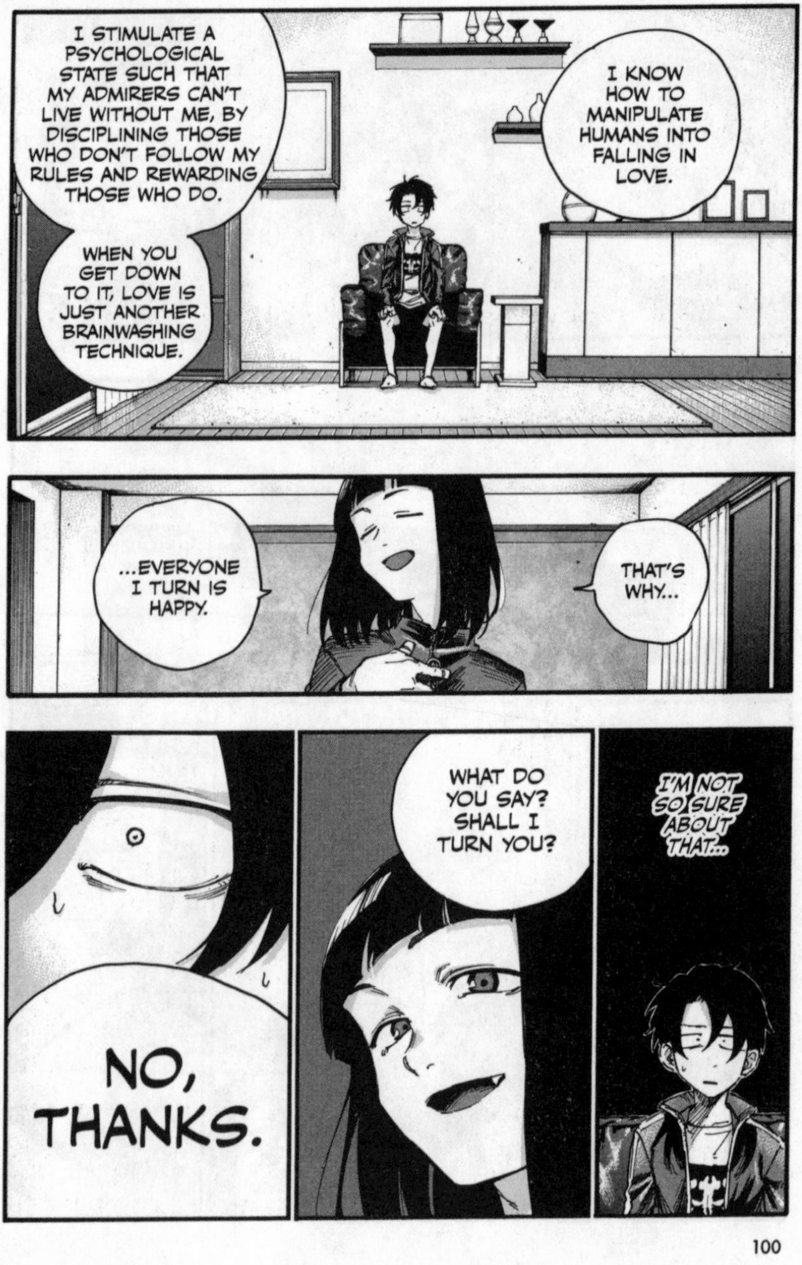
I KNOW HOW TO MANIPULATE HUMANS INTO FALLING IN LOVE.
I STIMULATE A PSYCHOLOGICAL STATE SUCH THAT MY ADMIRERS CAN'T LIVE WITHOUT ME, BY DISCIPLINING THOSE WHO DON'T FOLLOW MY RULES AND REWARDING THOSE WHO DO.
WHEN YOU GET DOWN TO IT, LOVE IS JUST ANOTHER BRAINWASHING TECHNIQUE.
THAT'S WHY...
...EVERYONE I TURN IS HAPPY.
I'M NOT SO SURE ABOUT THAT...
WHAT DO YOU SAY? SHALL I TURN YOU?
NO, THANKS.

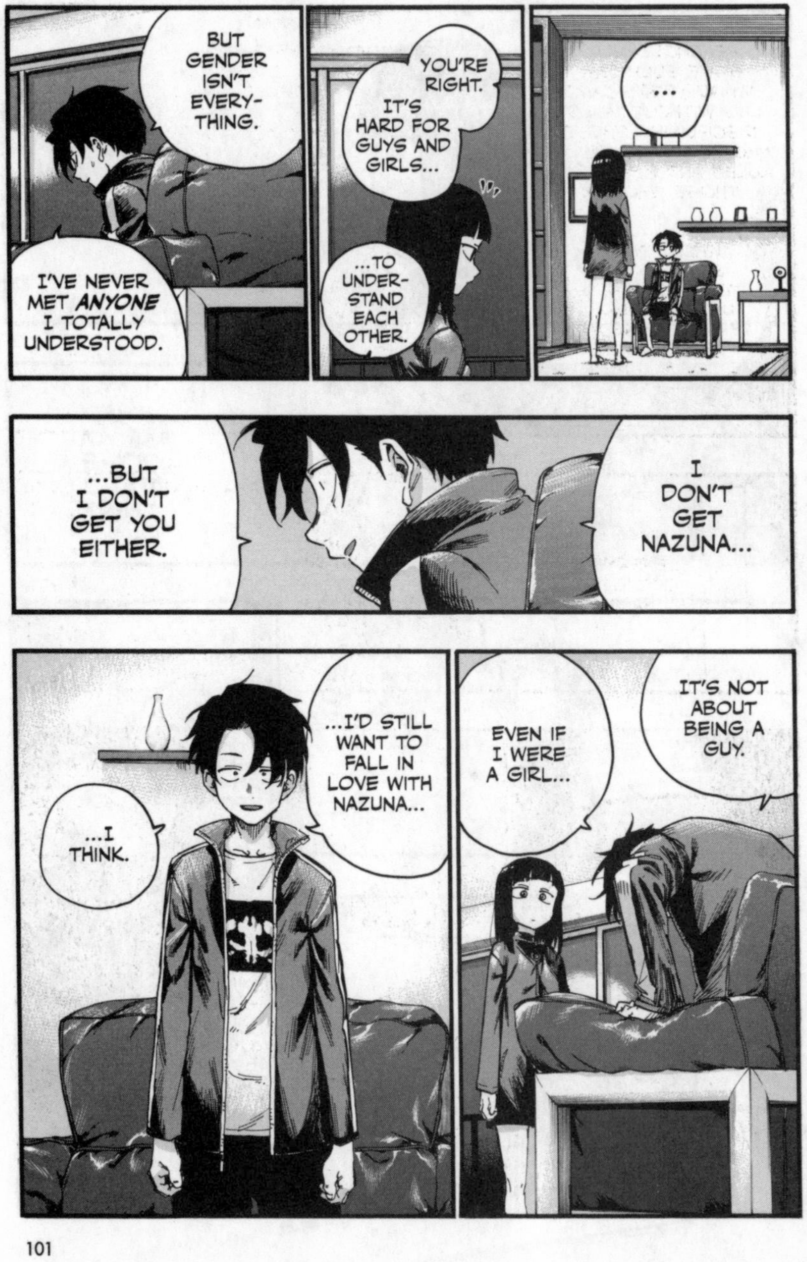
...
YOU'RE RIGHT. IT'S HARD FOR GUYS AND GIRLS...
...TO UNDERSTAND EACH OTHER.
BUT GENDER ISN'T EVERYTHING.
I'VE NEVER MET *ANYONE* I TOTALLY UNDERSTOOD.
I DON'T GET NAZUNA...
...BUT I DON'T GET YOU EITHER.
IT'S NOT ABOUT BEING A GUY.
EVEN IF I WERE A GIRL...
...I'D STILL WANT TO FALL IN LOVE WITH NAZUNA...
...I THINK.

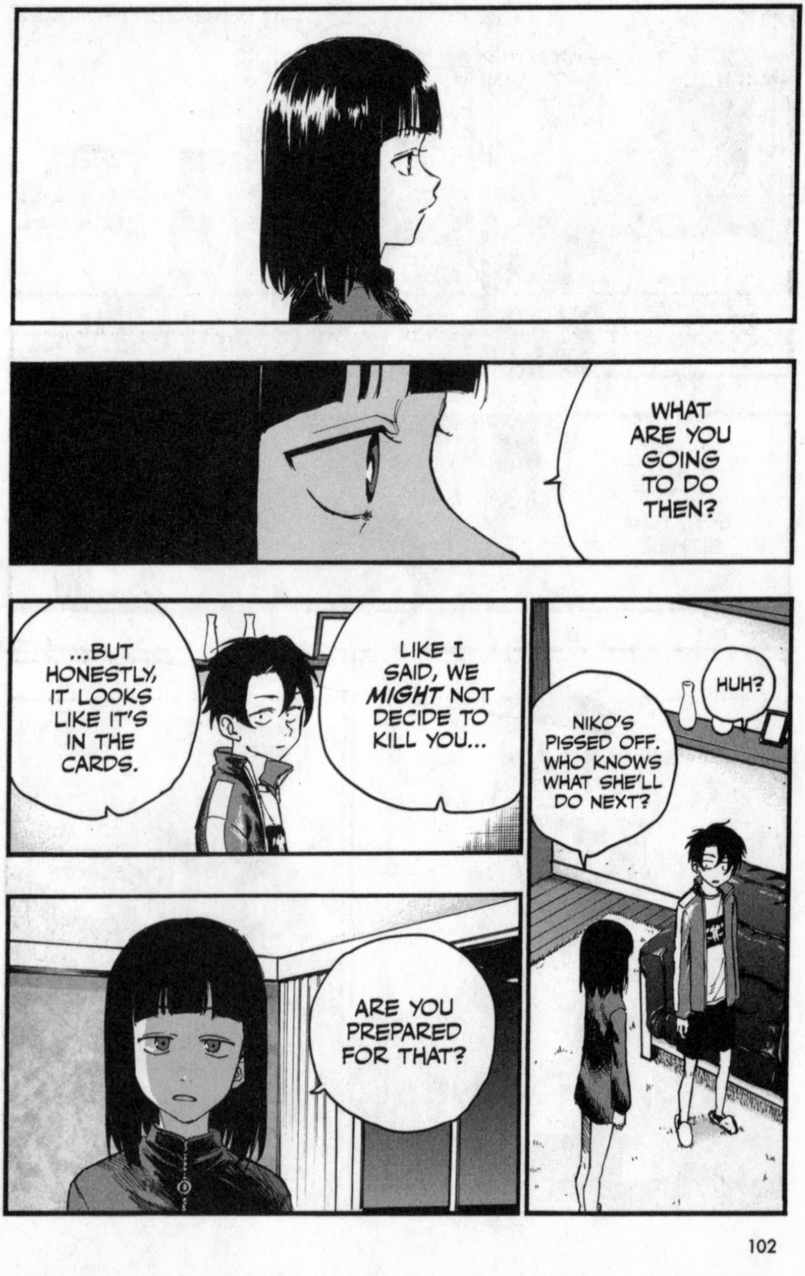
WHAT ARE YOU GOING TO DO THEN?
HUH?
NIKO'S PISSED OFF. WHO KNOWS WHAT SHE'LL DO NEXT?
LIKE I SAID, WE *MIGHT* NOT DECIDE TO KILL YOU...
...BUT HONESTLY, IT LOOKS LIKE IT'S IN THE CARDS.
ARE YOU PREPARED FOR THAT?

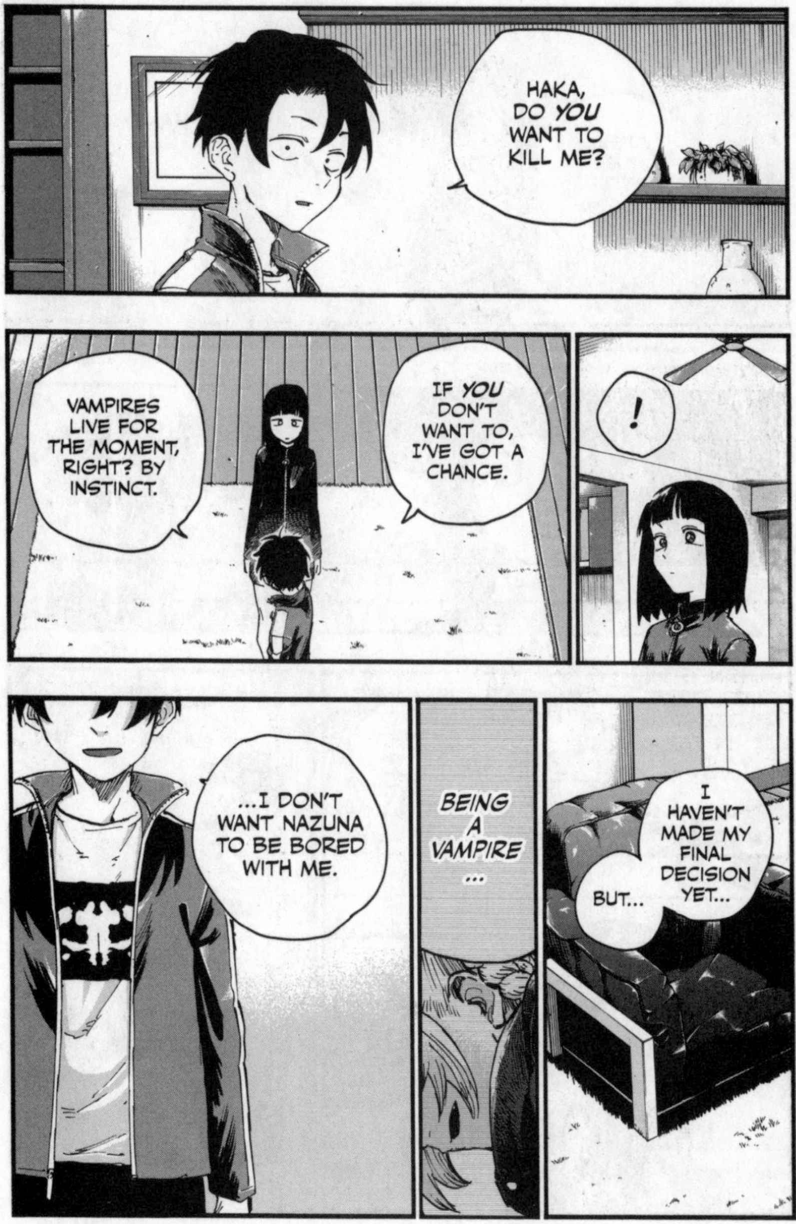
HAKA, DO *YOU* WANT TO KILL ME?
!
IF *YOU* DON'T WANT TO, I'VE GOT A CHANCE.
VAMPIRES LIVE FOR THE MOMENT, RIGHT? BY INSTINCT.
I HAVEN'T MADE MY FINAL DECISION YET...
BUT...
BEING A VAMPIRE ...
...I DON'T WANT NAZUNA TO BE BORED WITH ME.

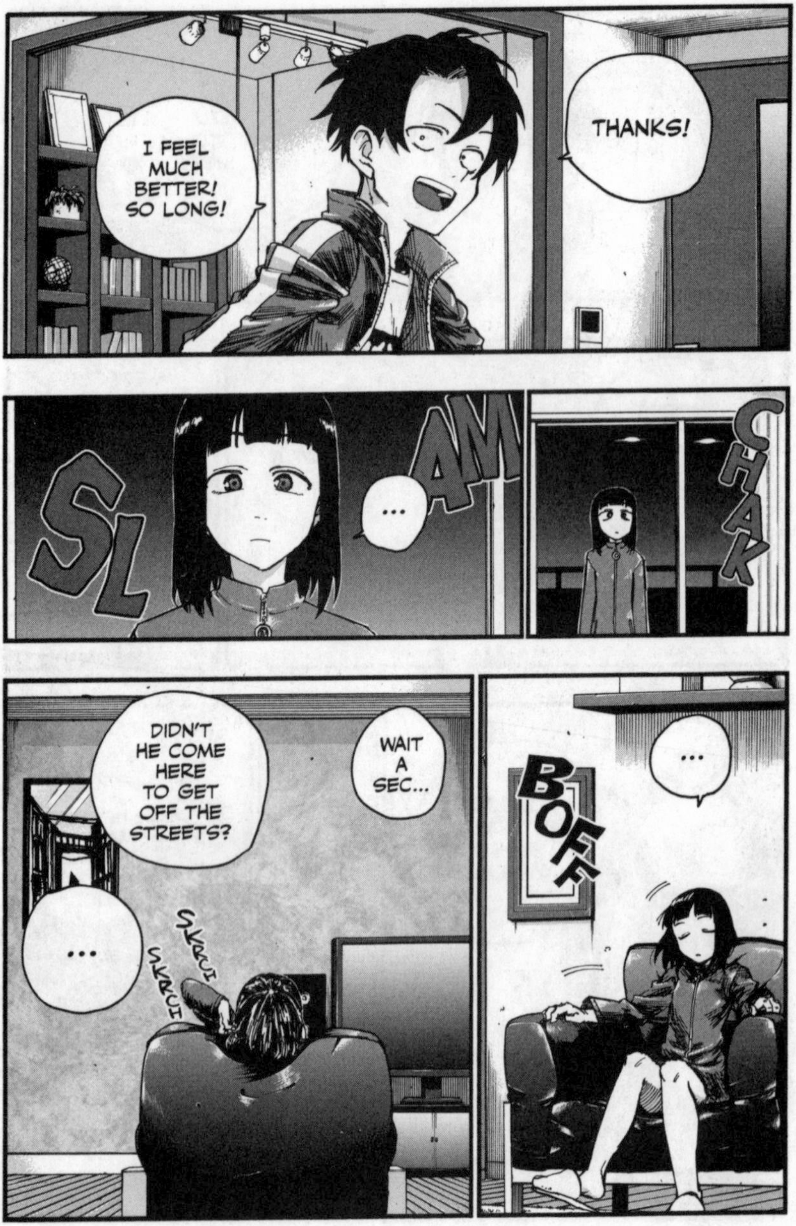
THANKS!
I FEEL MUCH BETTER! SO LONG!
CHAK
SLAM
...
...
BOFF
WAIT A SEC...
DIDN'T HE COME HERE TO GET OFF THE STREETS?
SKRCH SKRCH
...

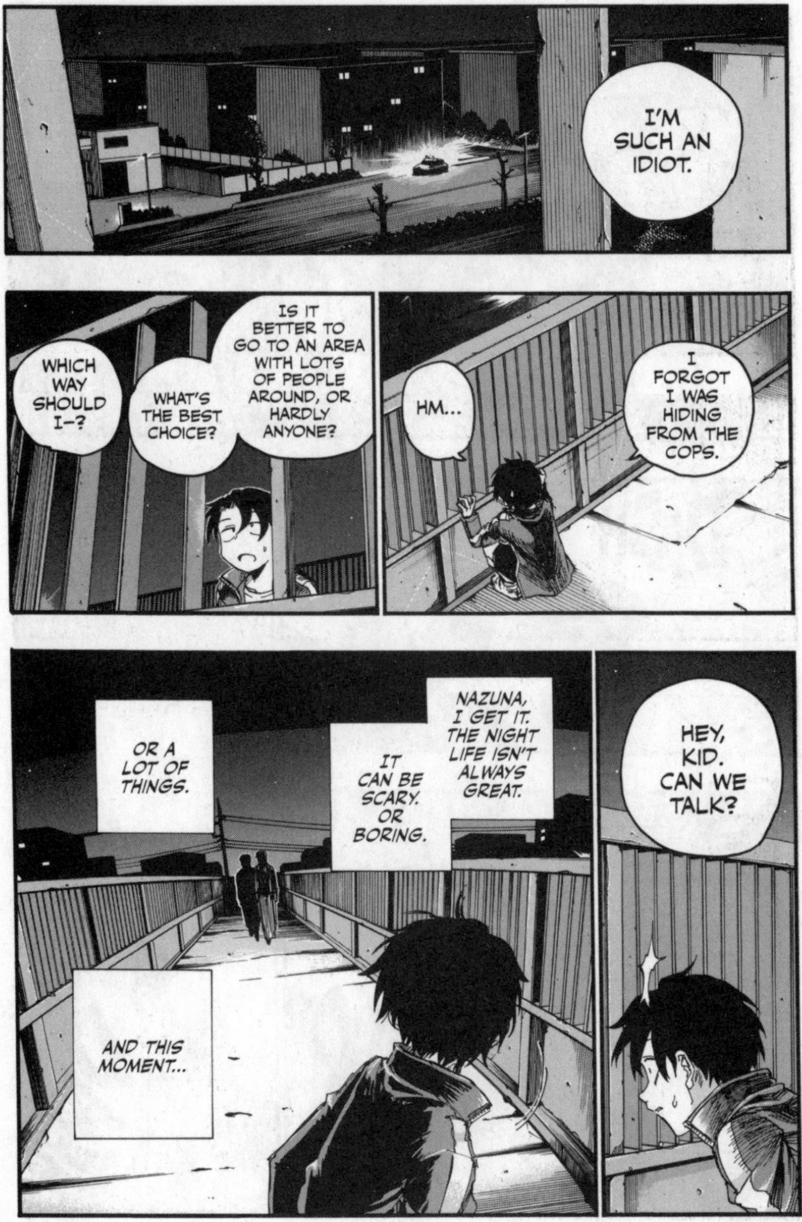
I'M SUCH AN IDIOT.
I FORGOT I WAS HIDING FROM THE COPS.
HM...
IS IT BETTER TO GO TO AN AREA WITH LOTS OF PEOPLE AROUND, OR HARDLY ANYONE?
WHAT'S THE BEST CHOICE?
WHICH WAY SHOULD I–?
HEY, KID. CAN WE TALK?
NAZUNA, I GET IT. THE NIGHT LIFE ISN'T ALWAYS GREAT.
IT CAN BE SCARY. OR BORING.
OR A LOT OF THINGS.
AND THIS MOMENT...

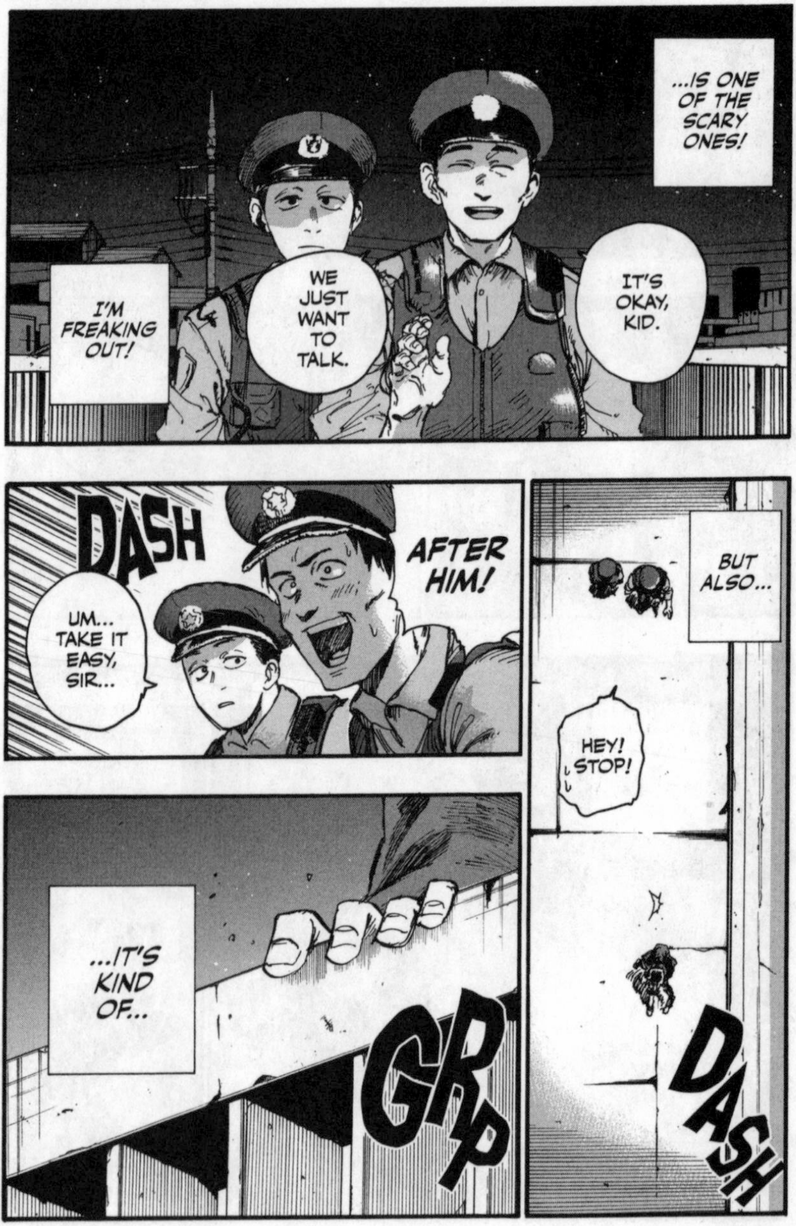
...IS ONE OF THE SCARY ONES!
IT'S OKAY, KID.
WE JUST WANT TO TALK.
I'M FREAKING OUT!
BUT ALSO...
HEY! STOP!
DASH
DASH
AFTER HIM!
UM... TAKE IT EASY, SIR...
...IT'S KIND OF...
GRP

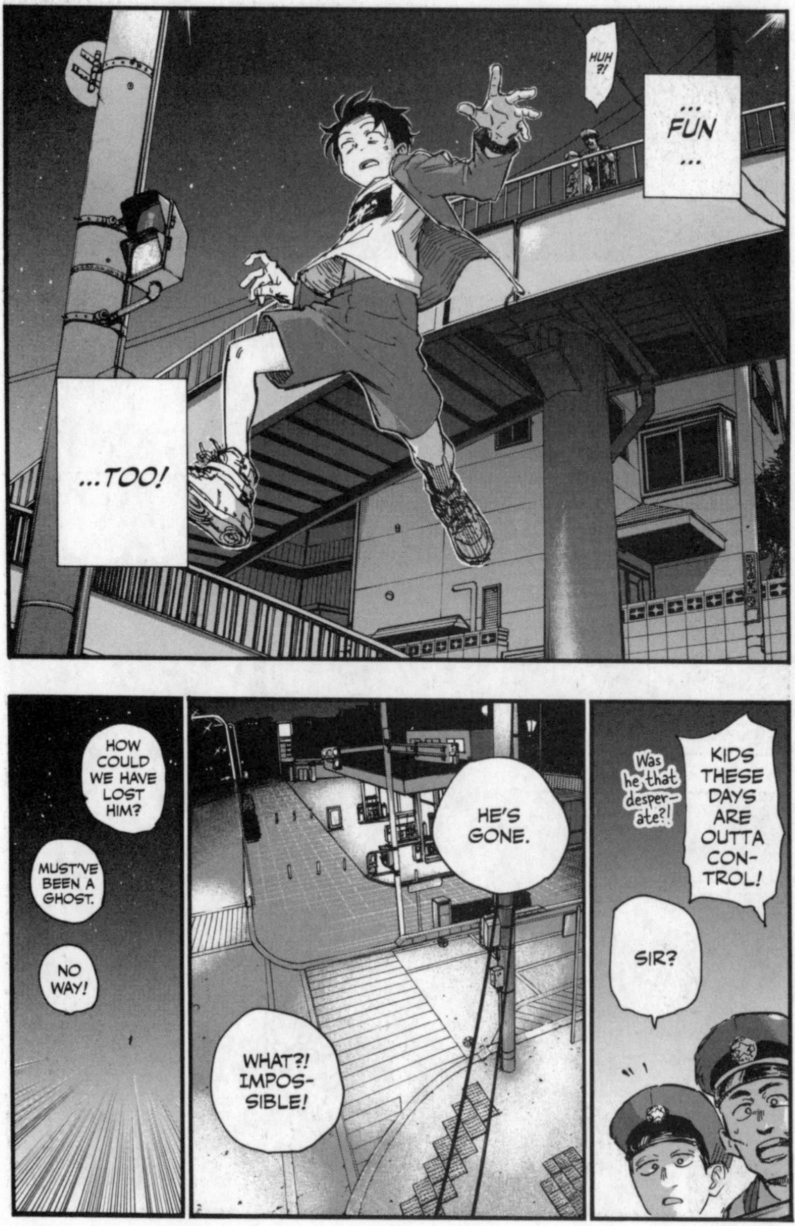
... FUN ...
HUH ?!
...TOO!
KIDS THESE DAYS ARE OUTTA CON-TROL!
Was he that desper-ate?!
SIR?
HE'S GONE.
WHAT?! IMPOS-SIBLE!
HOW COULD WE HAVE LOST HIM?
MUST'VE BEEN A GHOST.
NO WAY!

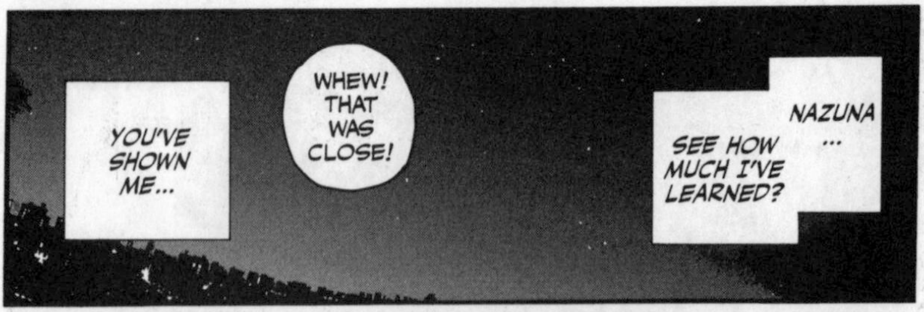
NAZUNA ... SEE HOW MUCH I'VE LEARNED?
WHEW! THAT WAS CLOSE!
YOU'VE SHOWN ME...

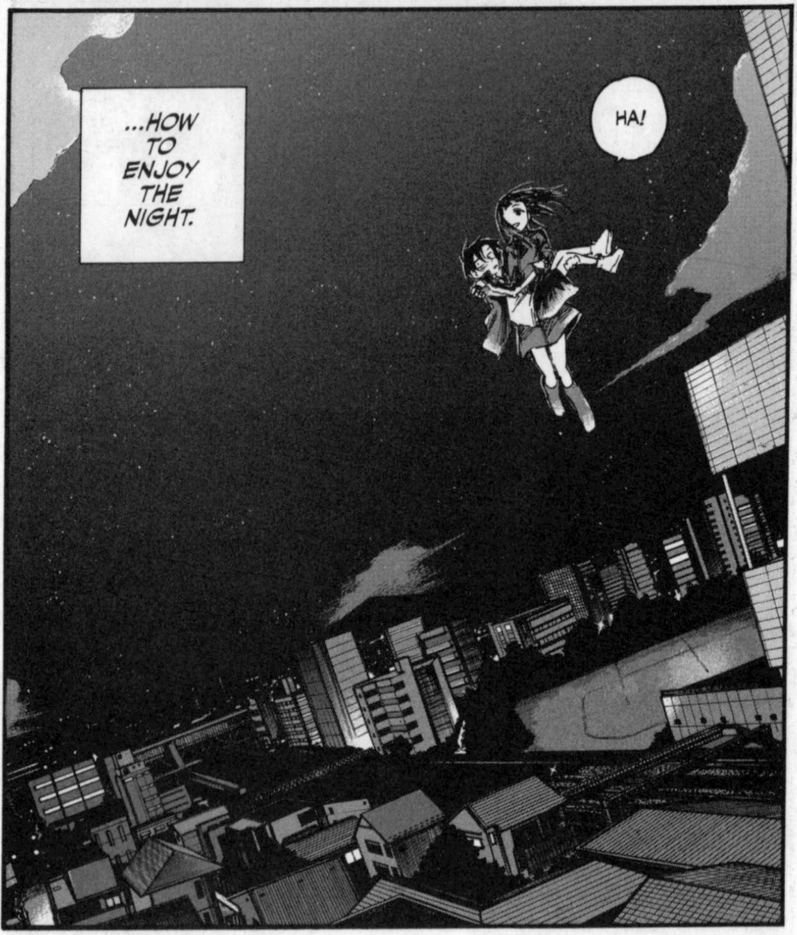
HA!
...HOW TO ENJOY THE NIGHT.

NIGHT 46: AS FRIENDS

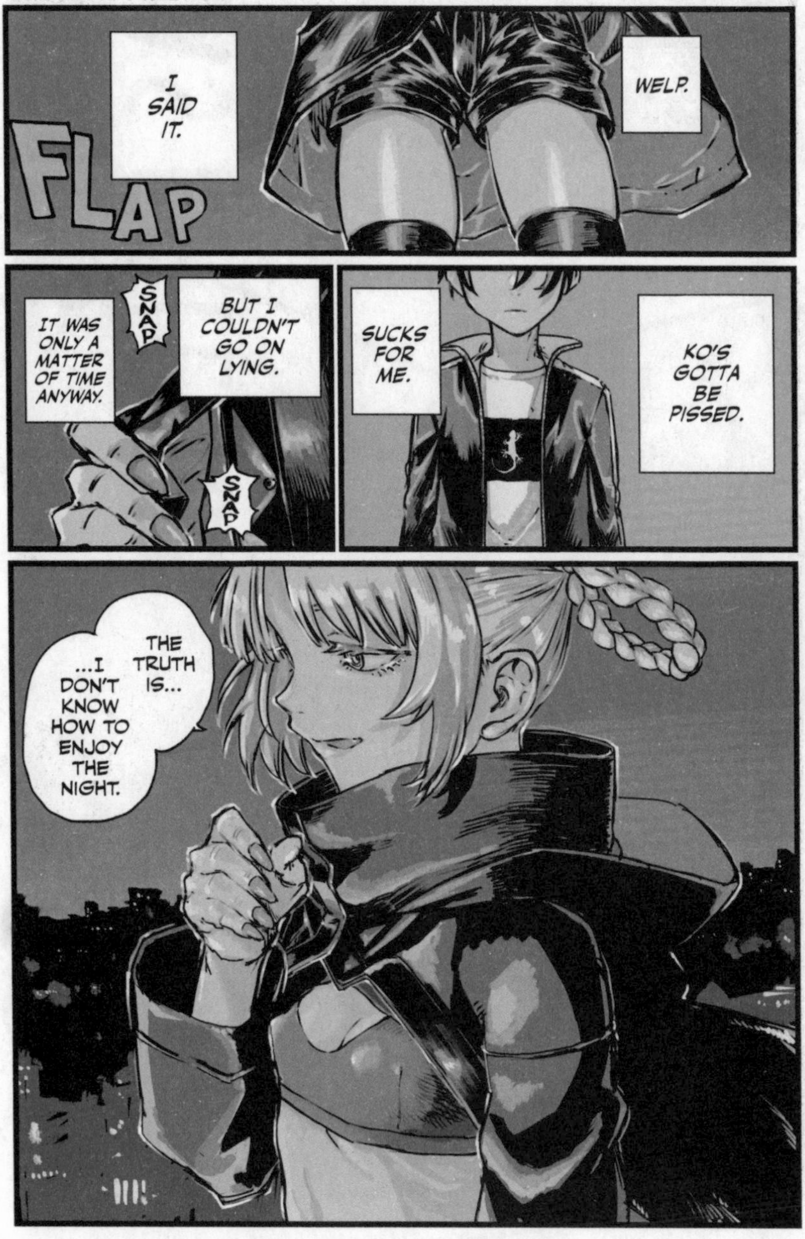
WELP.
I SAID IT.
FLAP
KO'S GOTTA BE PISSED.
SUCKS FOR ME.
BUT I COULDN'T GO ON LYING.
SNAP
IT WAS ONLY A MATTER OF TIME ANYWAY.
SNAP
THE TRUTH IS... ...I DON'T KNOW HOW TO ENJOY THE NIGHT.

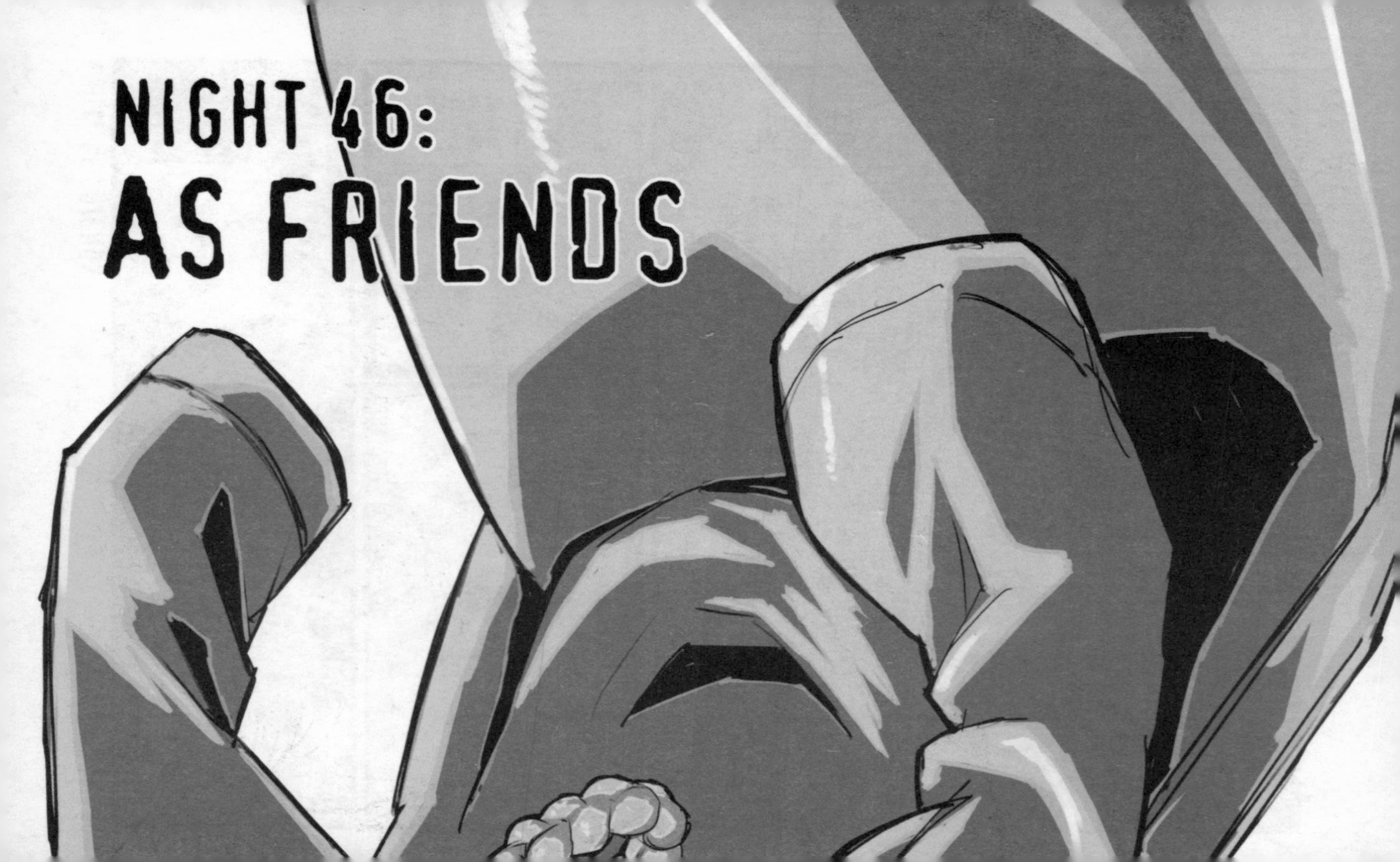
NIGHT 46:
AS FRIENDS

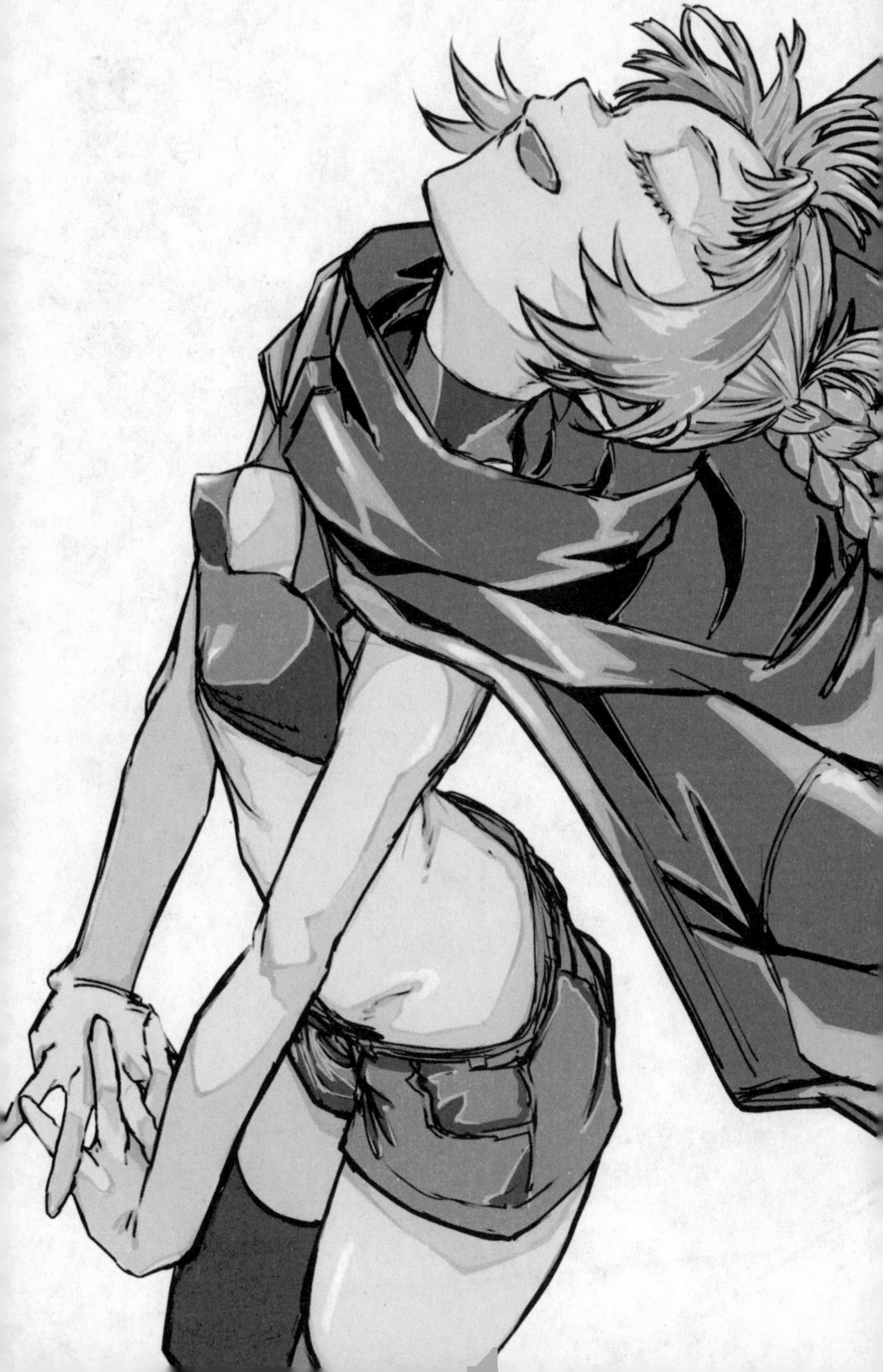

Call of the Night

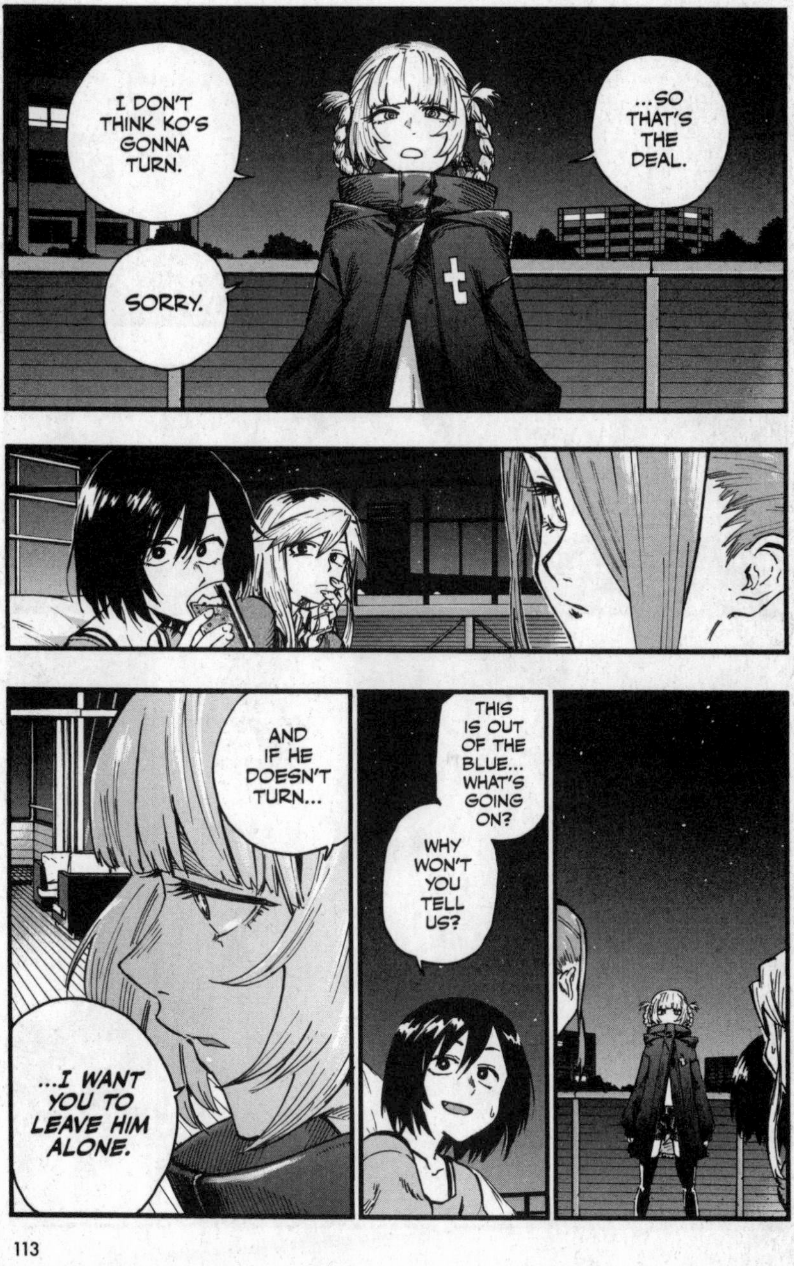
...SO THAT'S THE DEAL.
I DON'T THINK KO'S GONNA TURN.
SORRY.
THIS IS OUT OF THE BLUE... WHAT'S GOING ON?
WHY WON'T YOU TELL US?
AND IF HE DOESN'T TURN...
...I WANT YOU TO LEAVE HIM ALONE.

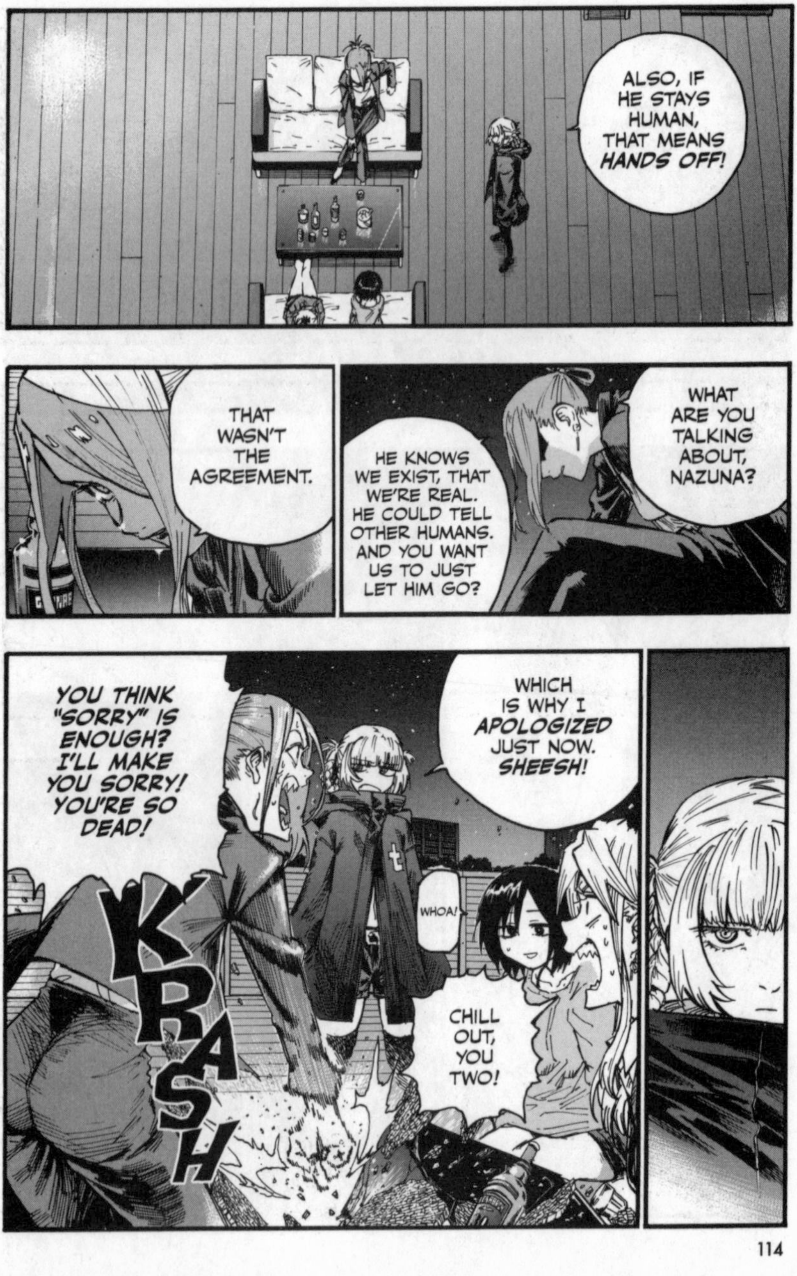
ALSO, IF HE STAYS HUMAN, THAT MEANS HANDS OFF!
WHAT ARE YOU TALKING ABOUT, NAZUNA?
HE KNOWS WE EXIST, THAT WE'RE REAL. HE COULD TELL OTHER HUMANS. AND YOU WANT US TO JUST LET HIM GO?
THAT WASN'T THE AGREEMENT.
WHICH IS WHY I APOLOGIZED JUST NOW. SHEESH!
YOU THINK "SORRY" IS ENOUGH? I'LL MAKE YOU SORRY! YOU'RE SO DEAD!
WHOA!
CHILL OUT, YOU TWO!
KRASH

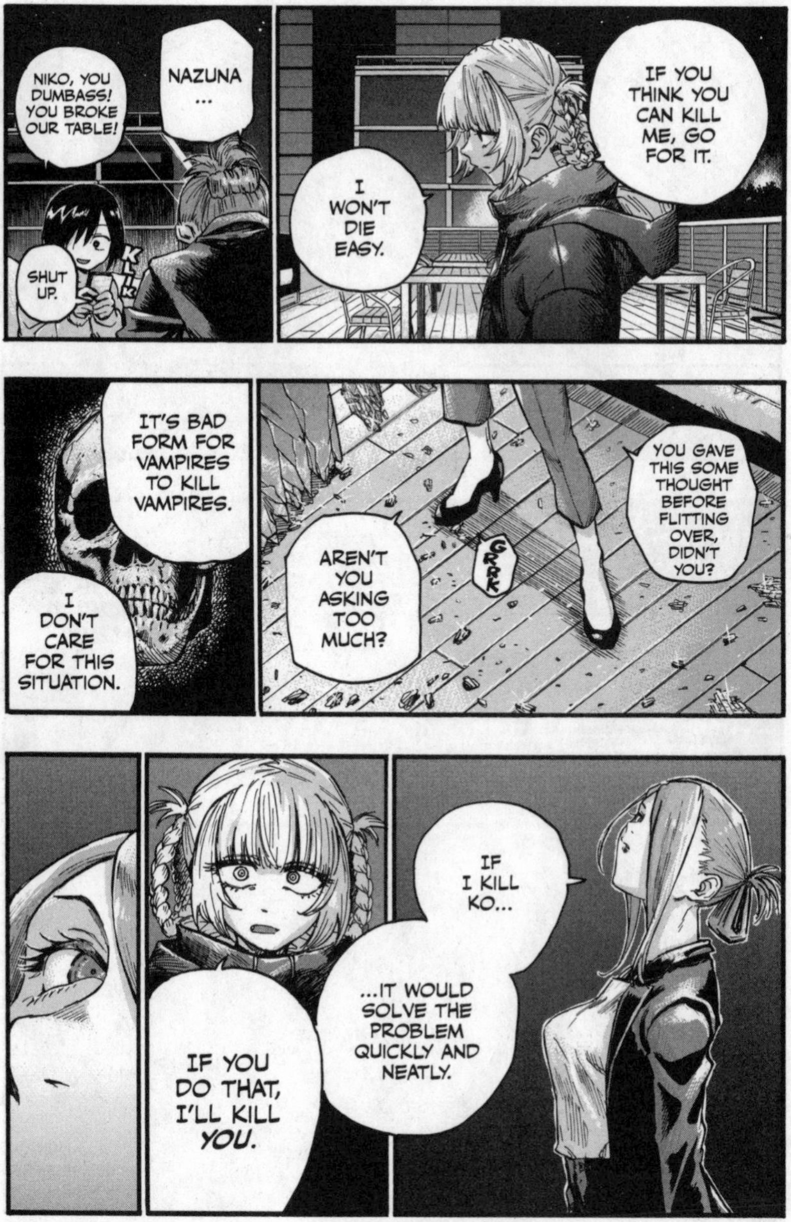
IF YOU THINK YOU CAN KILL ME, GO FOR IT.
I WON'T DIE EASY.
NAZUNA ...
NIKO, YOU DUMBASS! YOU BROKE OUR TABLE!
KLIK
SHUT UP.
YOU GAVE THIS SOME THOUGHT BEFORE FLITTING OVER, DIDN'T YOU?
GRRK
AREN'T YOU ASKING TOO MUCH?
IT'S BAD FORM FOR VAMPIRES TO KILL VAMPIRES.
I DON'T CARE FOR THIS SITUATION.
IF I KILL KO...
...IT WOULD SOLVE THE PROBLEM QUICKLY AND NEATLY.
IF YOU DO THAT, I'LL KILL *YOU*.

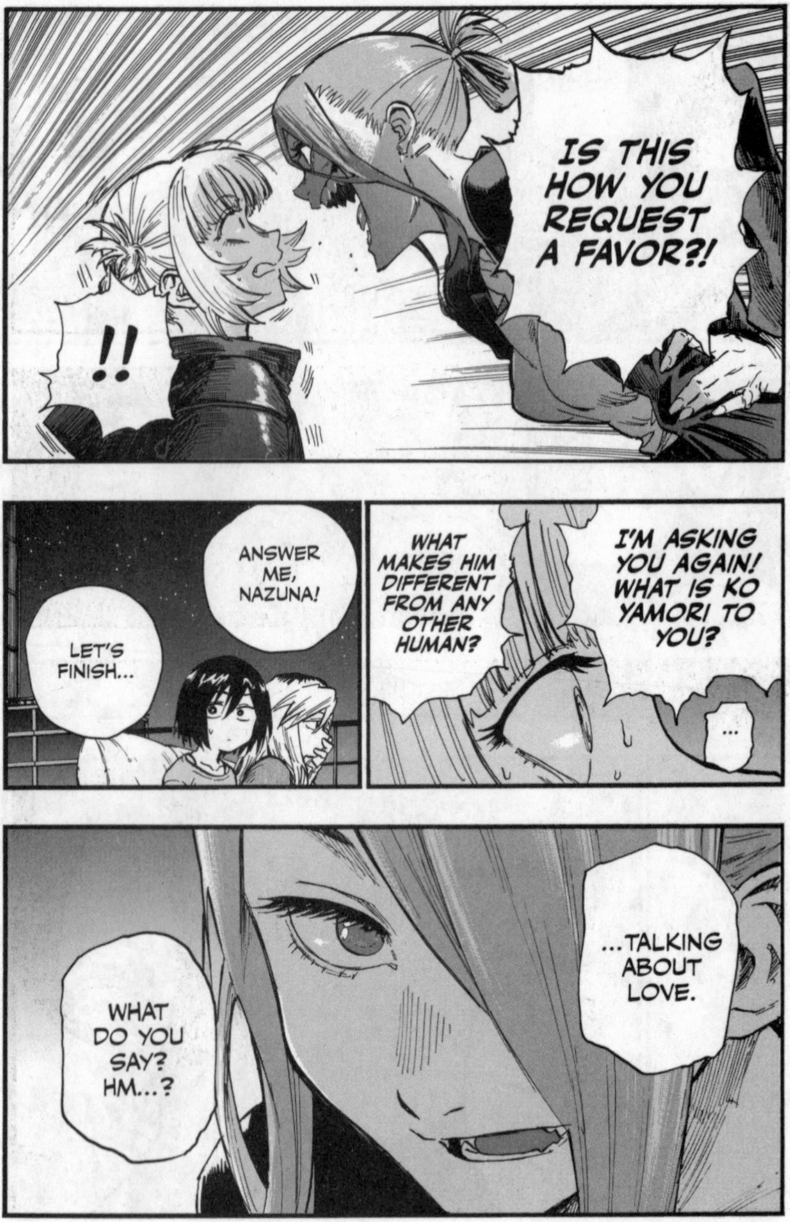
IS THIS HOW YOU REQUEST A FAVOR?!
!!
I'M ASKING YOU AGAIN! WHAT IS KO YAMORI TO YOU?
WHAT MAKES HIM DIFFERENT FROM ANY OTHER HUMAN?
...
ANSWER ME, NAZUNA!
LET'S FINISH...
...TALKING ABOUT LOVE.
WHAT DO YOU SAY? HM...?

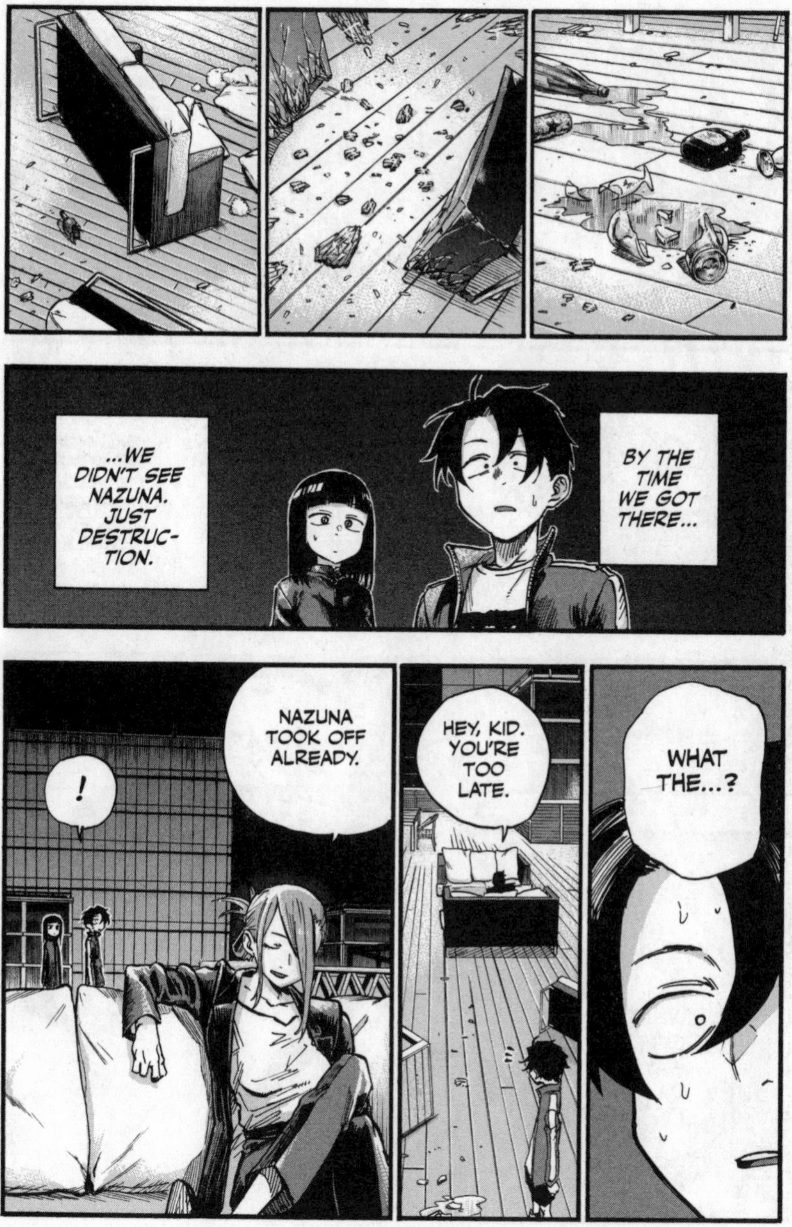
BY THE TIME WE GOT THERE...
...WE DIDN'T SEE NAZUNA. JUST DESTRUC-TION.
WHAT THE...?
HEY, KID. YOU'RE TOO LATE.
NAZUNA TOOK OFF ALREADY.
!

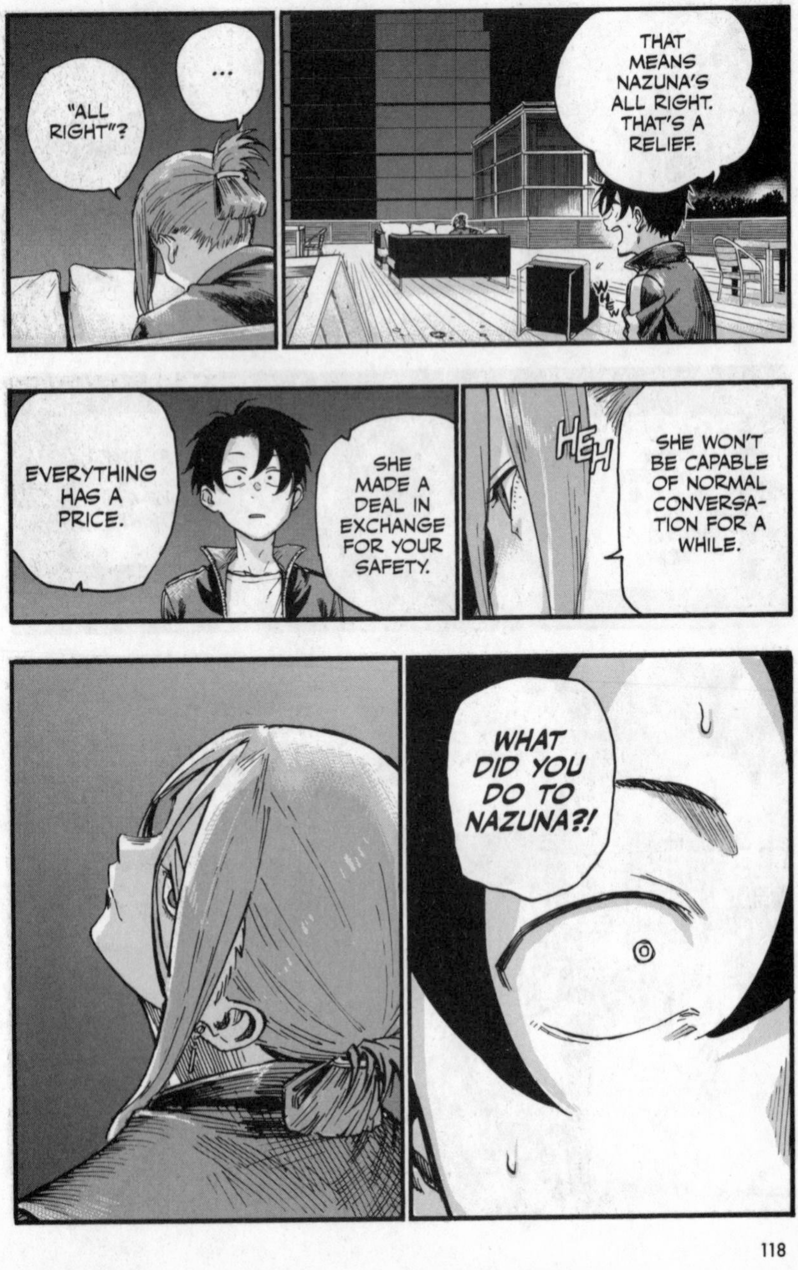
THAT MEANS NAZUNA'S ALL RIGHT. THAT'S A RELIEF.
WHEW
...
"ALL RIGHT"?
HEH
SHE WON'T BE CAPABLE OF NORMAL CONVERSA-TION FOR A WHILE.
SHE MADE A DEAL IN EXCHANGE FOR YOUR SAFETY.
EVERYTHING HAS A PRICE.
WHAT DID YOU DO TO NAZUNA?!

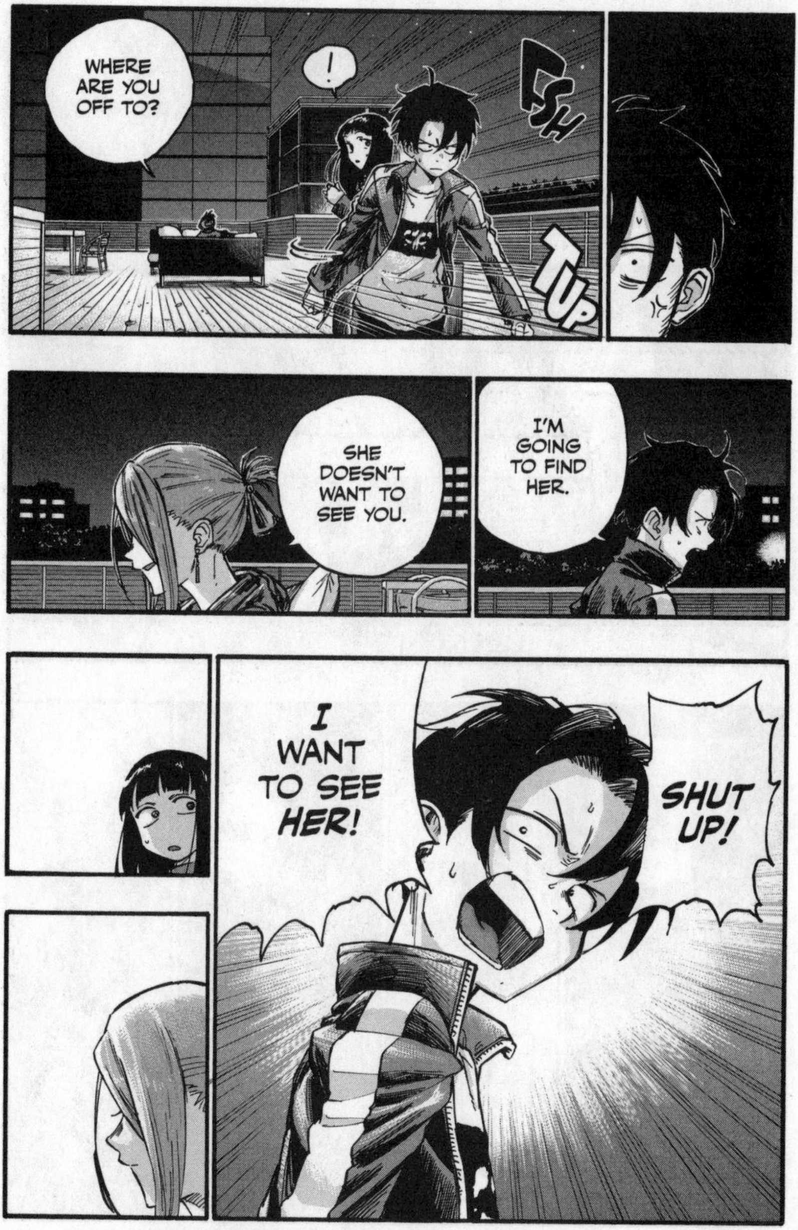
PSH
!
WHERE ARE YOU OFF TO?
TUP
I'M GOING TO FIND HER.
SHE DOESN'T WANT TO SEE YOU.
SHUT UP!
I WANT TO SEE HER!

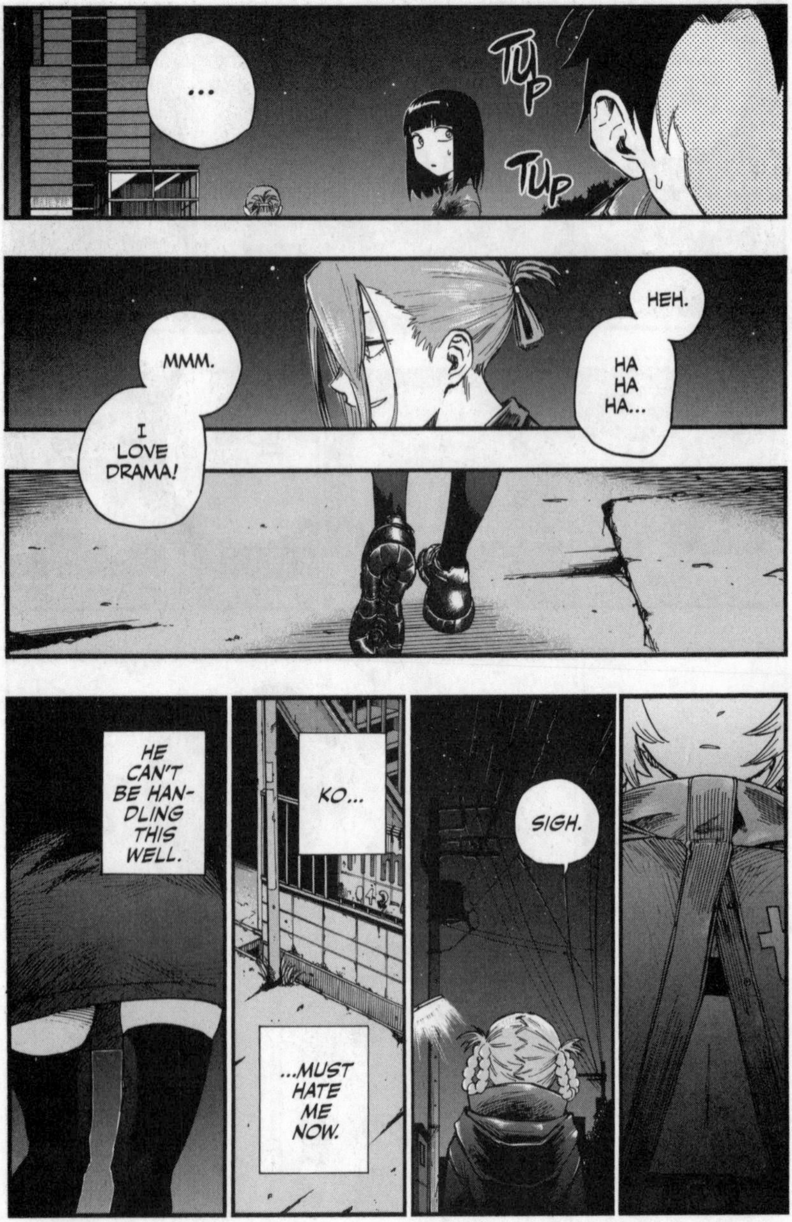
TUP
TUP
...
HEH.
HA HA HA...
MMM.
I LOVE DRAMA!
SIGH.
KO...
...MUST HATE ME NOW.
HE CAN'T BE HAN-DLING THIS WELL.

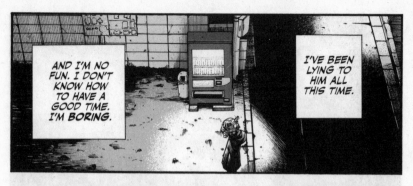

I'VE BEEN LYING TO HIM ALL THIS TIME.
AND I'M NO FUN. I DON'T KNOW HOW TO HAVE A GOOD TIME. I'M BORING.
GOING FOR WALKS.
DRINKING. PLAYING VIDEO GAMES.
JING
THAT'S ALL I DO.
JING
JING
JING
I TRIED TO ACT ALL COOL TO IMPRESS KO.
Asari
SUPER
ALCOHOL 300 ml
SUGAR CONTENT 0
I WONDER WHY...?

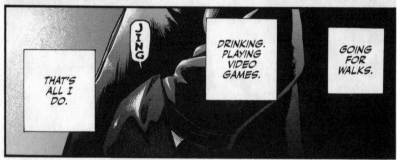

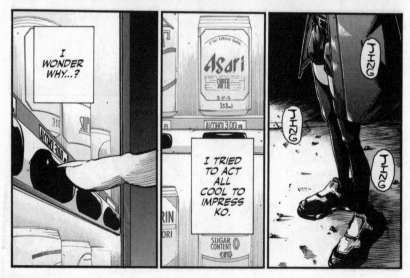

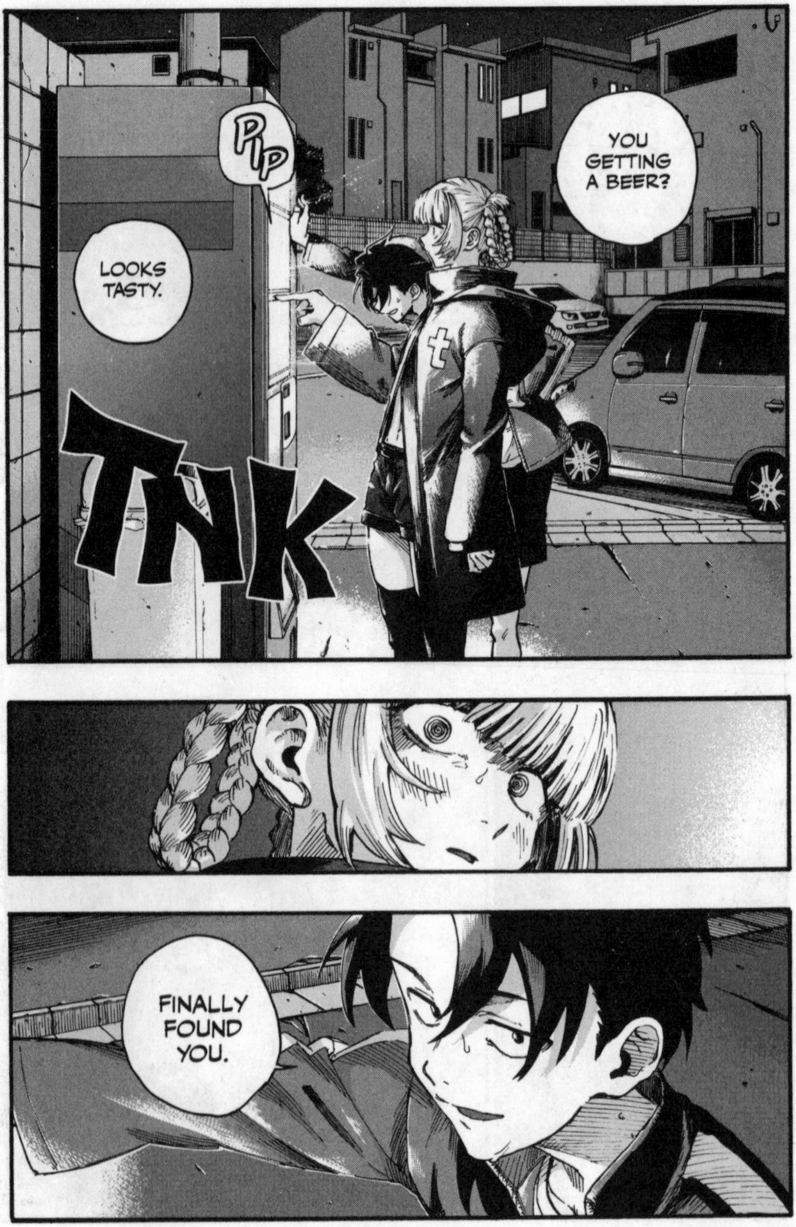
YOU GETTING A BEER?
PIP
LOOKS TASTY.
TNK
FINALLY FOUND YOU.

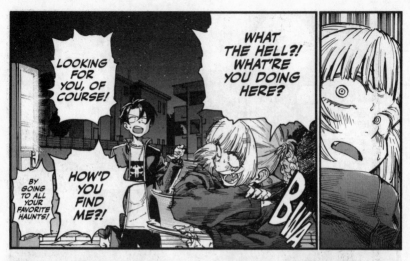

WHAT THE HELL?! WHAT'RE YOU DOING HERE?
LOOKING FOR YOU, OF COURSE!
BWA
HOW'D YOU FIND ME?!
BY GOING TO ALL YOUR FAVORITE HAUNTS!
WAIT A SEC...
...
WHAT?
YOU AREN'T HURT OR ANY-THING?
YOU'RE OKAY?
I'M FINE. DON'T WORRY ABOUT ME.
OKAY, OKAY. BUT NIKO SAID–

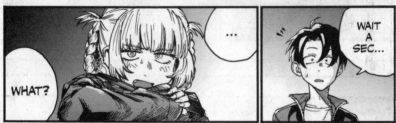

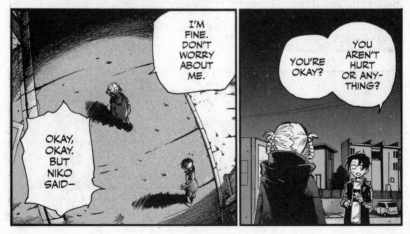

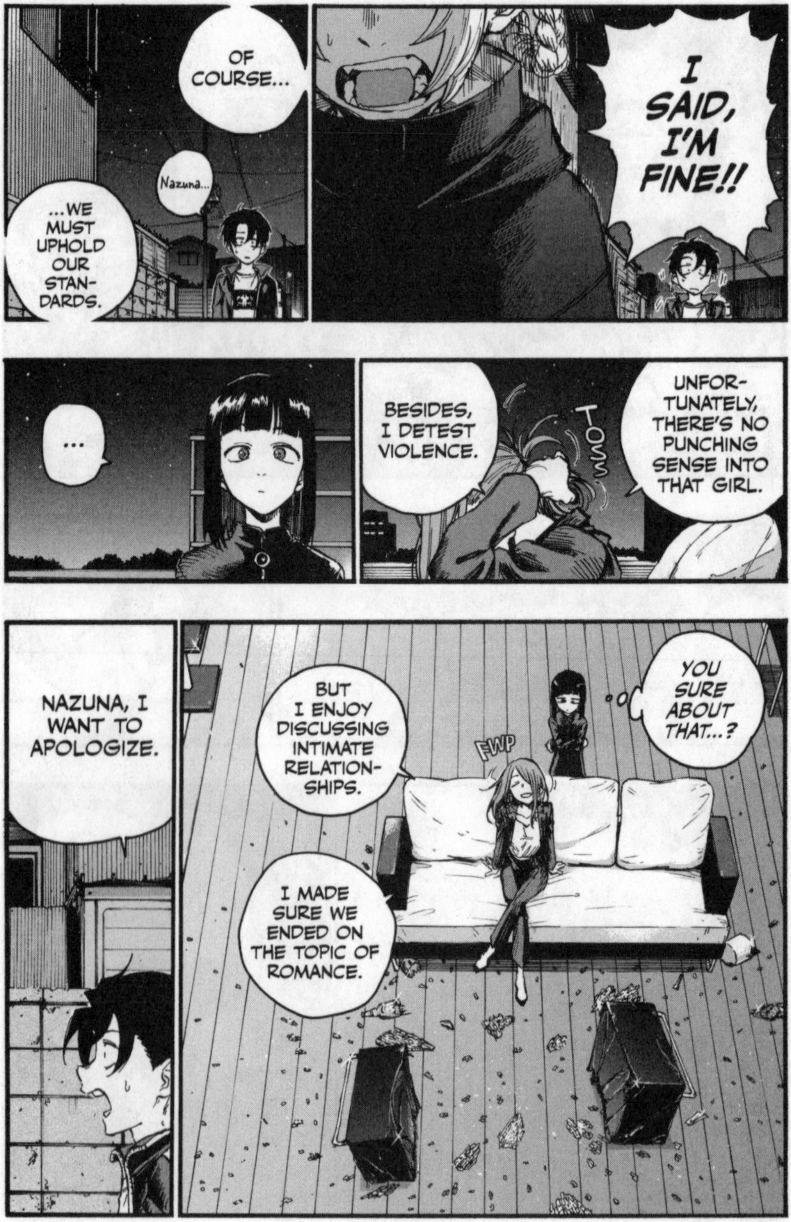
I SAID, I'M FINE!!
OF COURSE...
Nazuna...
...WE MUST UPHOLD OUR STAN-DARDS.
UNFOR-TUNATELY, THERE'S NO PUNCHING SENSE INTO THAT GIRL.
TOSS
BESIDES, I DETEST VIOLENCE.
...
YOU SURE ABOUT THAT...?
FWP
BUT I ENJOY DISCUSSING INTIMATE RELATION-SHIPS.
I MADE SURE WE ENDED ON THE TOPIC OF ROMANCE.
NAZUNA, I WANT TO APOLOGIZE.

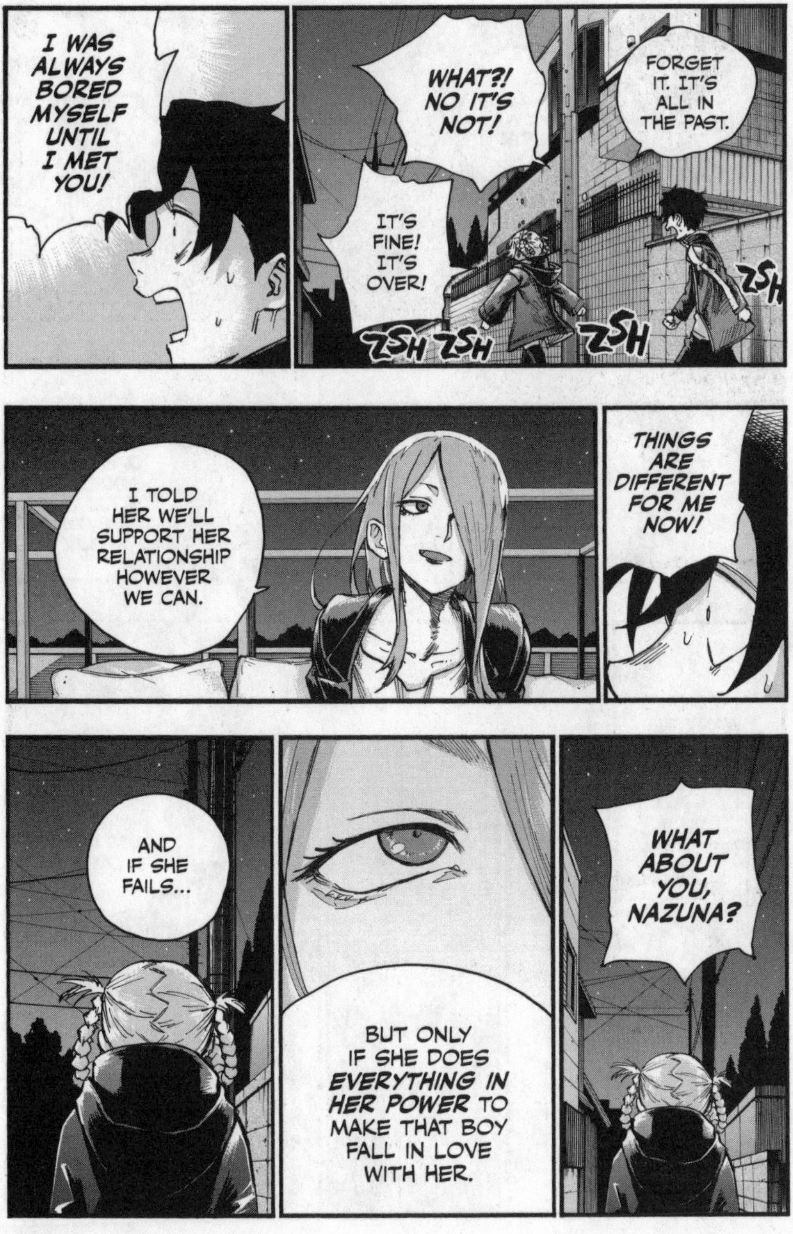
FORGET IT. IT'S ALL IN THE PAST.
WHAT?! NO IT'S NOT!
IT'S FINE! IT'S OVER!
ZSH
ZSH
ZSH ZSH
I WAS ALWAYS BORED MYSELF UNTIL I MET YOU!
THINGS ARE DIFFERENT FOR ME NOW!
I TOLD HER WE'LL SUPPORT HER RELATIONSHIP HOWEVER WE CAN.
WHAT ABOUT YOU, NAZUNA?
BUT ONLY IF SHE DOES EVERYTHING IN HER POWER TO MAKE THAT BOY FALL IN LOVE WITH HER.
AND IF SHE FAILS...

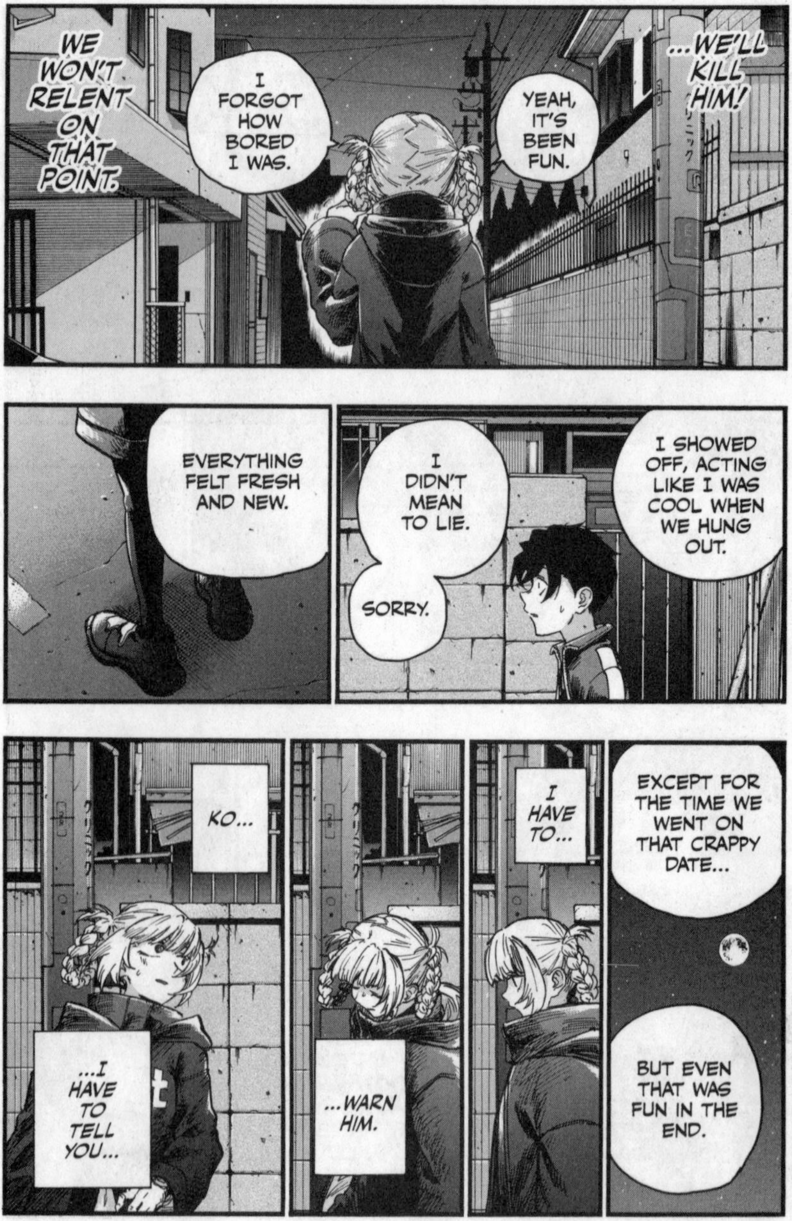
...WE'LL KILL HIM!
YEAH, IT'S BEEN FUN.
I FORGOT HOW BORED I WAS.
WE WON'T RELENT ON THAT POINT.
I SHOWED OFF, ACTING LIKE I WAS COOL WHEN WE HUNG OUT.
I DIDN'T MEAN TO LIE.
SORRY.
EVERYTHING FELT FRESH AND NEW.
EXCEPT FOR THE TIME WE WENT ON THAT CRAPPY DATE...
BUT EVEN THAT WAS FUN IN THE END.
I HAVE TO...
...WARN HIM.
KO...
...I HAVE TO TELL YOU...

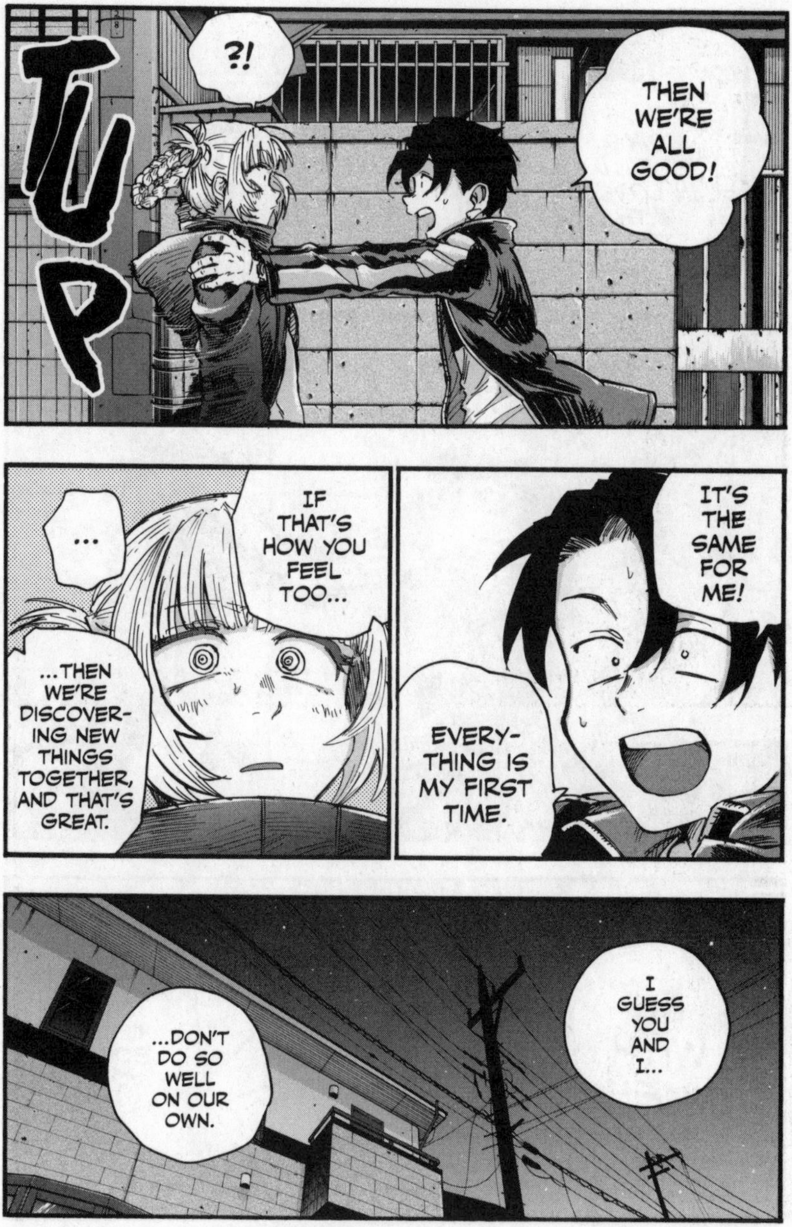
THEN WE'RE ALL GOOD!
?!
TUP
IT'S THE SAME FOR ME!
EVERY-THING IS MY FIRST TIME.
IF THAT'S HOW YOU FEEL TOO...
...
...THEN WE'RE DISCOVER-ING NEW THINGS TOGETHER, AND THAT'S GREAT.
I GUESS YOU AND I...
...DON'T DO SO WELL ON OUR OWN.

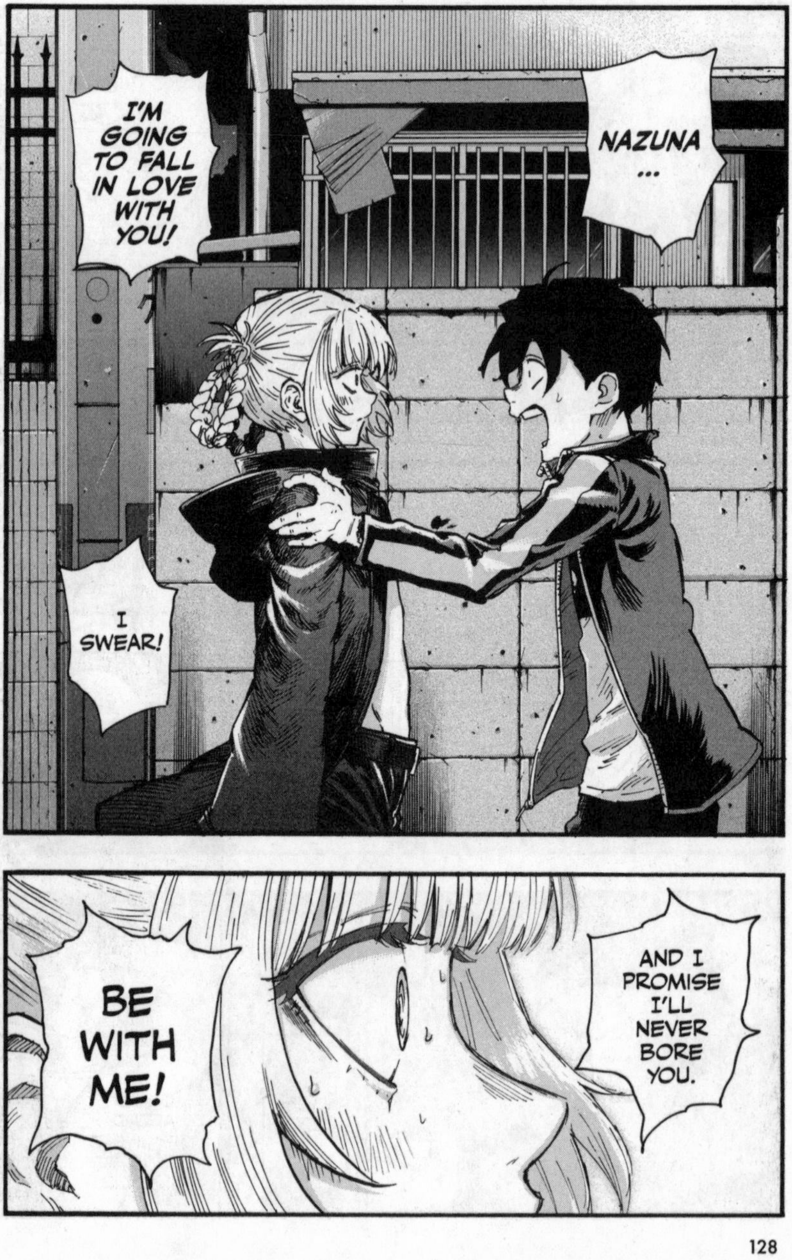
NAZUNA ...
I'M GOING TO FALL IN LOVE WITH YOU!
I SWEAR!
AND I PROMISE I'LL NEVER BORE YOU.
BE WITH ME!

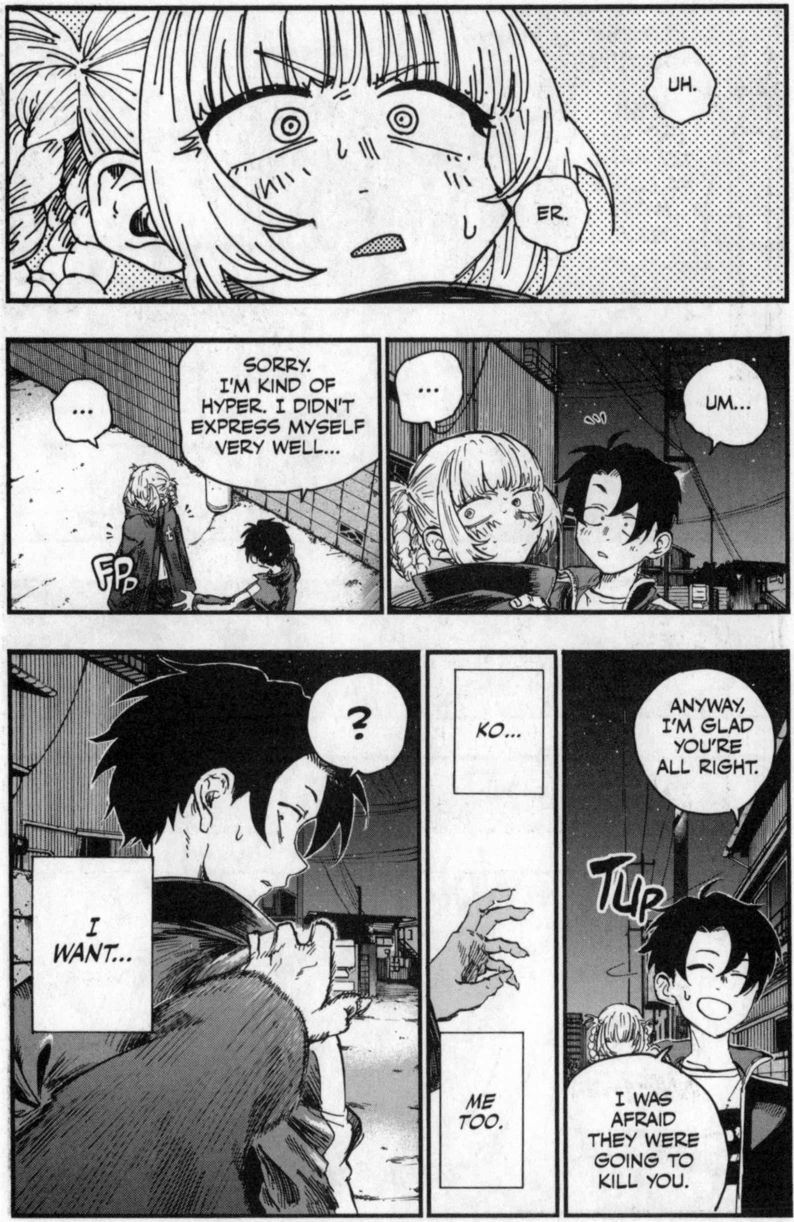
UH.
ER.
UM...
...
SORRY. I'M KIND OF HYPER. I DIDN'T EXPRESS MYSELF VERY WELL...
...
FPP
ANYWAY, I'M GLAD YOU'RE ALL RIGHT.
TUP
I WAS AFRAID THEY WERE GOING TO KILL YOU.
KO...
ME TOO.
?
I WANT...

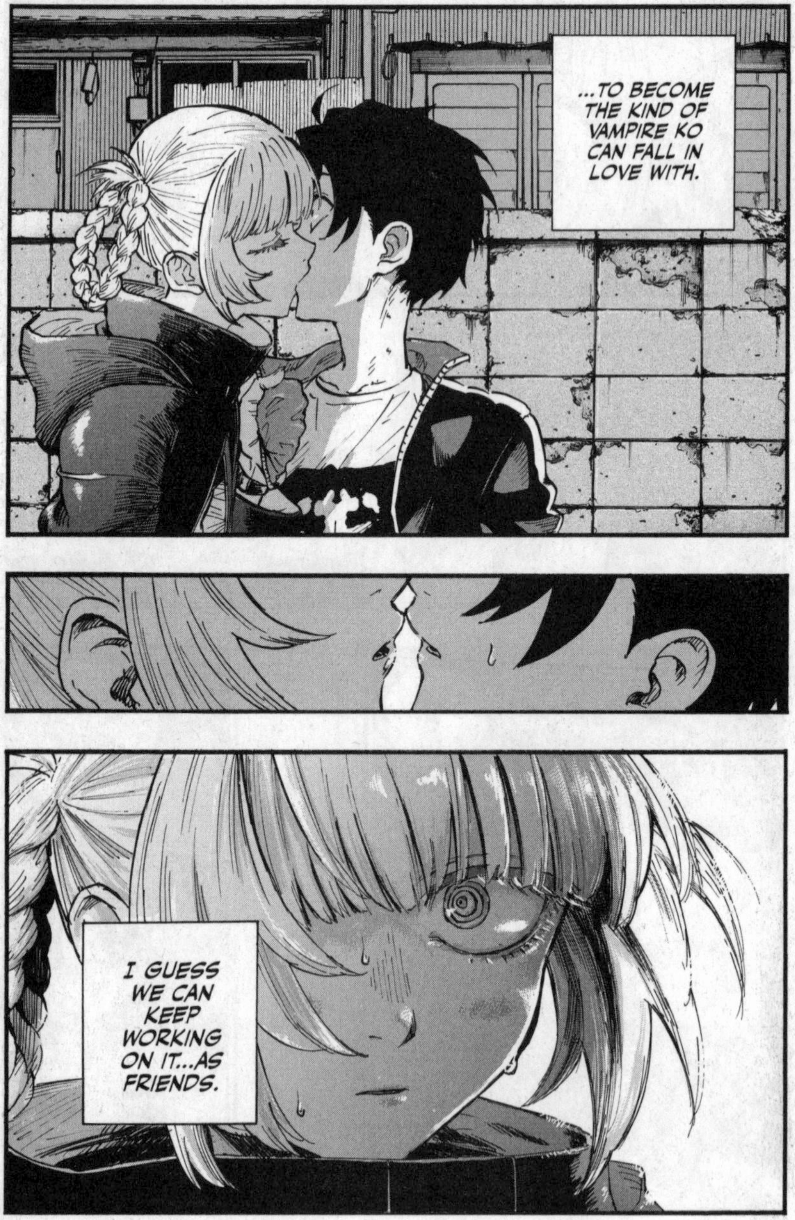
...TO BECOME THE KIND OF VAMPIRE KO CAN FALL IN LOVE WITH.
I GUESS WE CAN KEEP WORKING ON IT...AS FRIENDS.

Call of the Night

Call of the Night

NIGHT 47: YOU WANT TO TALK ABOUT KO, DON'T YOU?

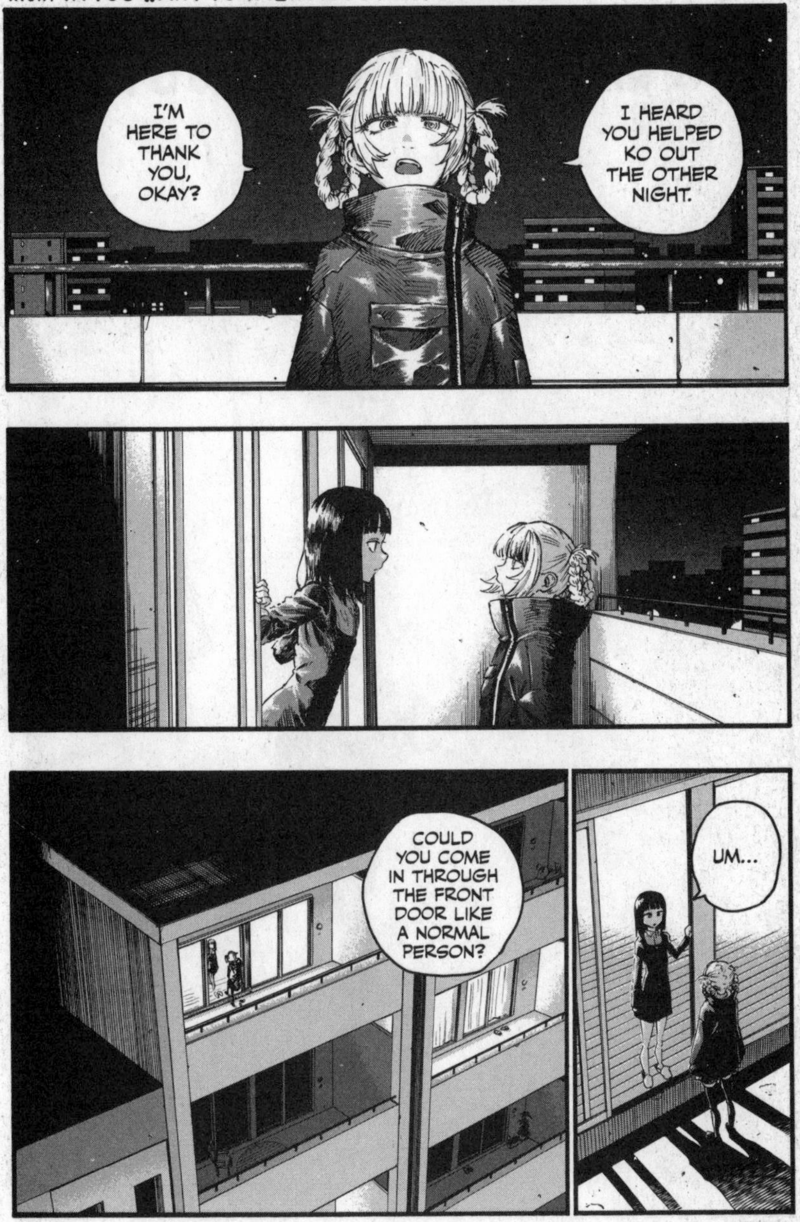
I HEARD YOU HELPED KO OUT THE OTHER NIGHT.
I'M HERE TO THANK YOU, OKAY?
UM...
COULD YOU COME IN THROUGH THE FRONT DOOR LIKE A NORMAL PERSON?

NIGHT 47:
YOU WANT TO TALK ABOUT KO, DON'T YOU?

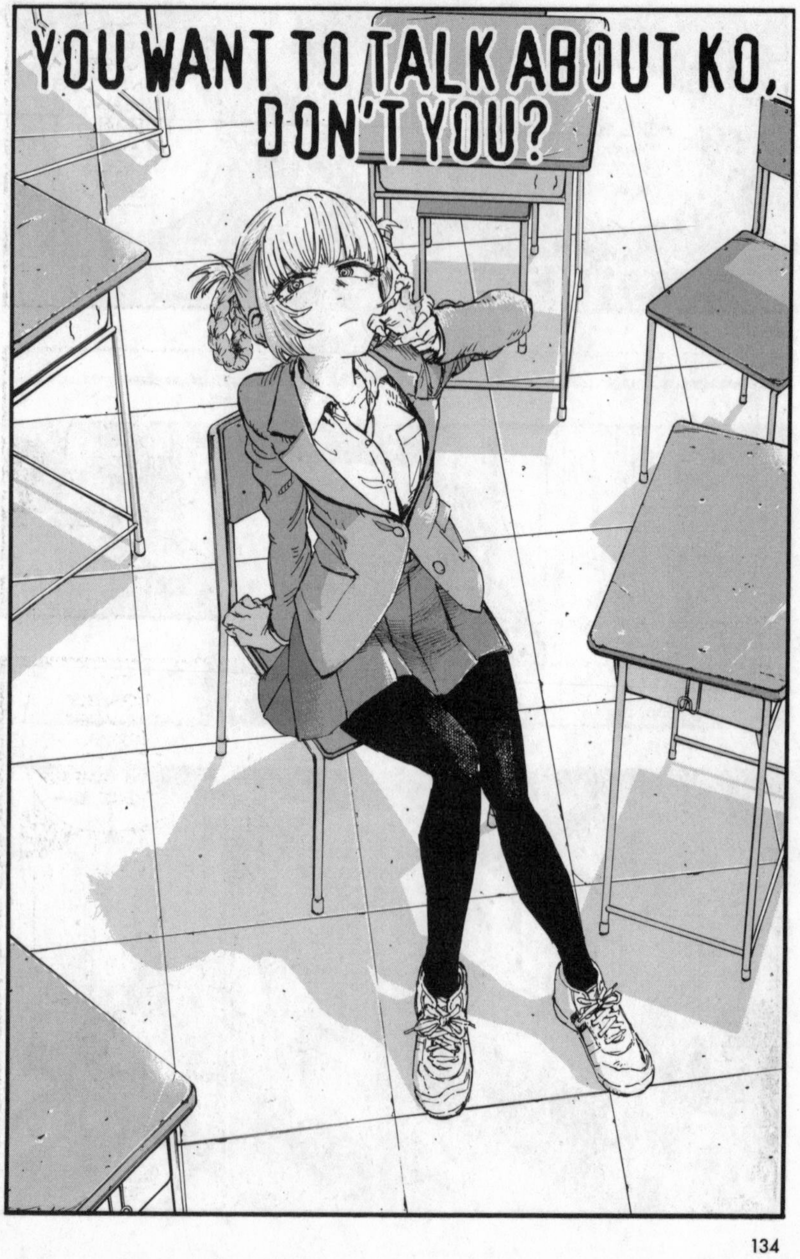

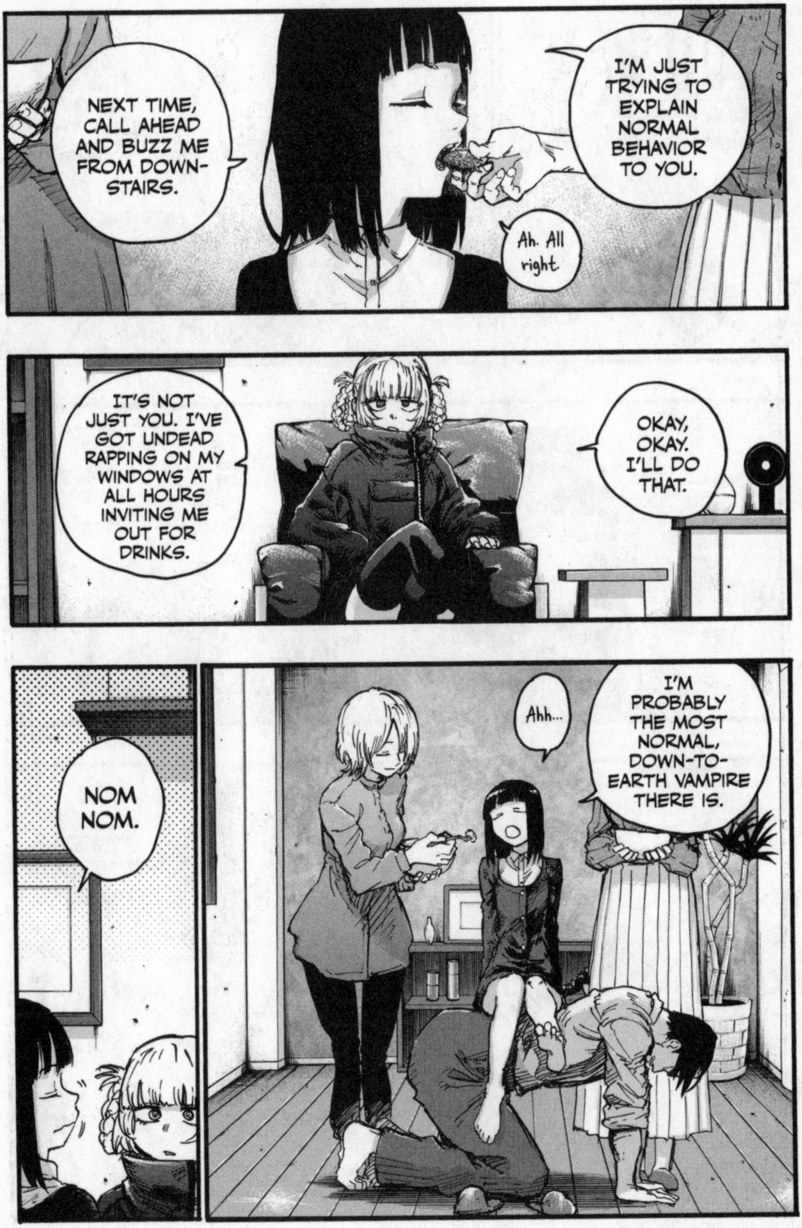

I'M JUST TRYING TO EXPLAIN NORMAL BEHAVIOR TO YOU.
Ah. All right.
NEXT TIME, CALL AHEAD AND BUZZ ME FROM DOWN-STAIRS.
OKAY, OKAY. I'LL DO THAT.
IT'S NOT JUST YOU. I'VE GOT UNDEAD RAPPING ON MY WINDOWS AT ALL HOURS INVITING ME OUT FOR DRINKS.
I'M PROBABLY THE MOST NORMAL, DOWN-TO-EARTH VAMPIRE THERE IS.
Ahh...
NOM NOM.

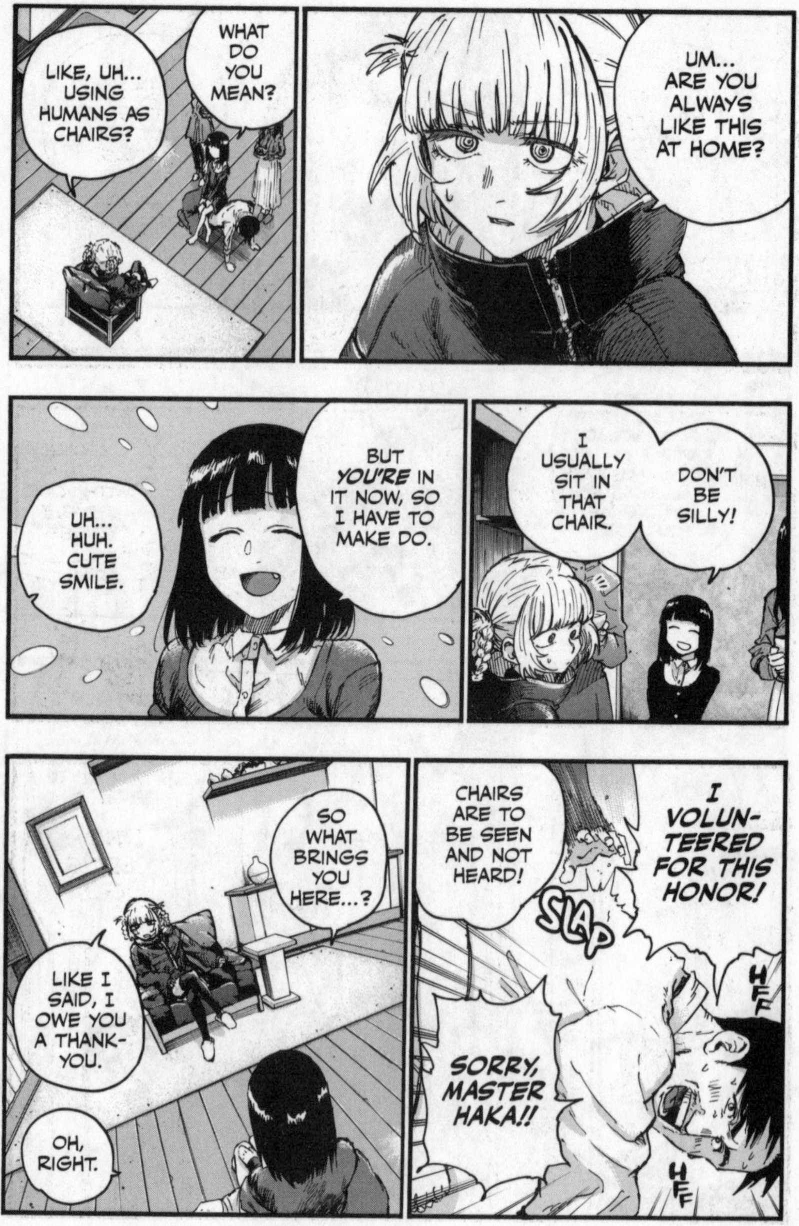
UM... ARE YOU ALWAYS LIKE THIS AT HOME?
WHAT DO YOU MEAN?
LIKE, UH... USING HUMANS AS CHAIRS?
DON'T BE SILLY!
I USUALLY SIT IN THAT CHAIR.
BUT *YOU'RE* IN IT NOW, SO I HAVE TO MAKE DO.
UH... HUH. CUTE SMILE.
I VOLUNTEERED FOR THIS HONOR!
CHAIRS ARE TO BE SEEN AND NOT HEARD!
SLAP
HFF
SORRY, MASTER HAKA!!
HFF
SO WHAT BRINGS YOU HERE...?
LIKE I SAID, I OWE YOU A THANK-YOU.
OH, RIGHT.

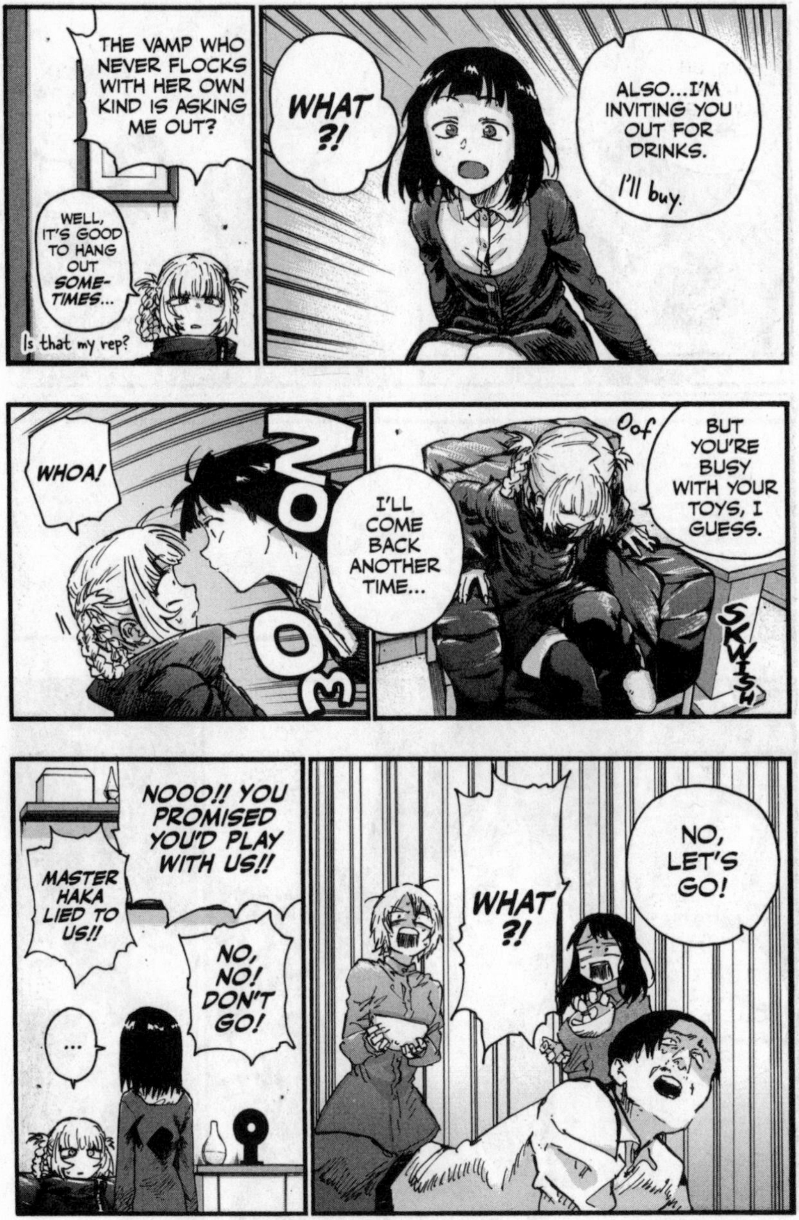
ALSO...I'M INVITING YOU OUT FOR DRINKS.
I'll buy.
WHAT ?!
THE VAMP WHO NEVER FLOCKS WITH HER OWN KIND IS ASKING ME OUT?
WELL, IT'S GOOD TO HANG OUT SOME-TIMES...
Is that my rep?
Oof
BUT YOU'RE BUSY WITH YOUR TOYS, I GUESS.
SKWISH
I'LL COME BACK ANOTHER TIME...
ZOOM
WHOA!
NO, LET'S GO!
WHAT ?!
NOOO!! YOU PROMISED YOU'D PLAY WITH US!!
MASTER HAKA LIED TO US!!
NO, NO! DON'T GO!
...

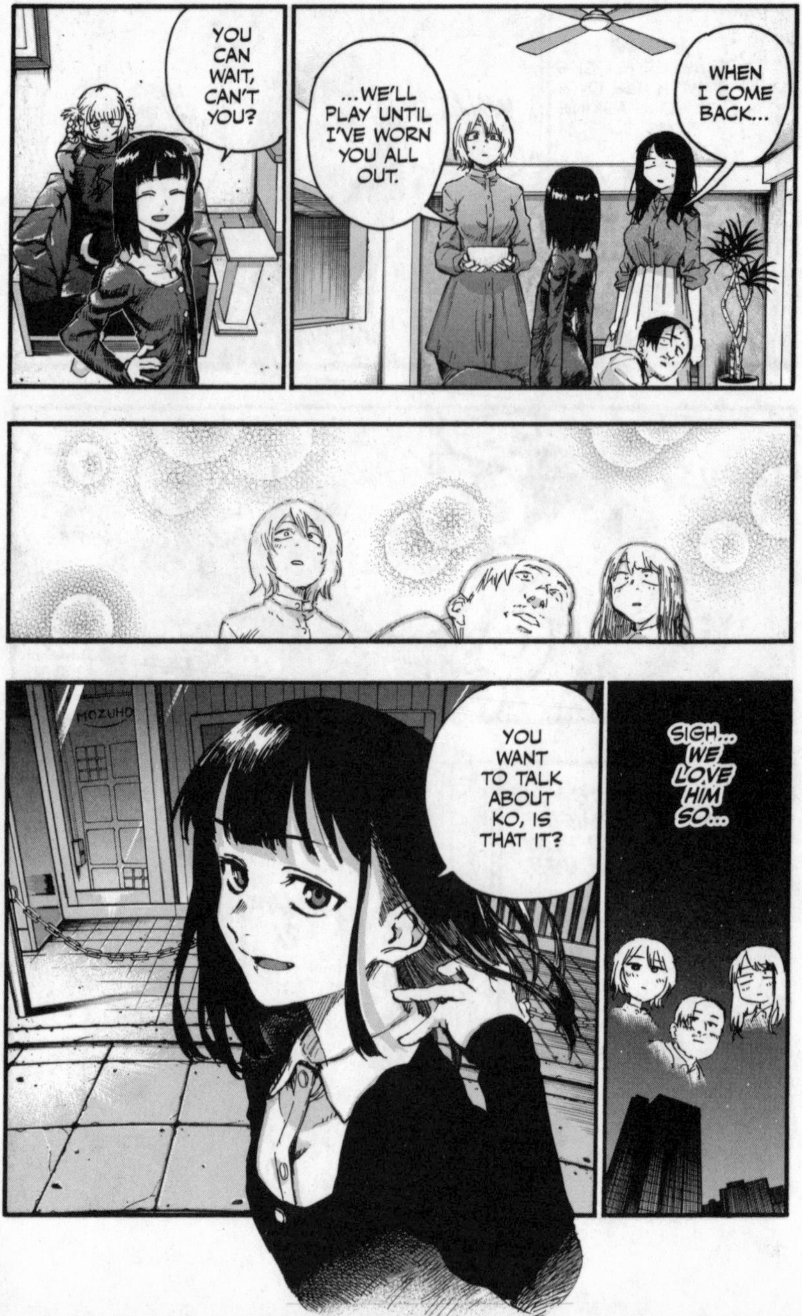
WHEN I COME BACK...
...WE'LL PLAY UNTIL I'VE WORN YOU ALL OUT.
YOU CAN WAIT, CAN'T YOU?
SIGH... WE LOVE HIM SO...
YOU WANT TO TALK ABOUT KO, IS THAT IT?
MOZUHO

HUH?! HA HA! WHAAAT?
WONDERING HOW I COULD TELL?
NO WAY! I JUST WANT A DRINKING BUDDY!
IS THAT SO?
YOU ALWAYS AVOID US, BUT TO-NIGHT...
...YOU CAME BY TO INVITE ME OUT.
YOU MUST HAVE AN ULTERIOR MOTIVE.
NIKO TOLD ME YOU PROMISED TO TURN YOUR BOY TOY.
IN THAT CASE, IT'S OBVIOUS WHY YOU'RE HERE.
YOU WANT MY HELP...
...
...TO MAKE KO FALL IN LOVE WITH YOU.
WELL ...
GREAT! BUT BEFORE WE GO DRINKING, LET'S MAKE A QUICK STOP.
WHERE?

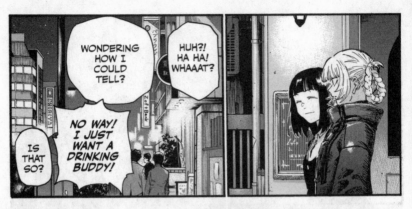

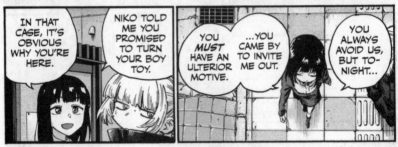

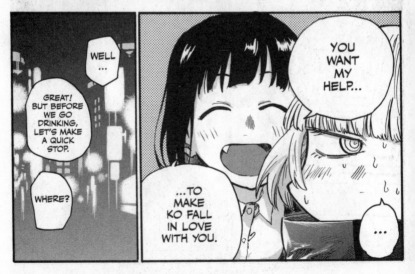

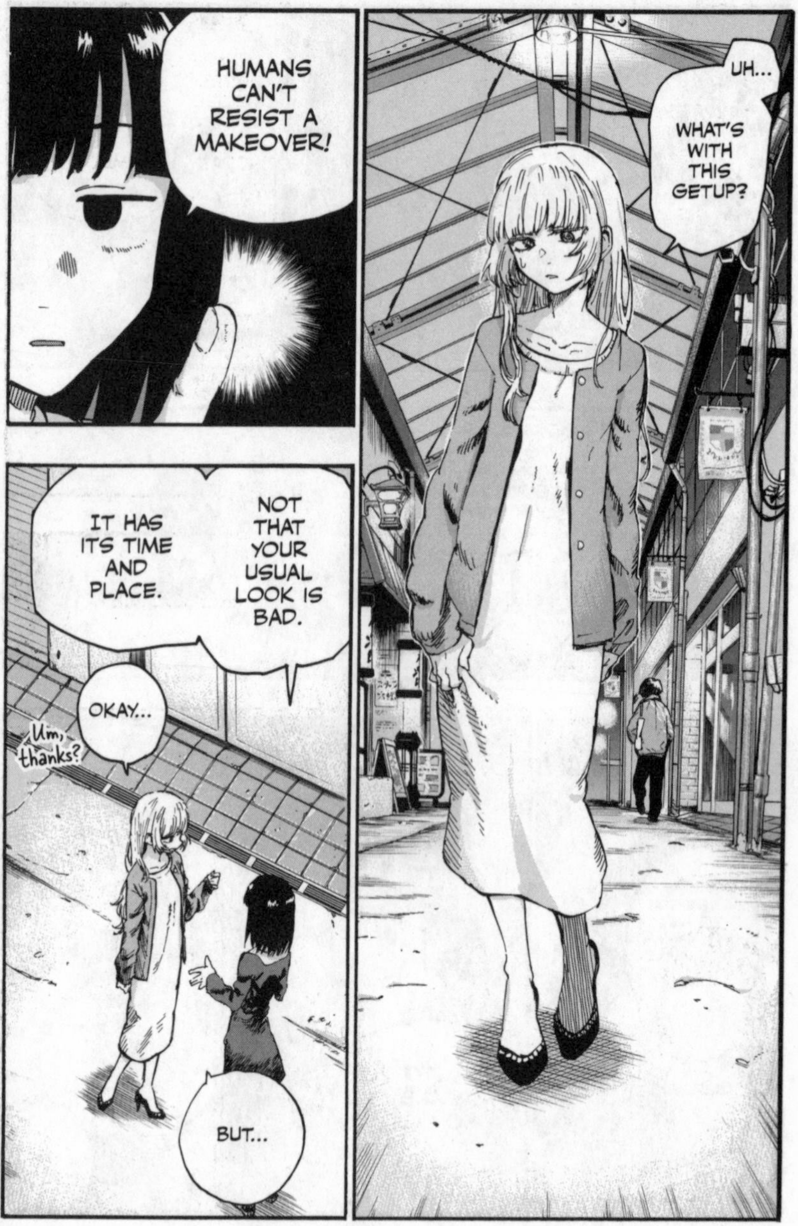
UH...
WHAT'S WITH THIS GETUP?
HUMANS CAN'T RESIST A MAKEOVER!
NOT THAT YOUR USUAL LOOK IS BAD.
IT HAS ITS TIME AND PLACE.
OKAY...
Um, thanks?
BUT...

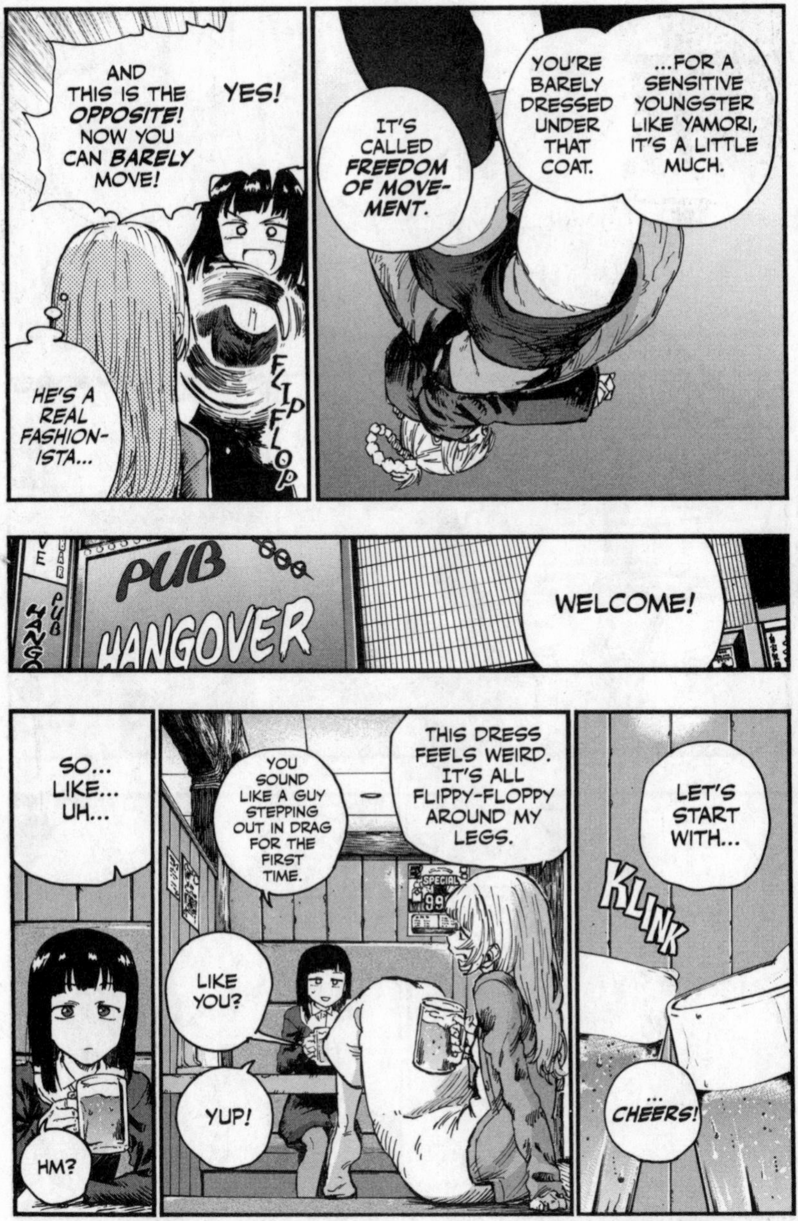
...FOR A SENSITIVE YOUNGSTER LIKE YAMORI, IT'S A LITTLE MUCH.
YOU'RE BARELY DRESSED UNDER THAT COAT.
IT'S CALLED *FREEDOM OF MOVEMENT*.
YES!
AND THIS IS THE *OPPOSITE!* NOW YOU CAN *BARELY* MOVE!
FLIP FLOP
HE'S A REAL FASHIONISTA...
WELCOME!
PUB
HANGOVER
LET'S START WITH...
KLINK
...CHEERS!
THIS DRESS FEELS WEIRD. IT'S ALL FLIPPY-FLOPPY AROUND MY LEGS.
YOU SOUND LIKE A GUY STEPPING OUT IN DRAG FOR THE FIRST TIME.
LIKE YOU?
YUP!
SO... LIKE... UH...
HM?

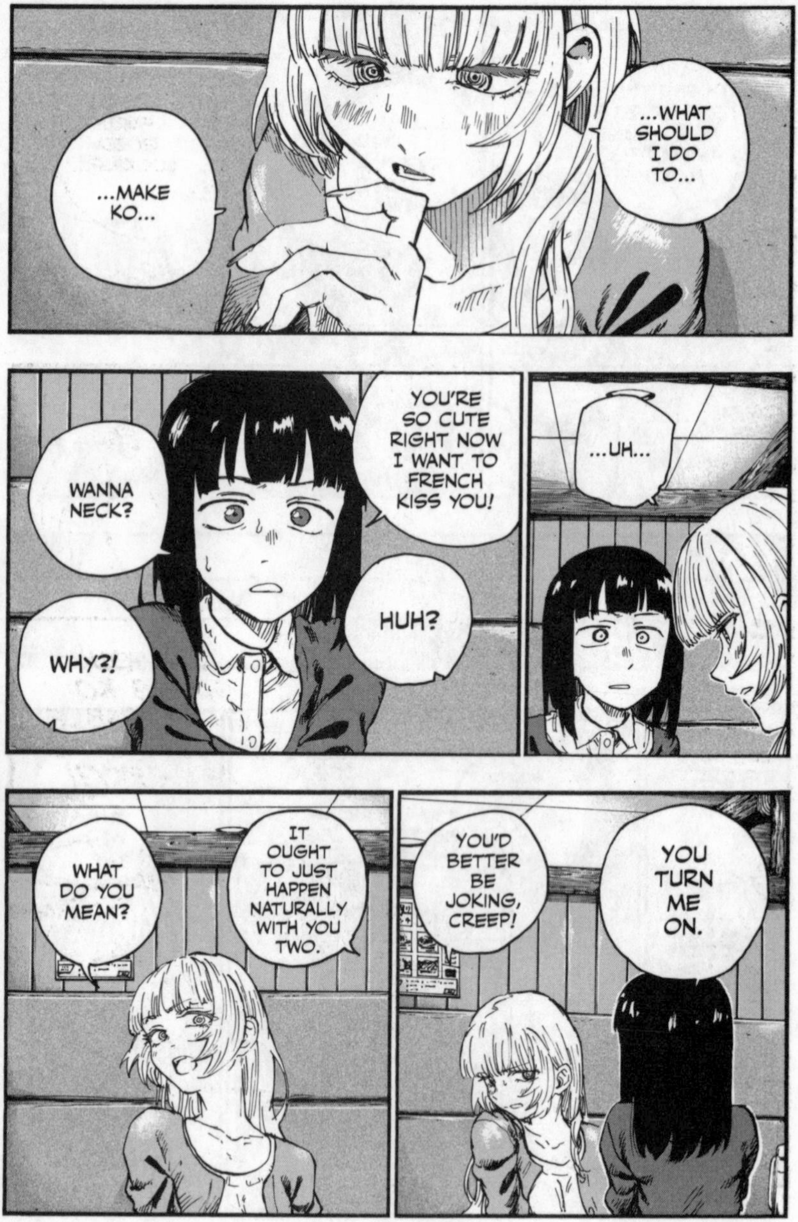
...WHAT SHOULD I DO TO...
...MAKE KO...
...UH...
YOU'RE SO CUTE RIGHT NOW I WANT TO FRENCH KISS YOU!
WANNA NECK?
HUH?
WHY?!
YOU TURN ME ON.
YOU'D BETTER BE JOKING, CREEP!
IT OUGHT TO JUST HAPPEN NATURALLY WITH YOU TWO.
WHAT DO YOU MEAN?

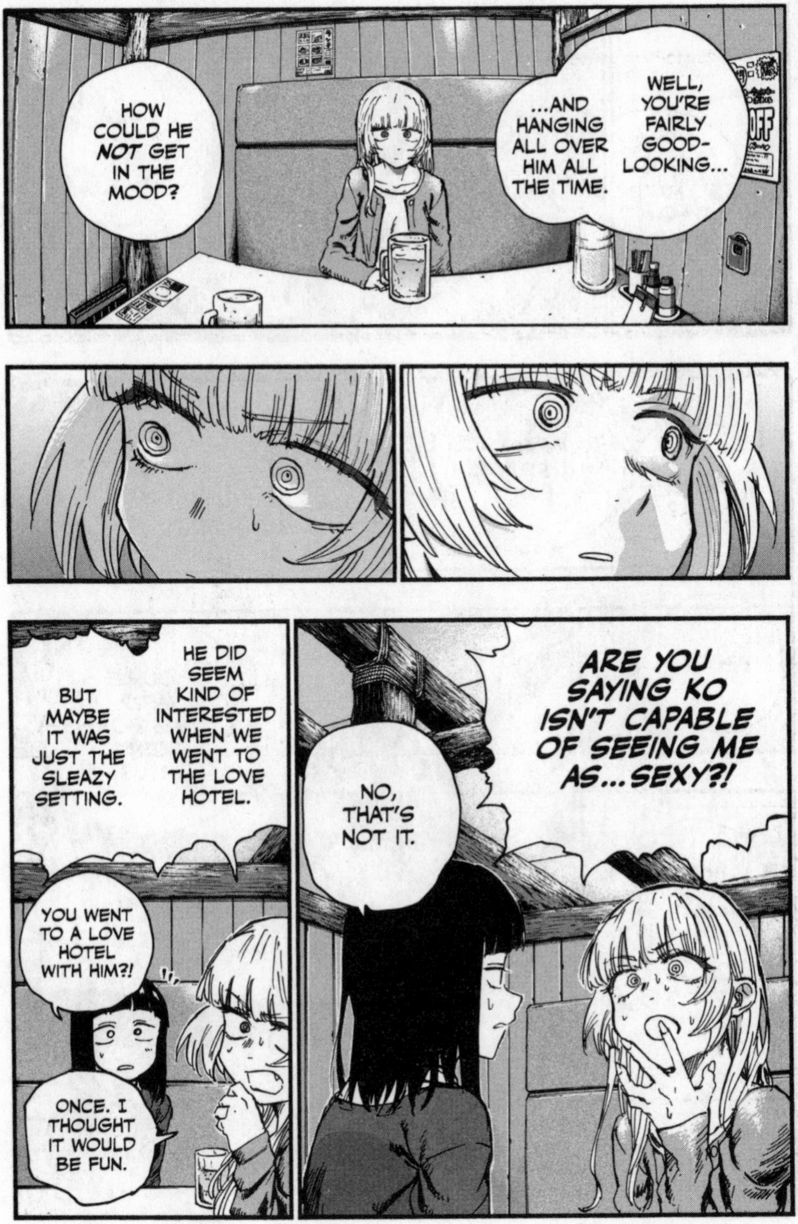
WELL, YOU'RE FAIRLY GOOD-LOOKING...
...AND HANGING ALL OVER HIM ALL THE TIME.
HOW COULD HE *NOT* GET IN THE MOOD?
ARE YOU SAYING KO ISN'T CAPABLE OF SEEING ME AS...SEXY?!
NO, THAT'S NOT IT.
HE DID SEEM KIND OF INTERESTED WHEN WE WENT TO THE LOVE HOTEL.
BUT MAYBE IT WAS JUST THE SLEAZY SETTING.
YOU WENT TO A LOVE HOTEL WITH HIM?!
ONCE. I THOUGHT IT WOULD BE FUN.

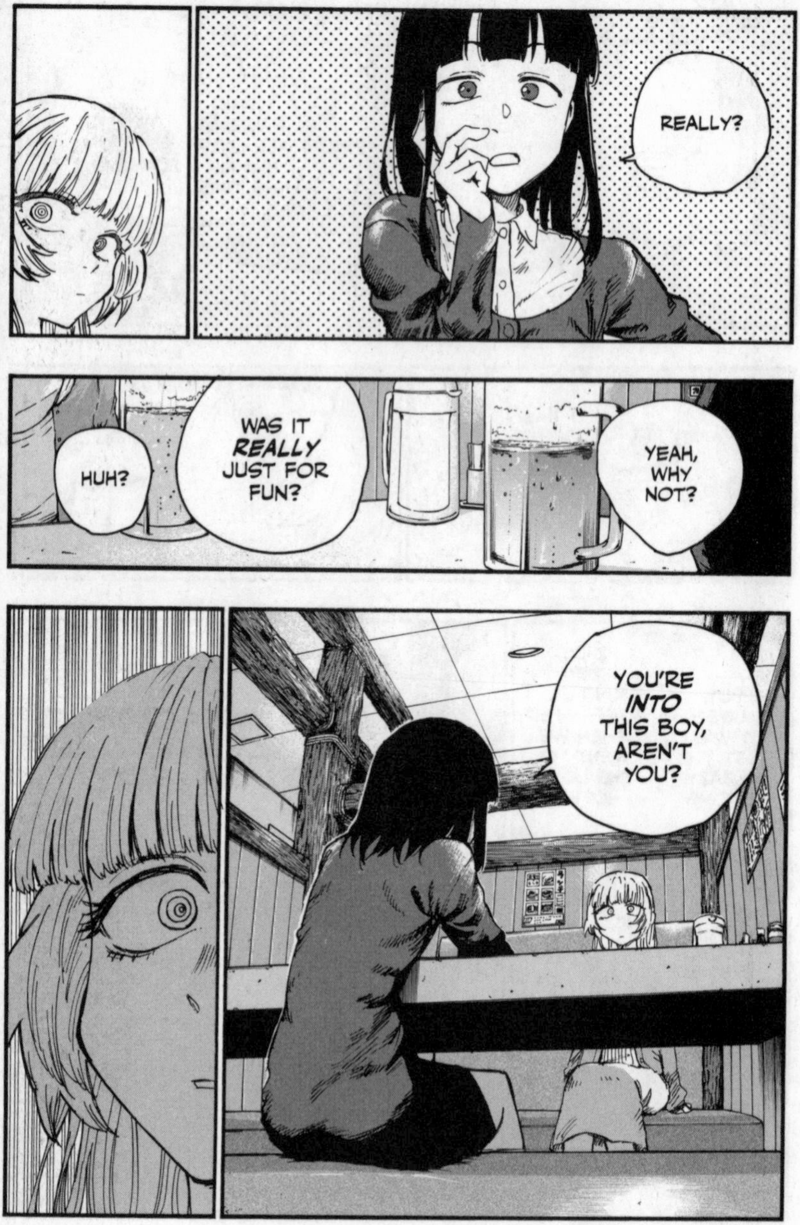
REALLY?
YEAH, WHY NOT?
WAS IT REALLY JUST FOR FUN?
HUH?
YOU'RE INTO THIS BOY, AREN'T YOU?

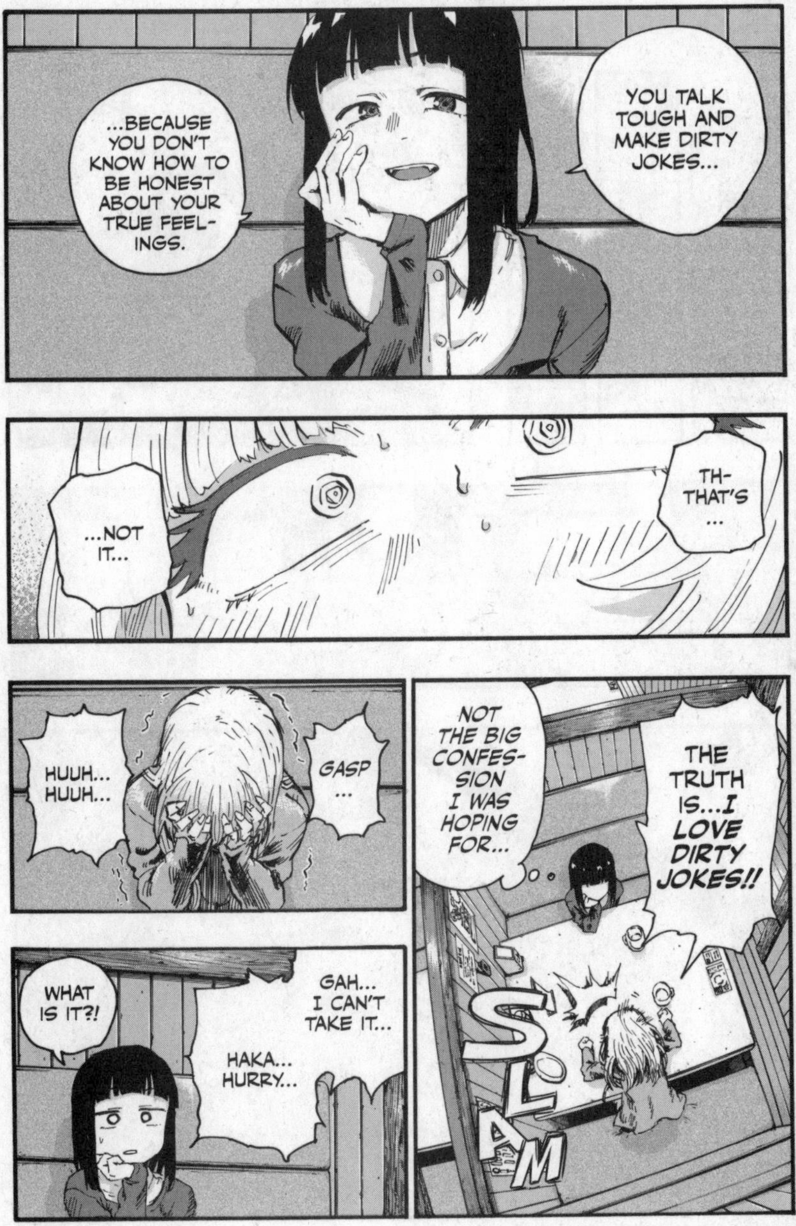
YOU TALK TOUGH AND MAKE DIRTY JOKES...
...BECAUSE YOU DON'T KNOW HOW TO BE HONEST ABOUT YOUR TRUE FEELINGS.
TH-THAT'S ...
...NOT IT...
THE TRUTH IS...I LOVE DIRTY JOKES!!
NOT THE BIG CONFESSION I WAS HOPING FOR...
SLAM
GASP ...
HUUH... HUUH...
GAH... I CAN'T TAKE IT...
HAKA... HURRY...
WHAT IS IT?!

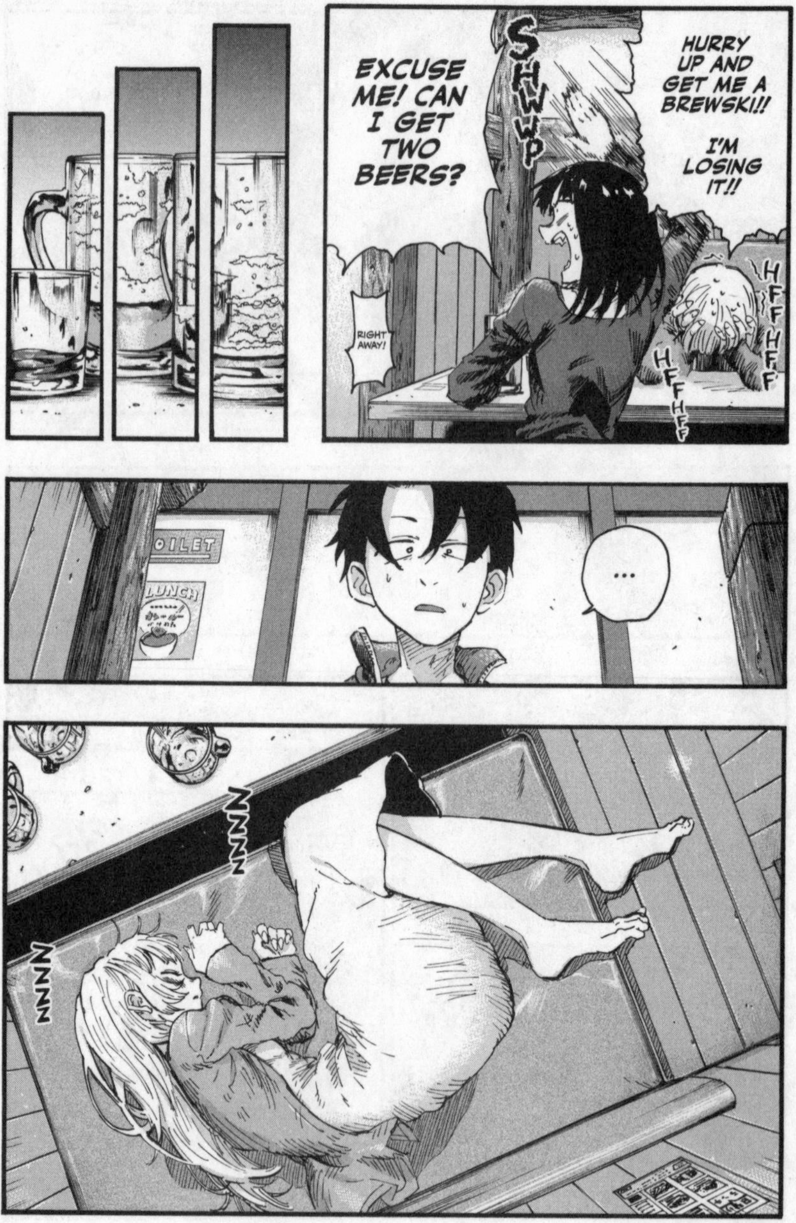
HURRY UP AND GET ME A BREWSKI!!
I'M LOSING IT!!
SHWWP
EXCUSE ME! CAN I GET TWO BEERS?
HFF HFF HFF
RIGHT AWAY!
HFF HFF HFF
OILET
LUNCH
...
ZZZZ
ZZZZ

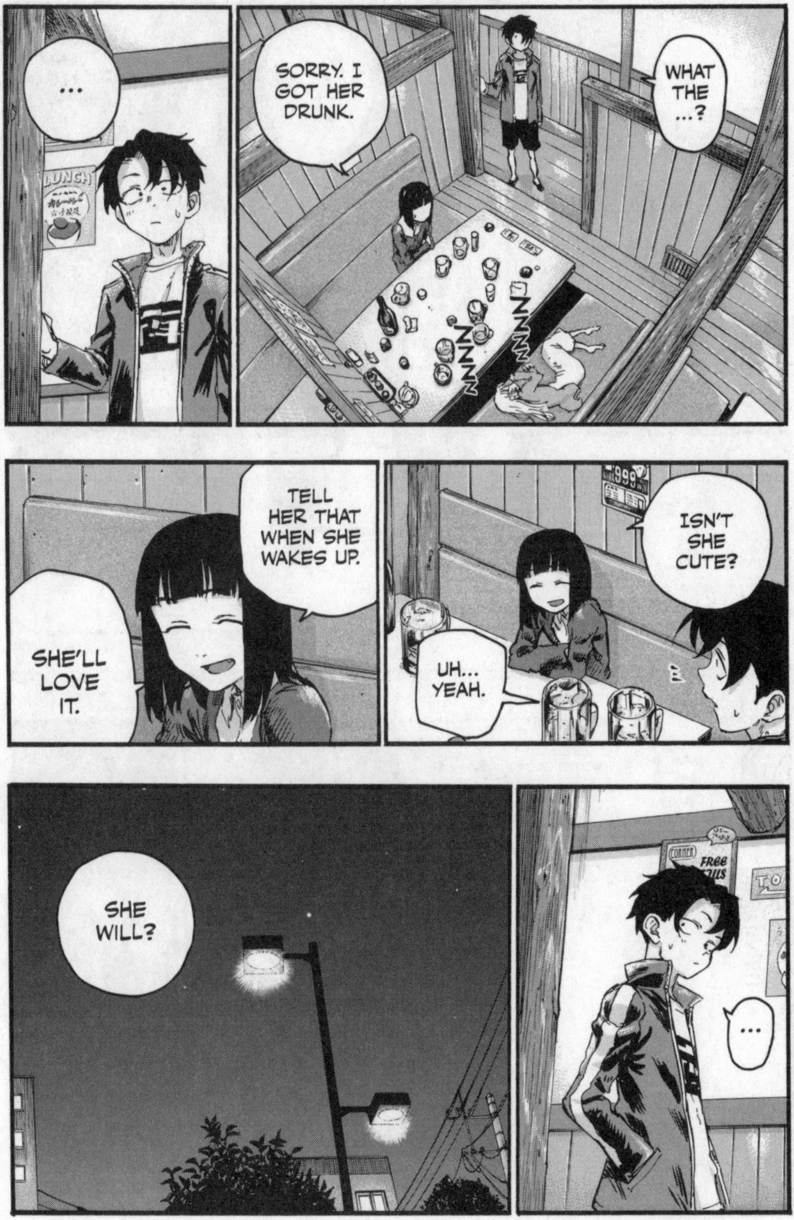
WHAT THE ...?
SORRY. I GOT HER DRUNK.
ZZZZ
ZZZZ
...
LUNCH
ISN'T SHE CUTE?
UH... YEAH.
TELL HER THAT WHEN SHE WAKES UP.
SHE'LL LOVE IT.
...
SHE WILL?

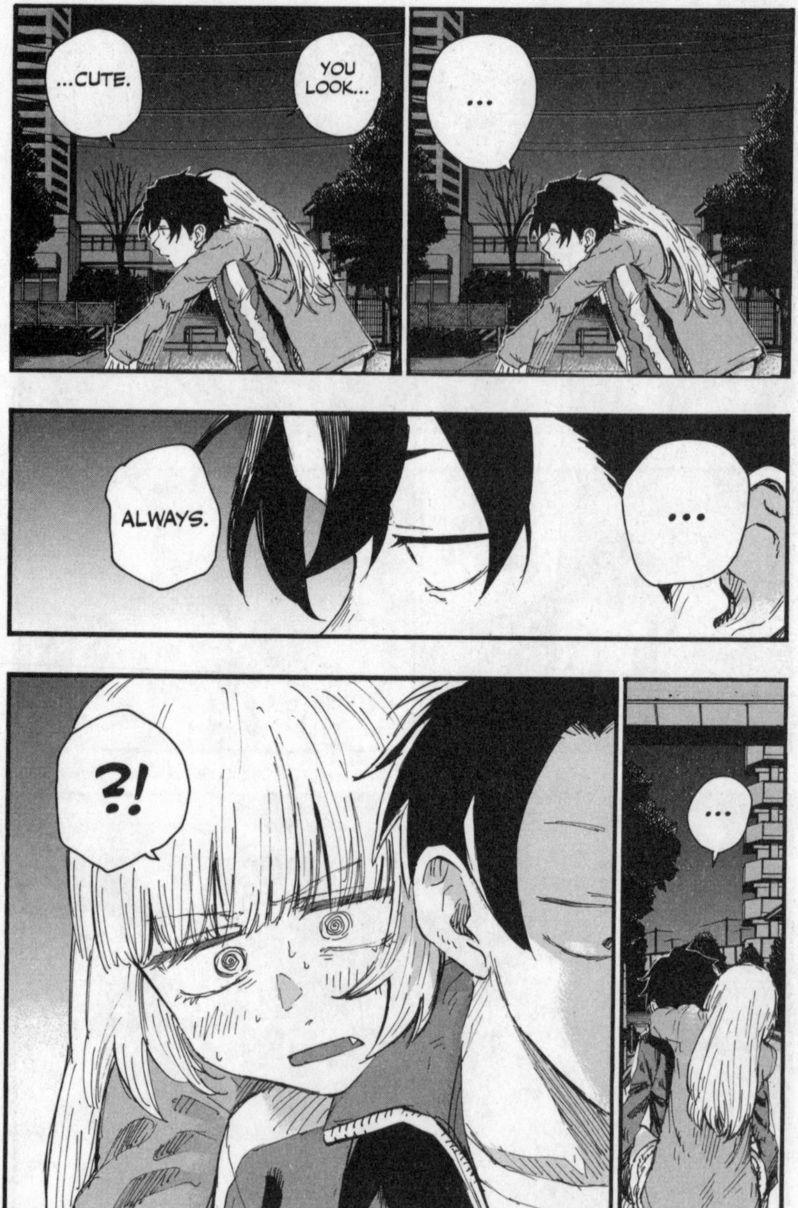
...
YOU LOOK...
...CUTE.
...
ALWAYS.
...
?!

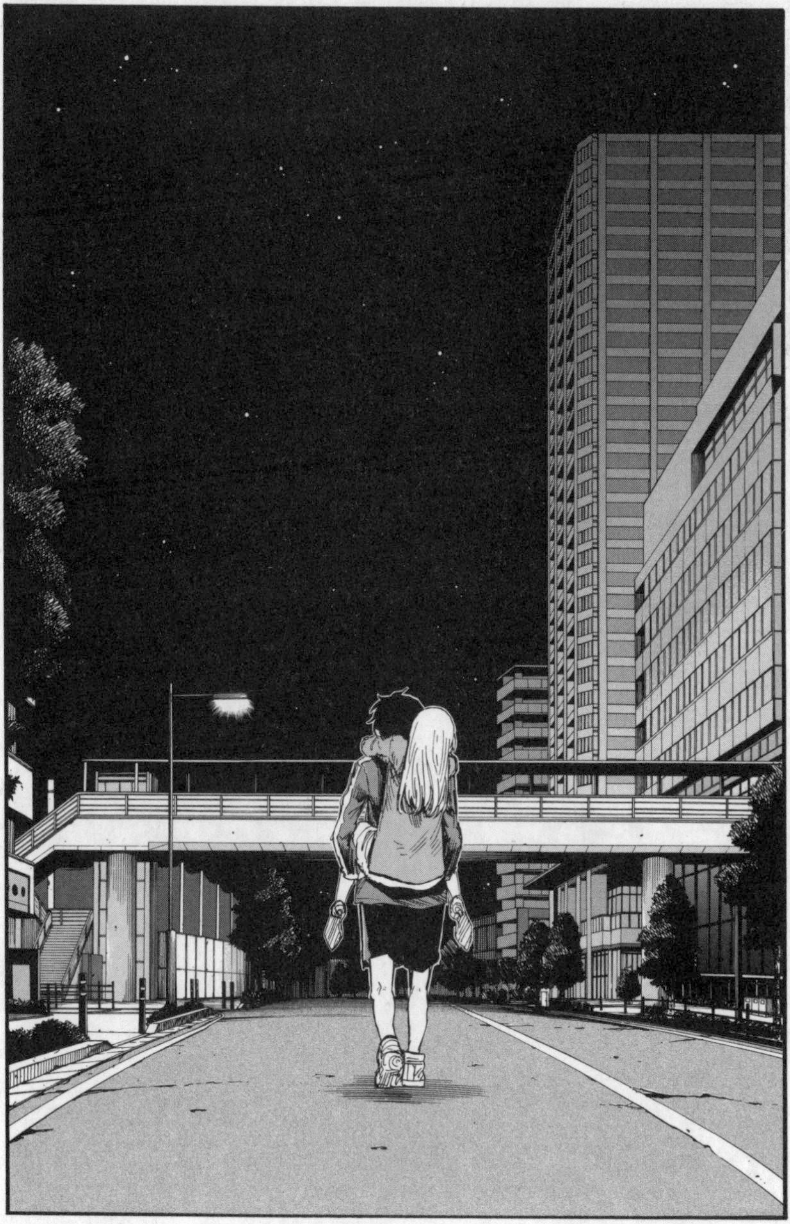

Call of the Night

NIGHT 48: WHY?

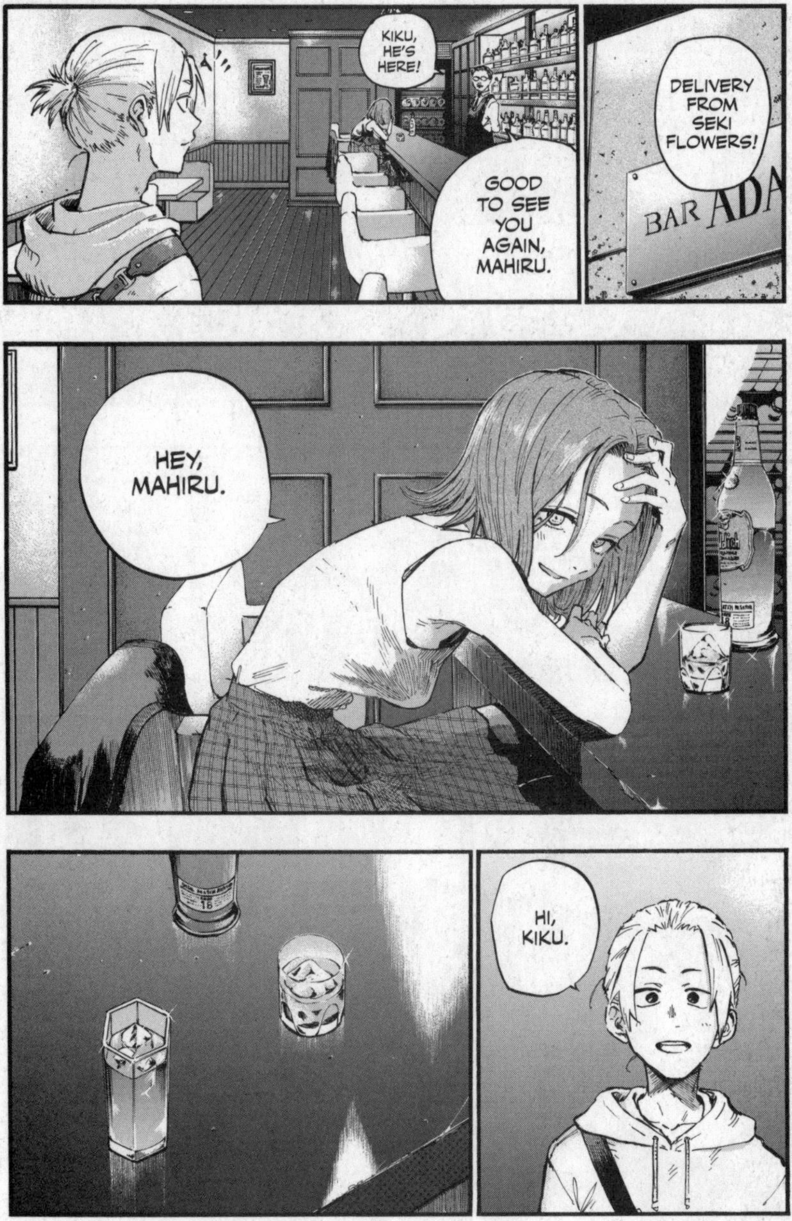
DELIVERY FROM SEKI FLOWERS!
BAR ADA
GOOD TO SEE YOU AGAIN, MAHIRU.
KIKU, HE'S HERE!
HEY, MAHIRU.
HI, KIKU.

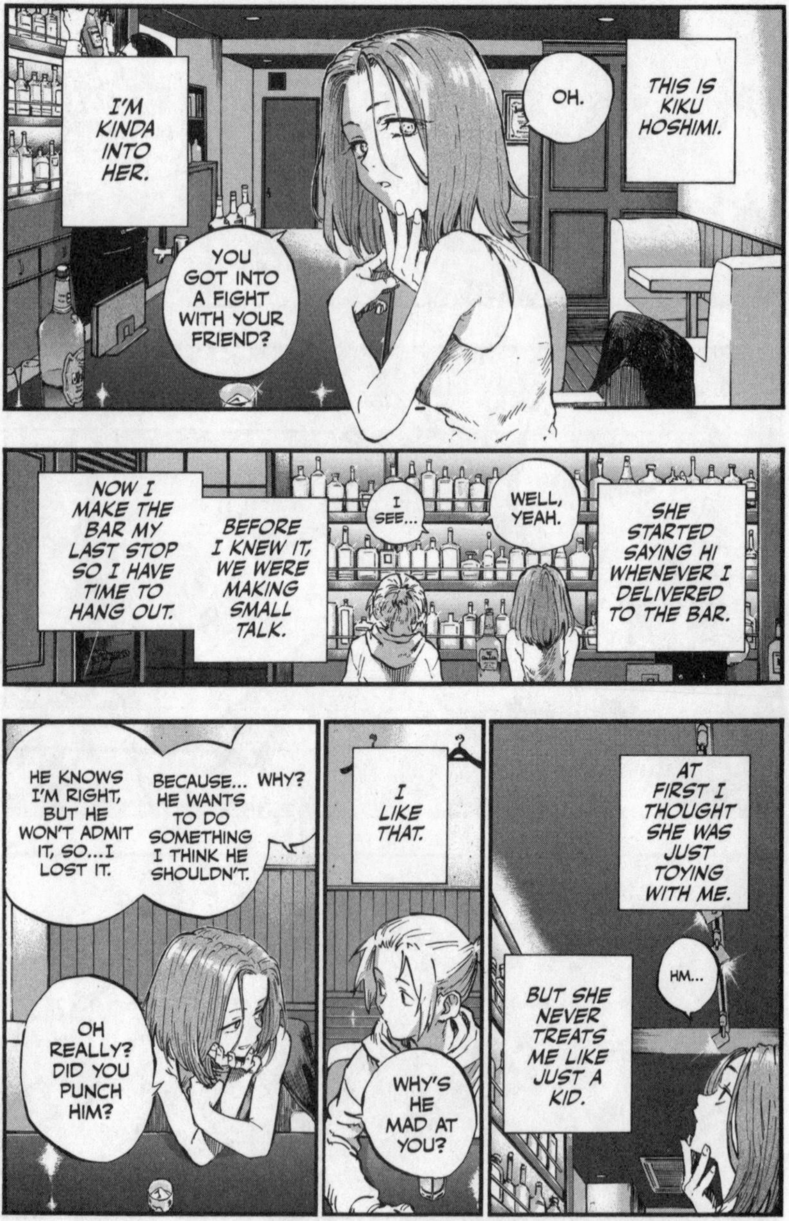
THIS IS KIKU HOSHIMI.
OH.
I'M KINDA INTO HER.
YOU GOT INTO A FIGHT WITH YOUR FRIEND?
SHE STARTED SAYING HI WHENEVER I DELIVERED TO THE BAR.
WELL, YEAH.
I SEE...
BEFORE I KNEW IT, WE WERE MAKING SMALL TALK.
NOW I MAKE THE BAR MY LAST STOP SO I HAVE TIME TO HANG OUT.
AT FIRST I THOUGHT SHE WAS JUST TOYING WITH ME.
HM...
BUT SHE NEVER TREATS ME LIKE JUST A KID.
I LIKE THAT.
WHY'S HE MAD AT YOU?
WHY?
BECAUSE... HE WANTS TO DO SOMETHING I THINK HE SHOULDN'T.
HE KNOWS I'M RIGHT, BUT HE WON'T ADMIT IT, SO...I LOST IT.
OH REALLY? DID YOU PUNCH HIM?

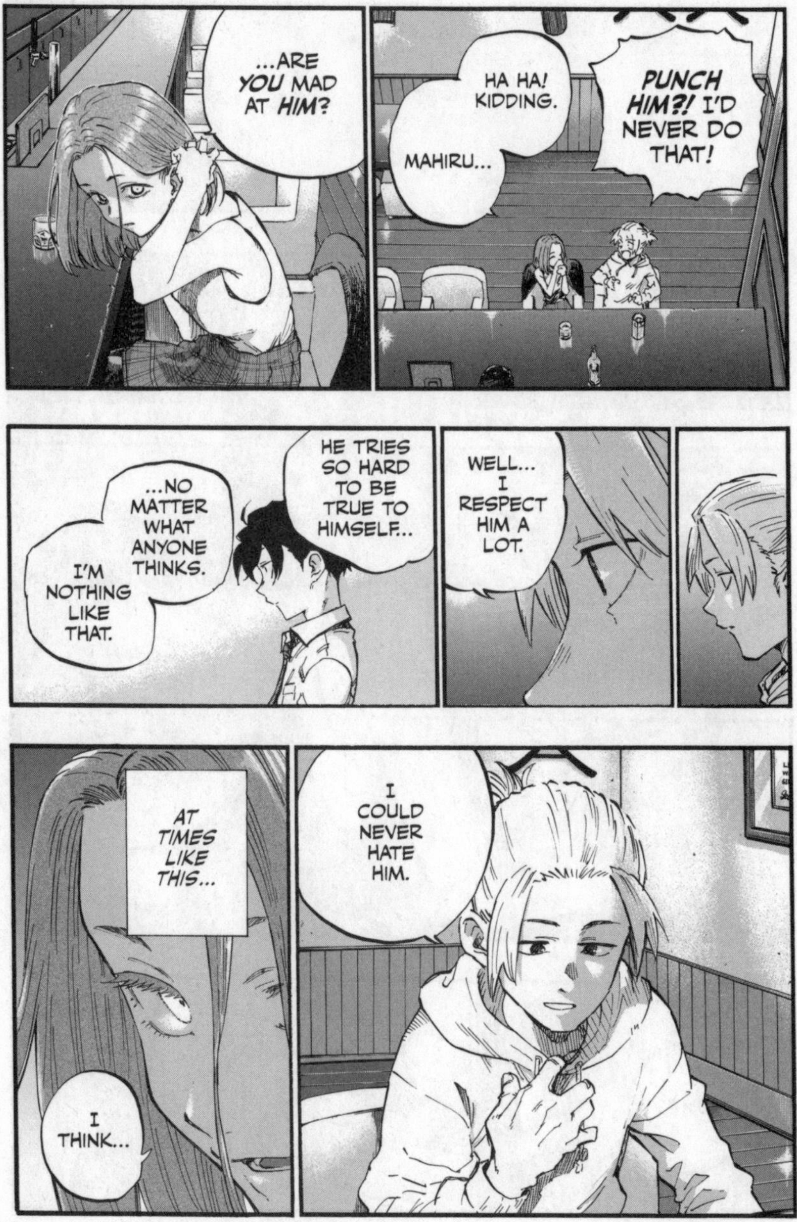
PUNCH HIM?! I'D NEVER DO THAT!
HA HA! KIDDING.
MAHIRU...
...ARE YOU MAD AT HIM?
WELL... I RESPECT HIM A LOT.
HE TRIES SO HARD TO BE TRUE TO HIMSELF...
...NO MATTER WHAT ANYONE THINKS.
I'M NOTHING LIKE THAT.
I COULD NEVER HATE HIM.
AT TIMES LIKE THIS...
I THINK...

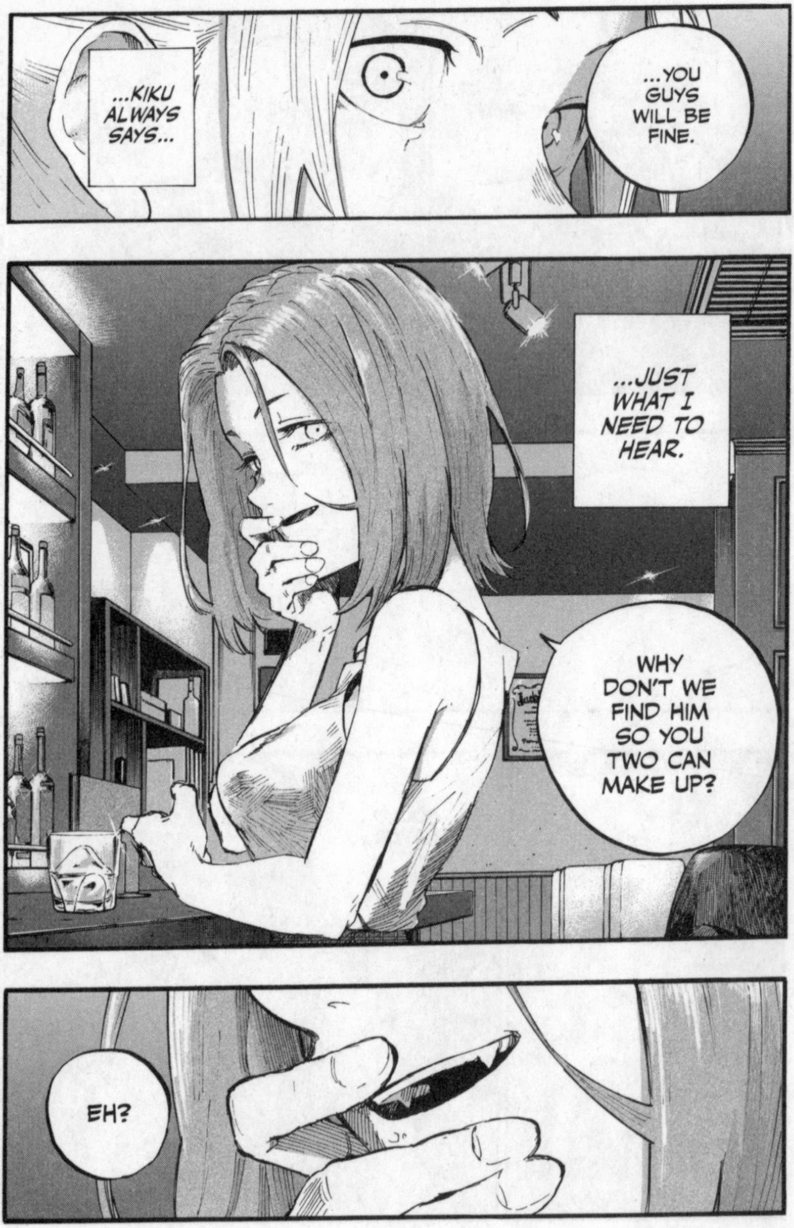
...YOU GUYS WILL BE FINE.
...KIKU ALWAYS SAYS...
...JUST WHAT I NEED TO HEAR.
WHY DON'T WE FIND HIM SO YOU TWO CAN MAKE UP?
EH?

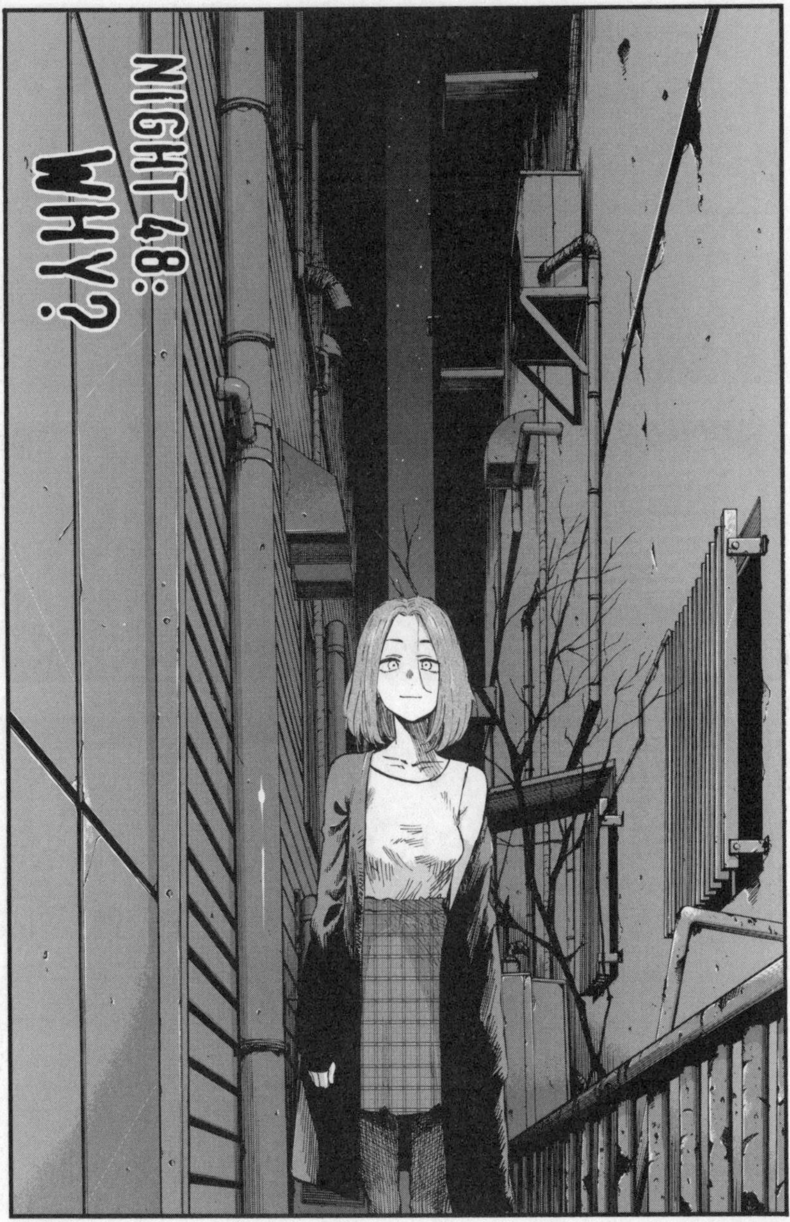
NIGHT 48:
WHY?

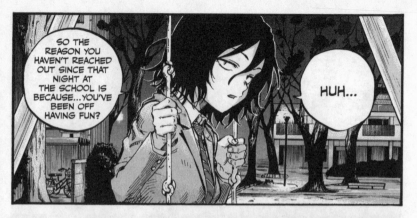

HUH...
SO THE REASON YOU HAVEN'T REACHED OUT SINCE THAT NIGHT AT THE SCHOOL IS BECAUSE...YOU'VE BEEN OFF HAVING FUN?
...
KREAK
A-ARE YOU MAD?
WHO, ME? IT'S JUST...
...YOU WERE OFF CHASING A GIRL...
...WHILE YOUR CHILDHOOD FRIEND WAS SCARED AND HURT.
...
STAB
STAB
I... I'M SORRY.
IT'S OKAY.
Really.
KRAK

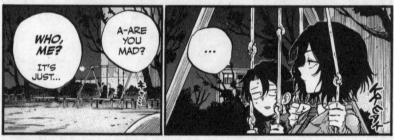

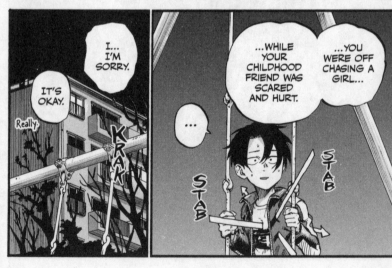

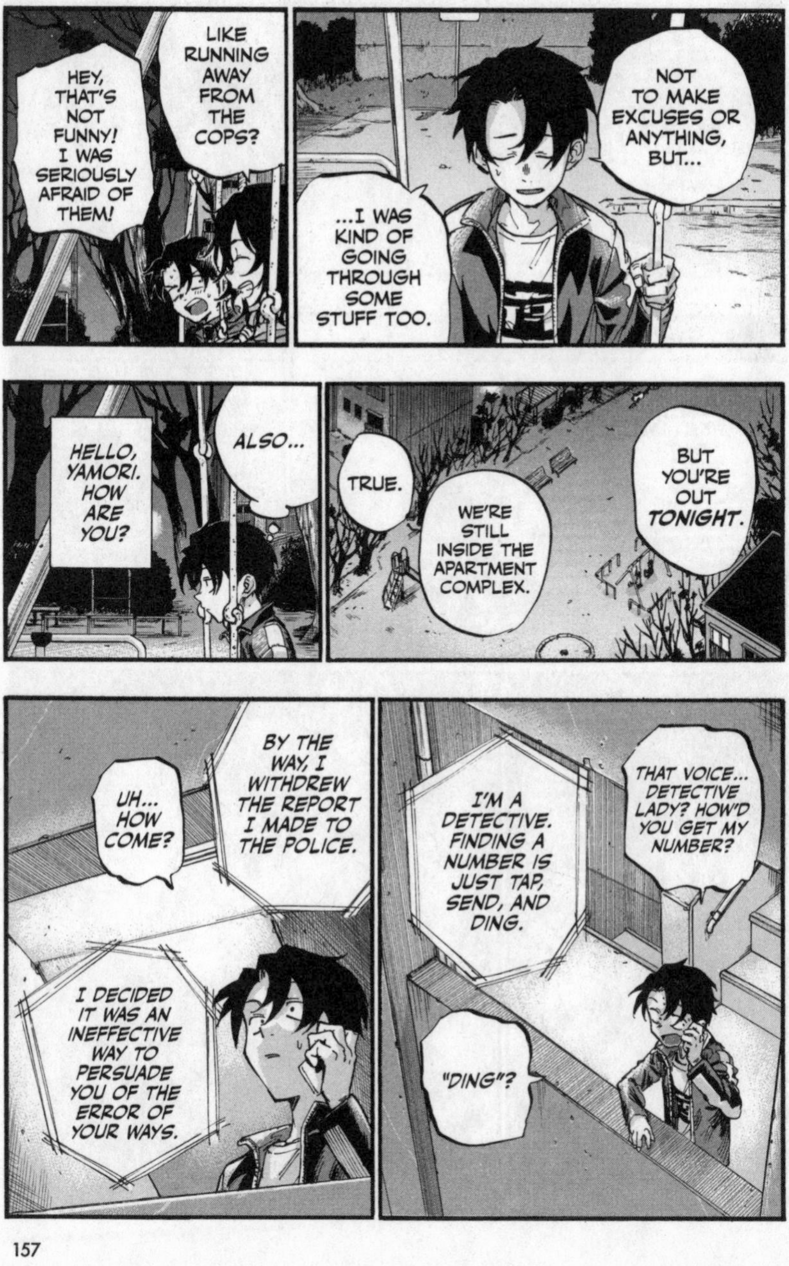
NOT TO MAKE EXCUSES OR ANYTHING, BUT...
...I WAS KIND OF GOING THROUGH SOME STUFF TOO.
LIKE RUNNING AWAY FROM THE COPS?
HEY, THAT'S NOT FUNNY! I WAS SERIOUSLY AFRAID OF THEM!
BUT YOU'RE OUT *TONIGHT*.
WE'RE STILL INSIDE THE APARTMENT COMPLEX.
TRUE.
ALSO...
HELLO, YAMORI. HOW ARE YOU?
THAT VOICE... DETECTIVE LADY? HOW'D YOU GET MY NUMBER?
I'M A DETECTIVE. FINDING A NUMBER IS JUST TAP, SEND, AND DING.
"DING"?
BY THE WAY, I WITHDREW THE REPORT I MADE TO THE POLICE.
UH... HOW COME?
I DECIDED IT WAS AN INEFFECTIVE WAY TO PERSUADE YOU OF THE ERROR OF YOUR WAYS.

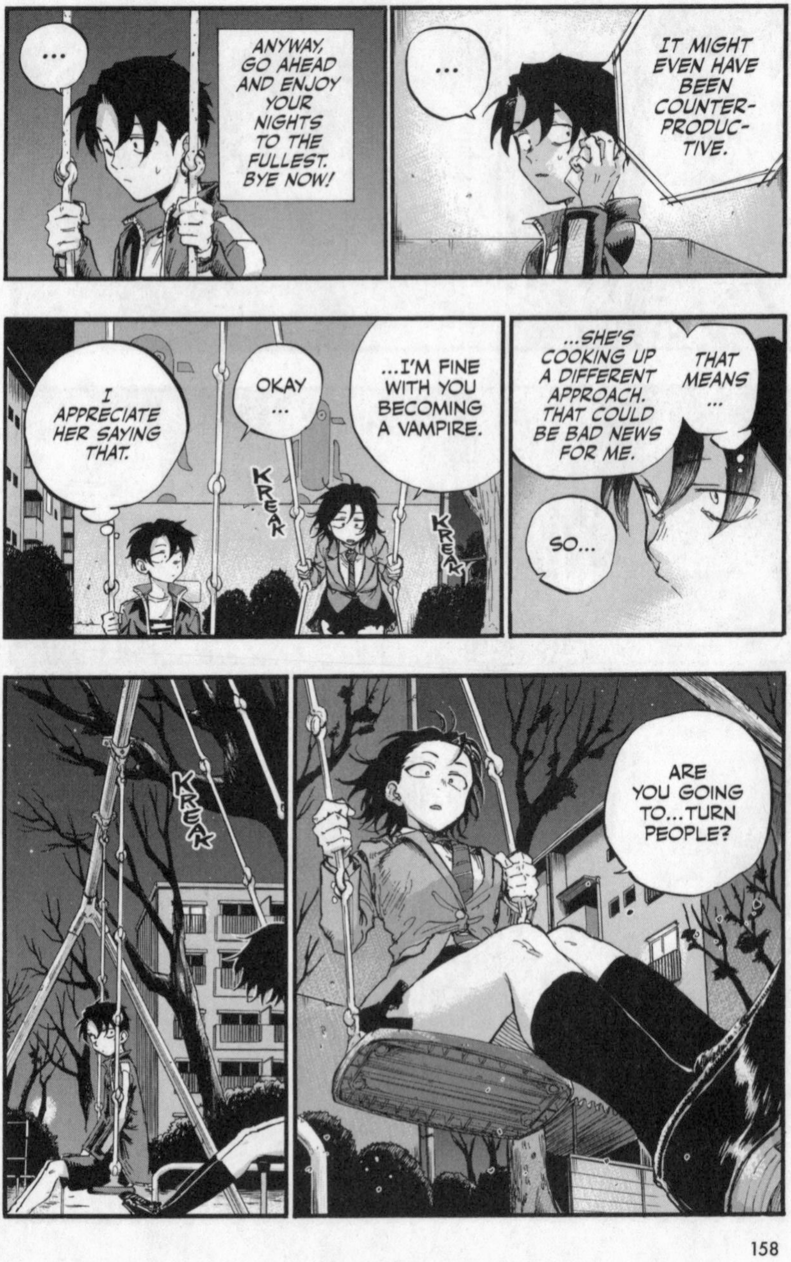
IT MIGHT EVEN HAVE BEEN COUNTER-PRODUCTIVE.
...
ANYWAY, GO AHEAD AND ENJOY YOUR NIGHTS TO THE FULLEST. BYE NOW!
...
THAT MEANS...
...SHE'S COOKING UP A DIFFERENT APPROACH. THAT COULD BE BAD NEWS FOR ME.
SO...
...I'M FINE WITH YOU BECOMING A VAMPIRE.
KREAK
OKAY...
KREAK
I APPRECIATE HER SAYING THAT.
ARE YOU GOING TO...TURN PEOPLE?
KREAK

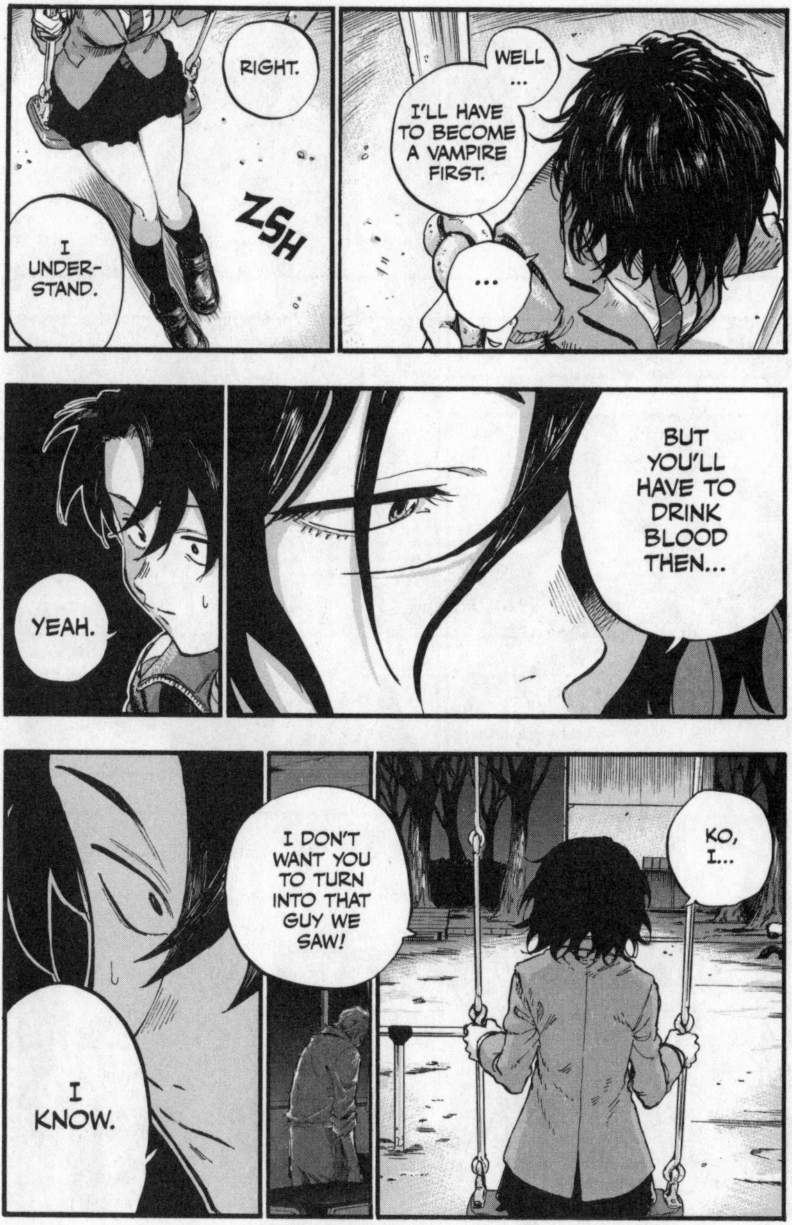
WELL ...
I'LL HAVE TO BECOME A VAMPIRE FIRST.
...
RIGHT.
ZSH
I UNDER-STAND.
BUT YOU'LL HAVE TO DRINK BLOOD THEN...
YEAH.
KO, I...
I DON'T WANT YOU TO TURN INTO THAT GUY WE SAW!
I KNOW.

HA HA!

SO I'LL BE THE FIRST TO LET YOU DRINK MY BLOOD!

DON'T FALL IN LOVE WITH ME THOUGH.

EW, NO WAY!

OH...

KO!

160

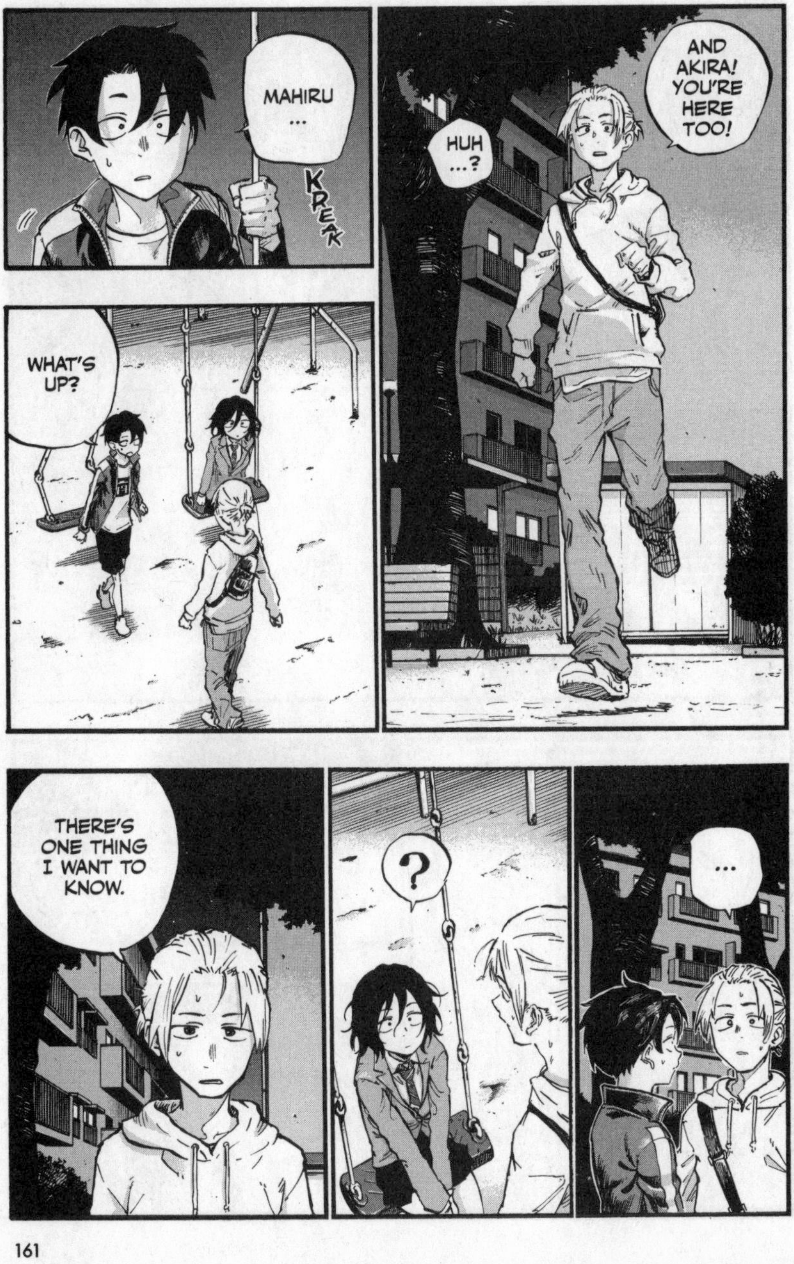
AND AKIRA! YOU'RE HERE TOO!
HUH ...?
MAHIRU ...
KREAK
WHAT'S UP?
...
?
THERE'S ONE THING I WANT TO KNOW.

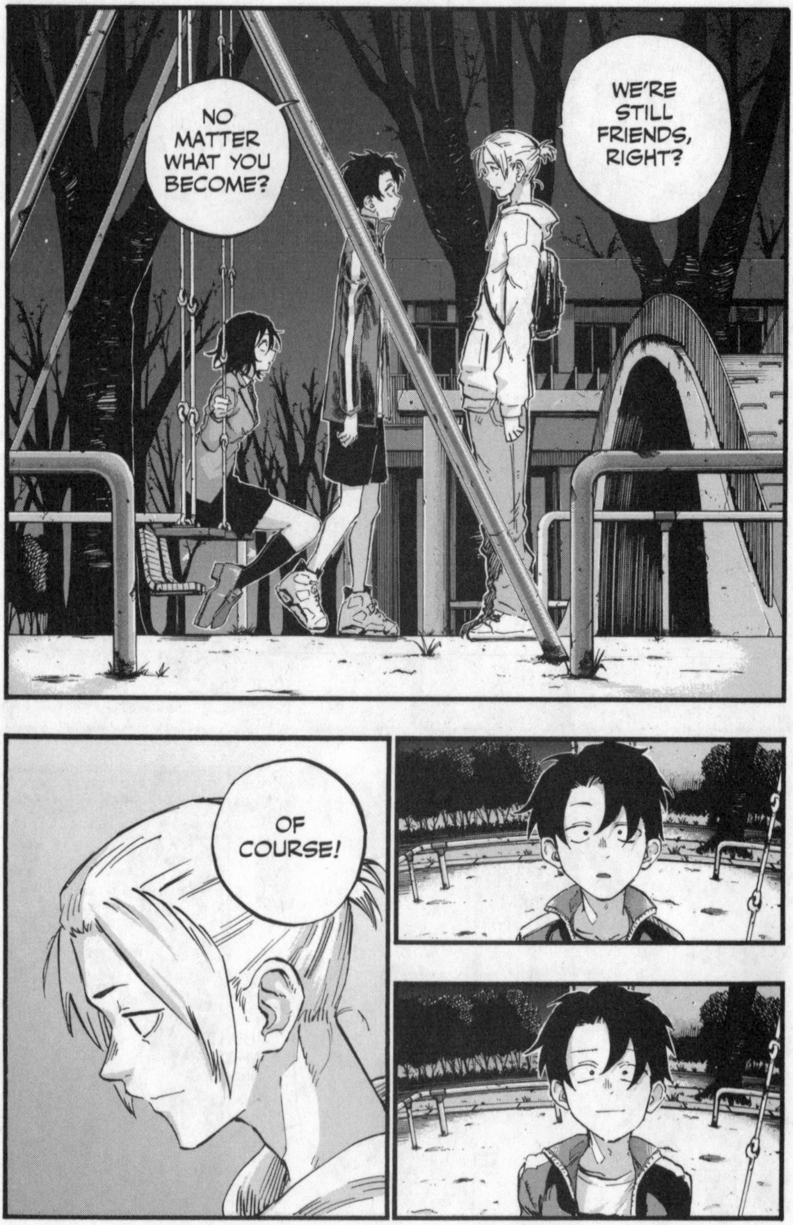
WE'RE STILL FRIENDS, RIGHT?
NO MATTER WHAT YOU BECOME?
OF COURSE!

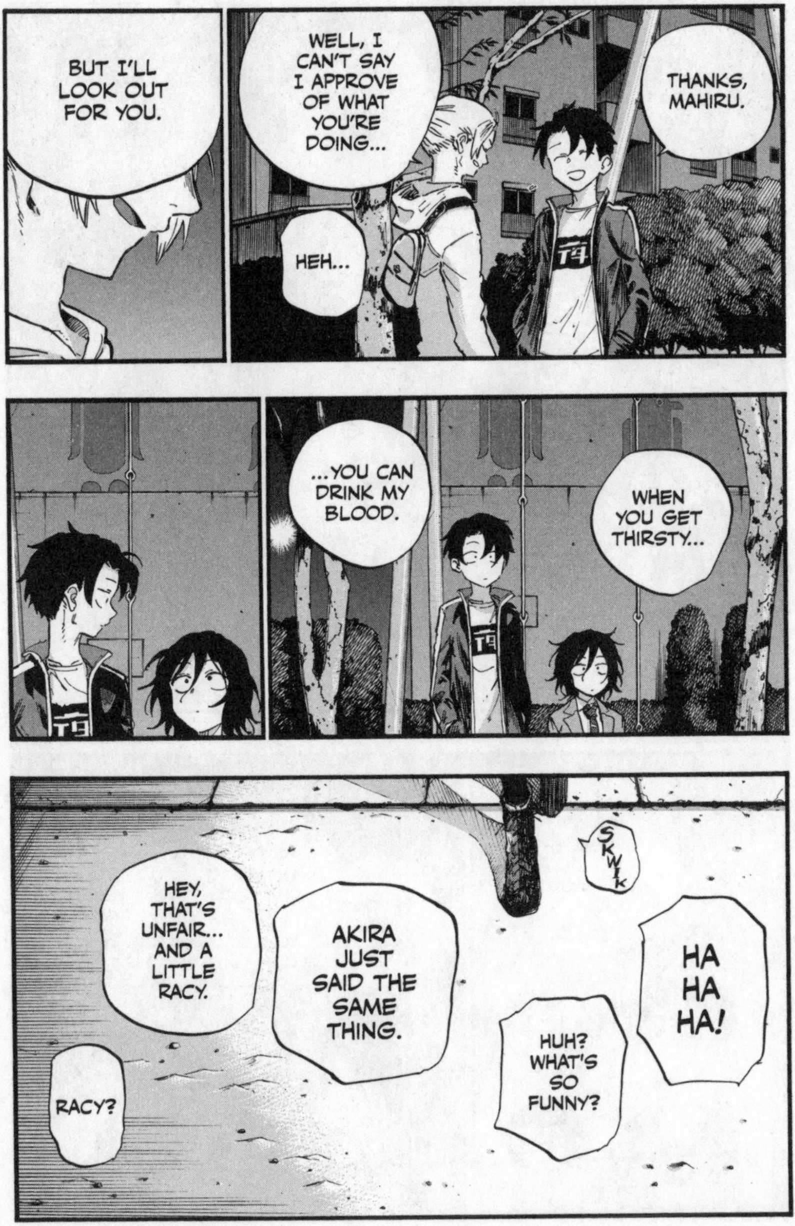
THANKS, MAHIRU.
WELL, I CAN'T SAY I APPROVE OF WHAT YOU'RE DOING...
HEH...
BUT I'LL LOOK OUT FOR YOU.
WHEN YOU GET THIRSTY...
...YOU CAN DRINK MY BLOOD.
SKWIK
HA HA HA!
HUH? WHAT'S SO FUNNY?
AKIRA JUST SAID THE SAME THING.
HEY, THAT'S UNFAIR... AND A LITTLE RACY.
RACY?

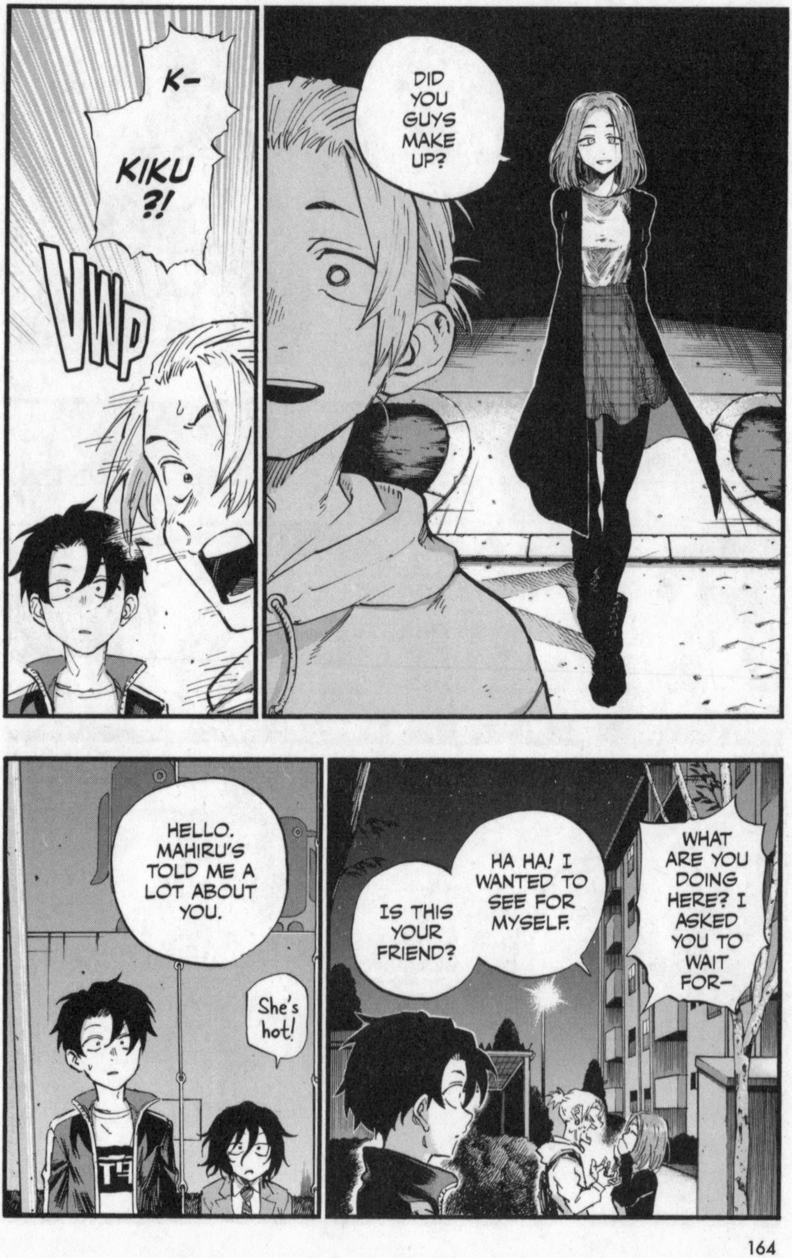
DID YOU GUYS MAKE UP?
K-
KIKU ?!
VWP
WHAT ARE YOU DOING HERE? I ASKED YOU TO WAIT FOR-
HA HA! I WANTED TO SEE FOR MYSELF.
IS THIS YOUR FRIEND?
HELLO. MAHIRU'S TOLD ME A LOT ABOUT YOU.
She's hot!

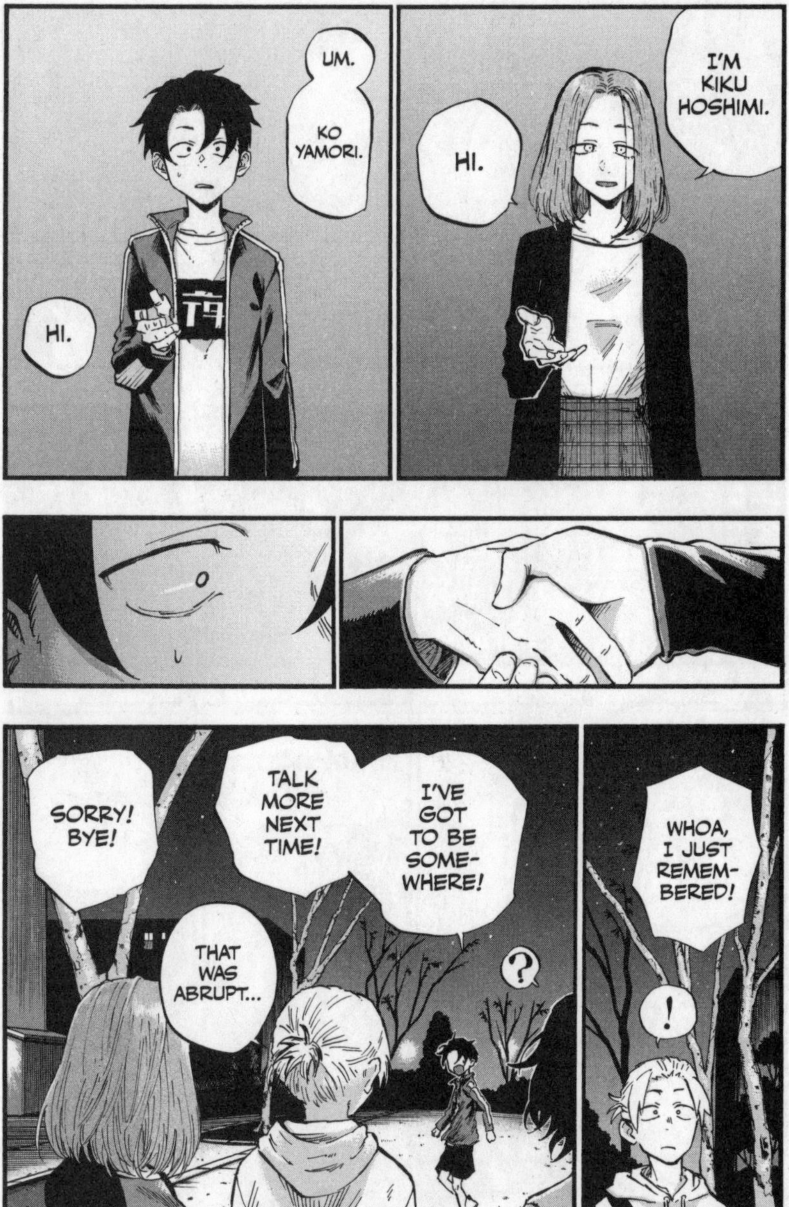
I'M KIKU HOSHIMI.
HI.
UM.
KO YAMORI.
HI.
WHOA, I JUST REMEMBERED!
!
I'VE GOT TO BE SOME-WHERE!
TALK MORE NEXT TIME!
SORRY! BYE!
?
THAT WAS ABRUPT...

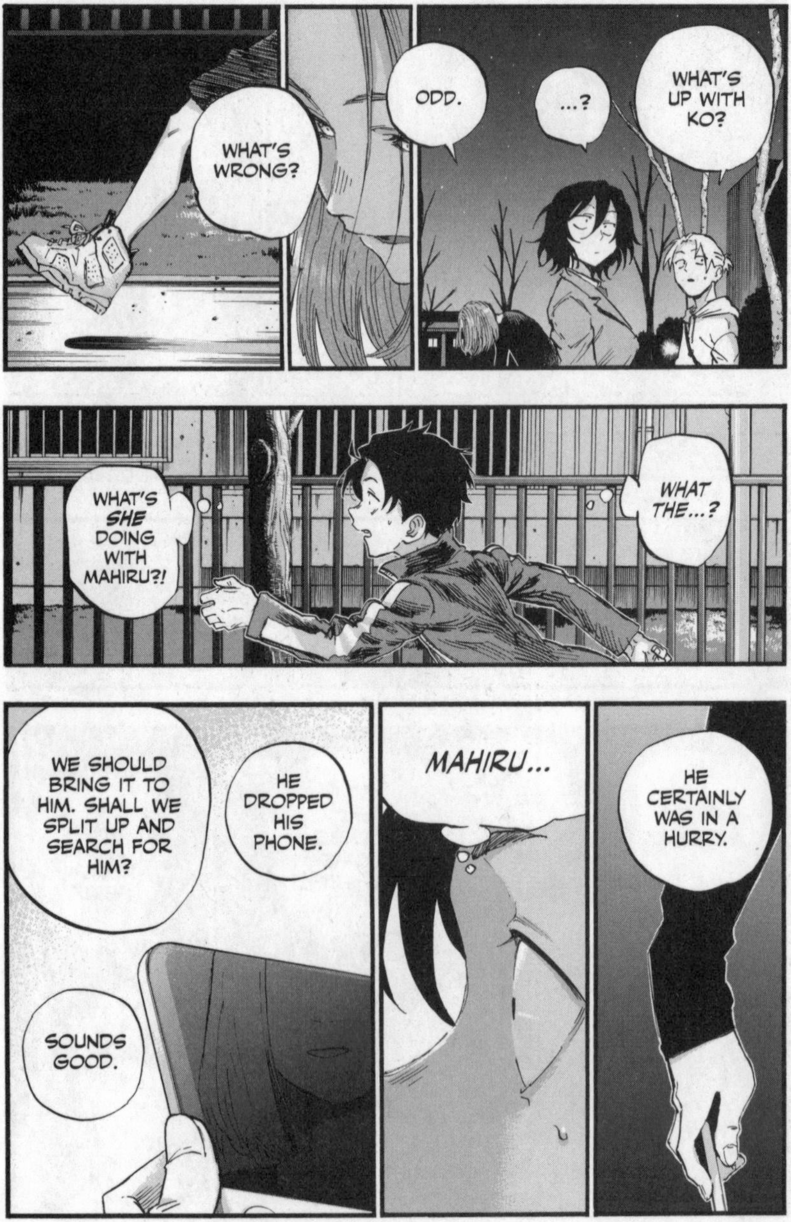
WHAT'S UP WITH KO?
...?
ODD.
WHAT'S WRONG?
WHAT THE...?
WHAT'S SHE DOING WITH MAHIRU?!
HE CERTAINLY WAS IN A HURRY.
MAHIRU...
HE DROPPED HIS PHONE.
WE SHOULD BRING IT TO HIM. SHALL WE SPLIT UP AND SEARCH FOR HIM?
SOUNDS GOOD.

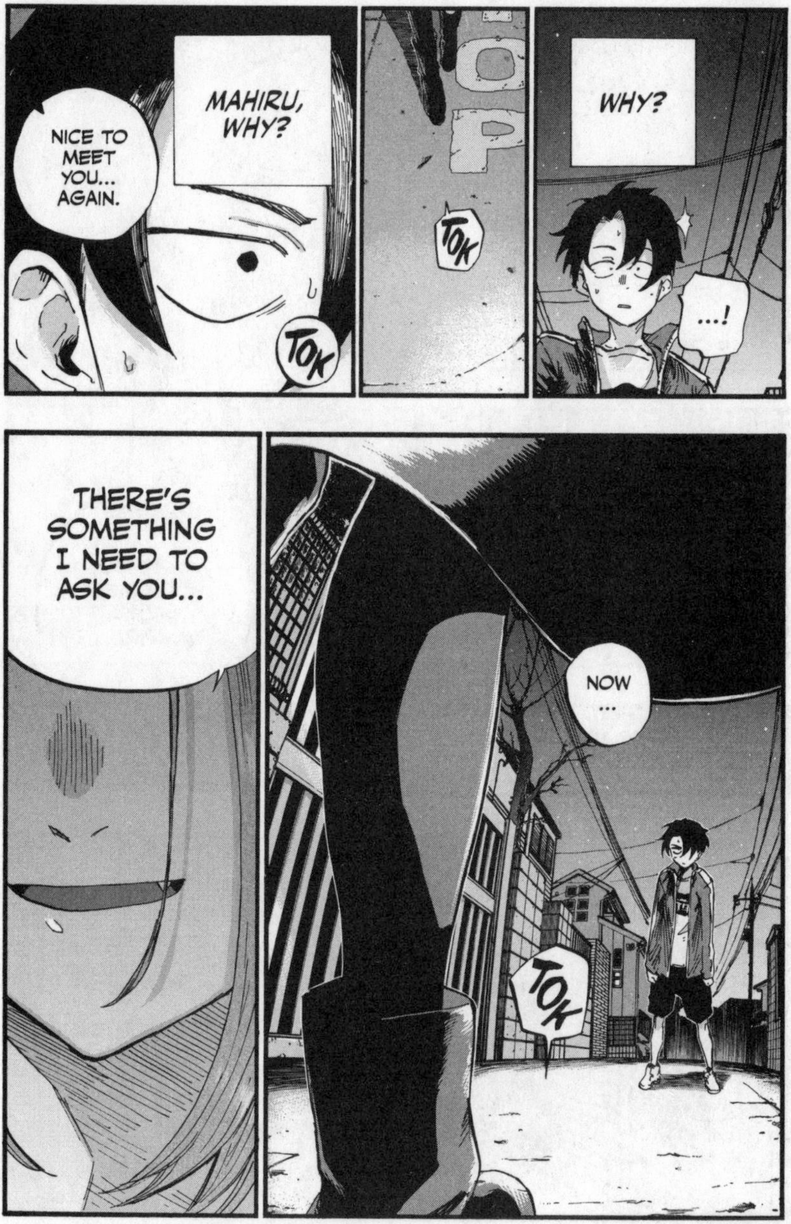
WHY?
...!
TOK
MAHIRU, WHY?
NICE TO MEET YOU... AGAIN.
TOK
NOW ...
TOK
THERE'S SOMETHING I NEED TO ASK YOU...

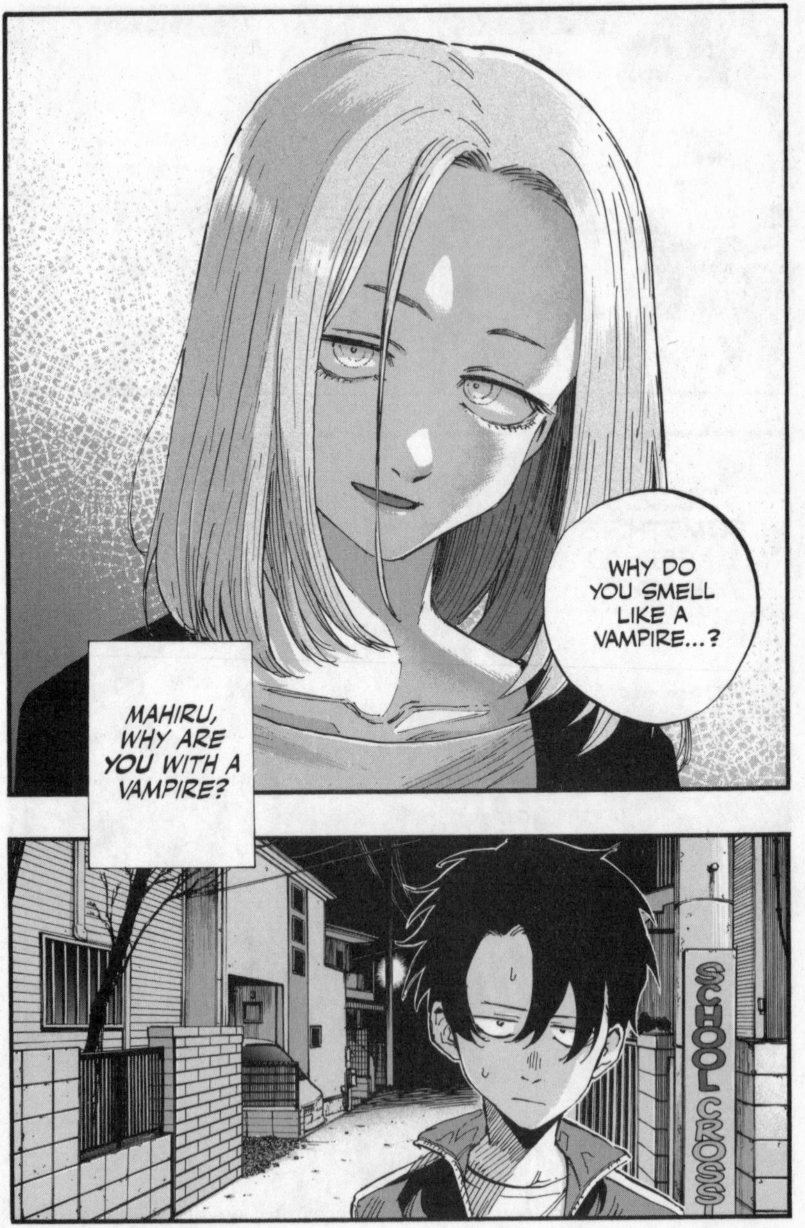
WHY DO YOU SMELL LIKE A VAMPIRE...?
MAHIRU, WHY ARE YOU WITH A VAMPIRE?
SCHOOL CROSS

NIGHT 49: DIDN'T YOU HEAR ME?

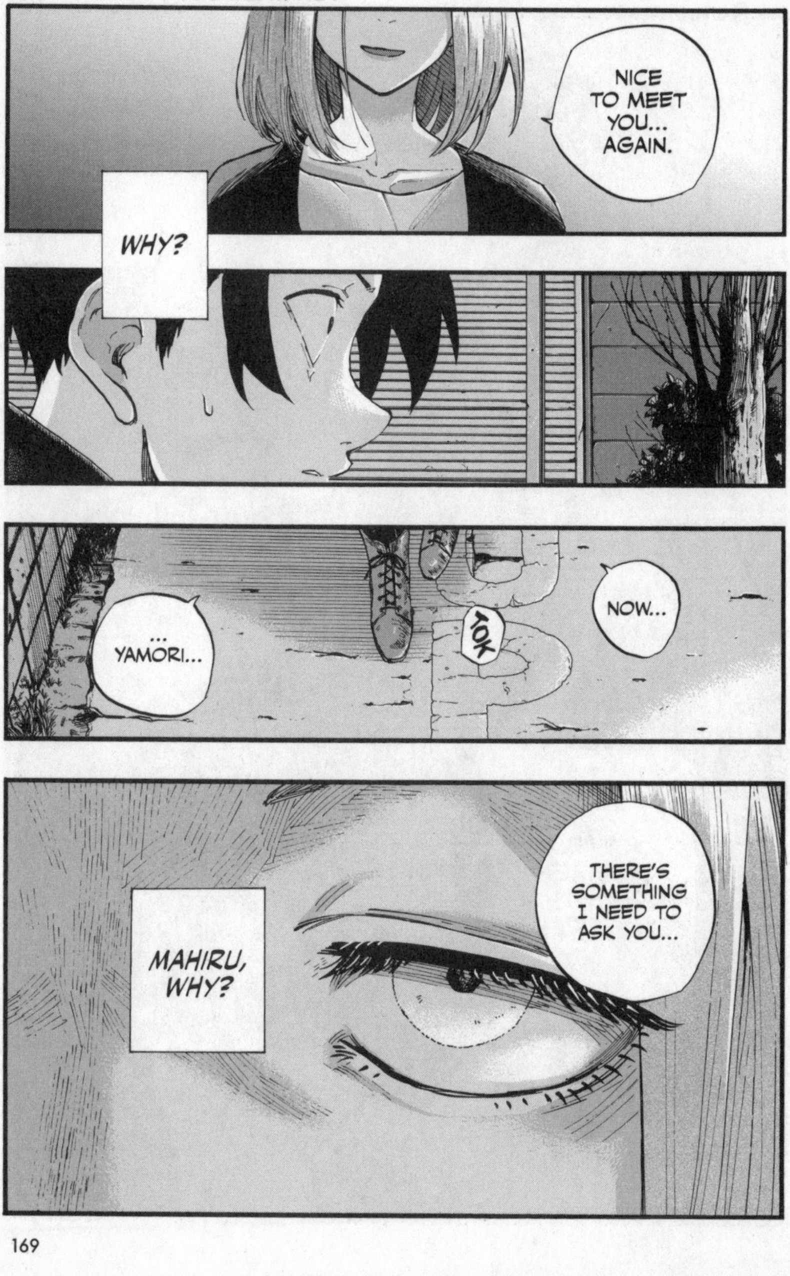

NICE TO MEET YOU... AGAIN.
WHY?
NOW...
TOK
... YAMORI...
THERE'S SOMETHING I NEED TO ASK YOU...
MAHIRU, WHY?

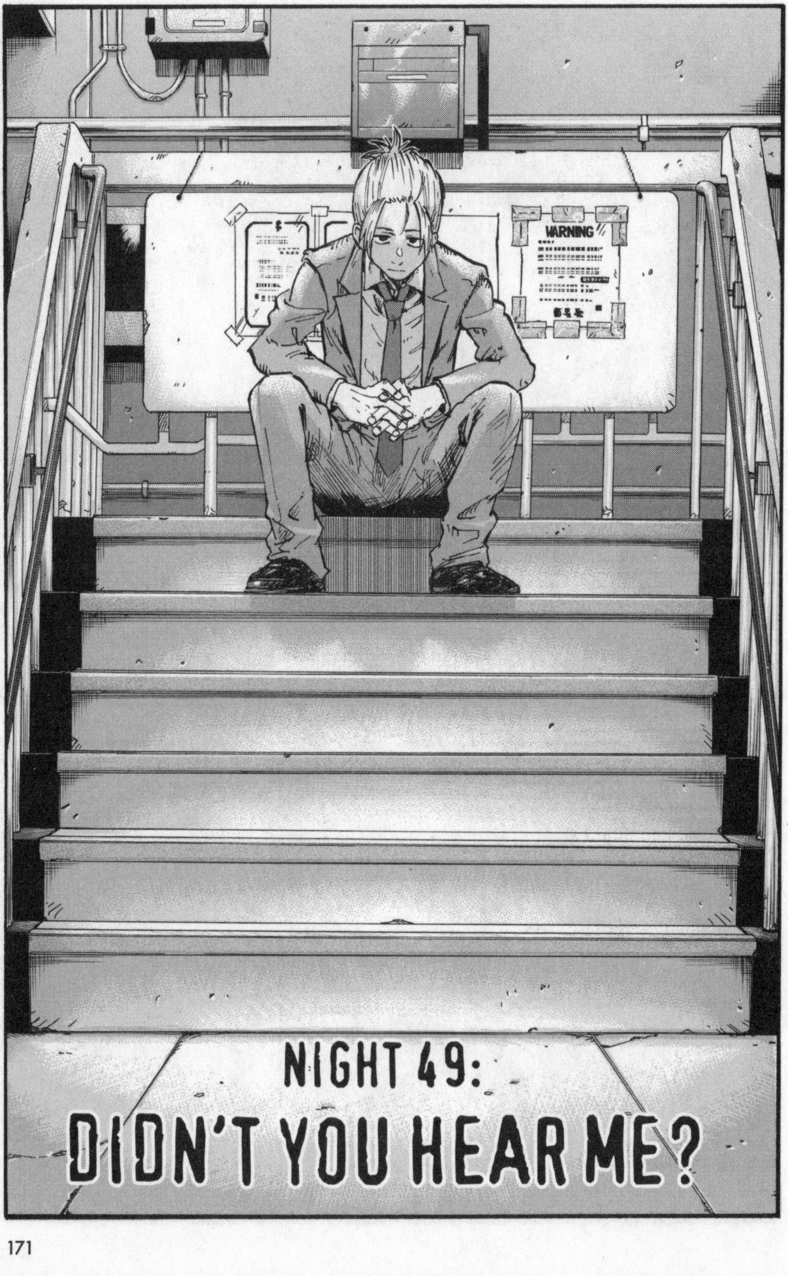
WARNING
NIGHT 49:
DIDN'T YOU HEAR ME?

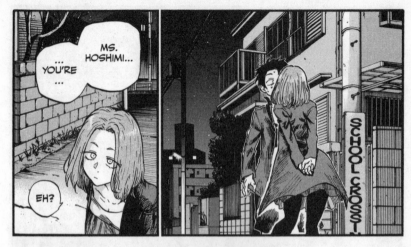

MS. HOSHIMI... ...YOU'RE...
EH?
...A VAMPIRE, AREN'T YOU?
I'M THE ONE ASKING THE QUESTIONS HERE!
DOES MAHIRU KNOW?
!

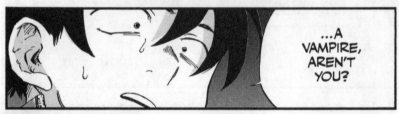

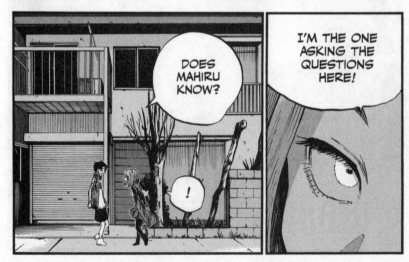

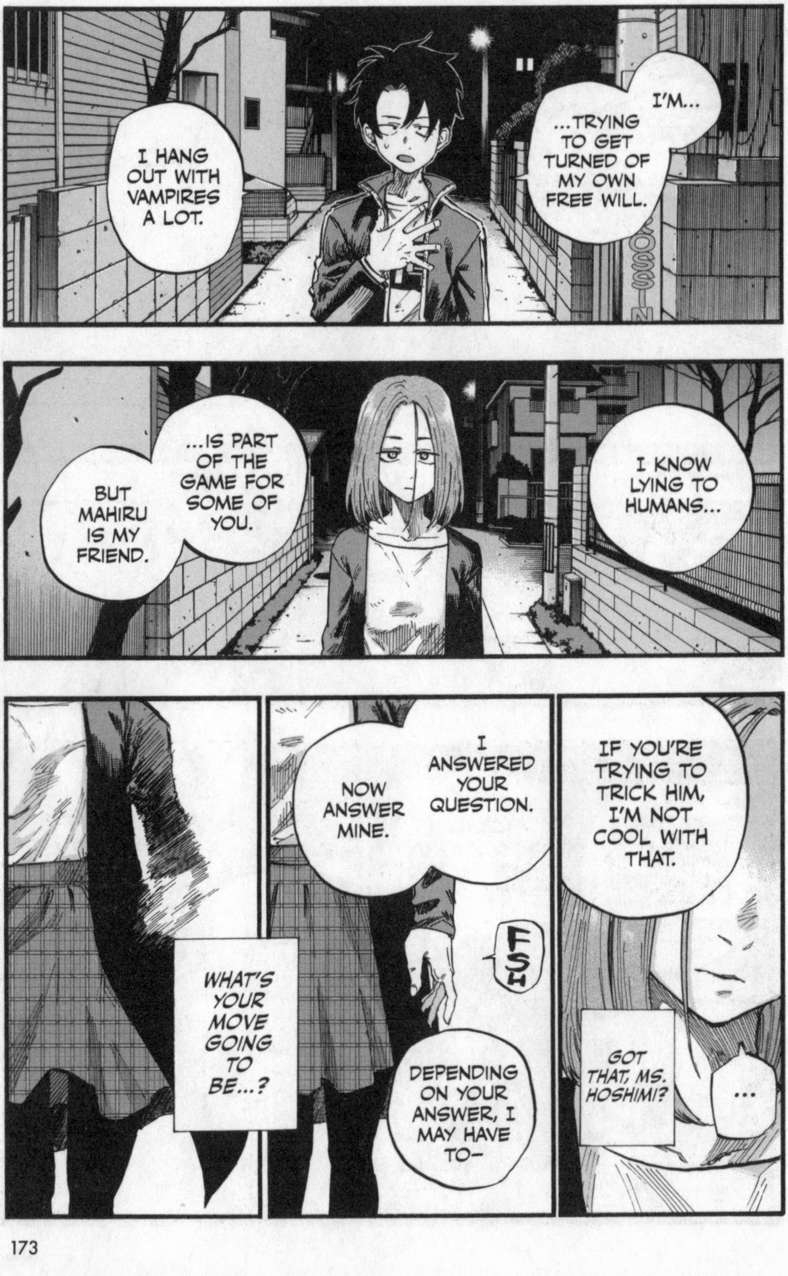
I'M... ...TRYING TO GET TURNED OF MY OWN FREE WILL.
I HANG OUT WITH VAMPIRES A LOT.
I KNOW LYING TO HUMANS...
...IS PART OF THE GAME FOR SOME OF YOU.
BUT MAHIRU IS MY FRIEND.
IF YOU'RE TRYING TO TRICK HIM, I'M NOT COOL WITH THAT.
...
GOT THAT, MS. HOSHIMI?
I ANSWERED YOUR QUESTION.
NOW ANSWER MINE.
FSH
DEPENDING ON YOUR ANSWER, I MAY HAVE TO–
WHAT'S YOUR MOVE GOING TO BE...?

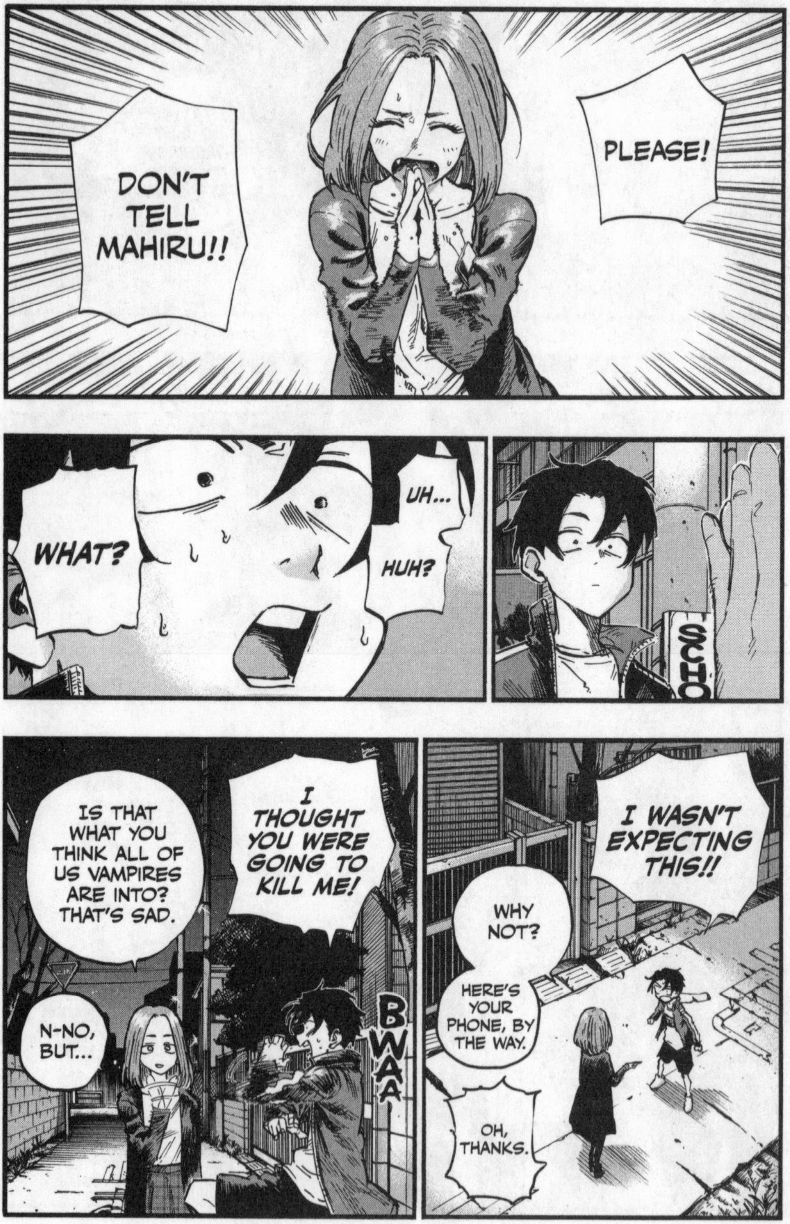
DON'T TELL MAHIRU!!
PLEASE!
WHAT?
UH...
HUH?
SCHO
IS THAT WHAT YOU THINK ALL OF US VAMPIRES ARE INTO? THAT'S SAD.
I THOUGHT YOU WERE GOING TO KILL ME!
BWAA
N-NO, BUT...
I WASN'T EXPECTING THIS!!
WHY NOT?
HERE'S YOUR PHONE, BY THE WAY.
OH, THANKS.

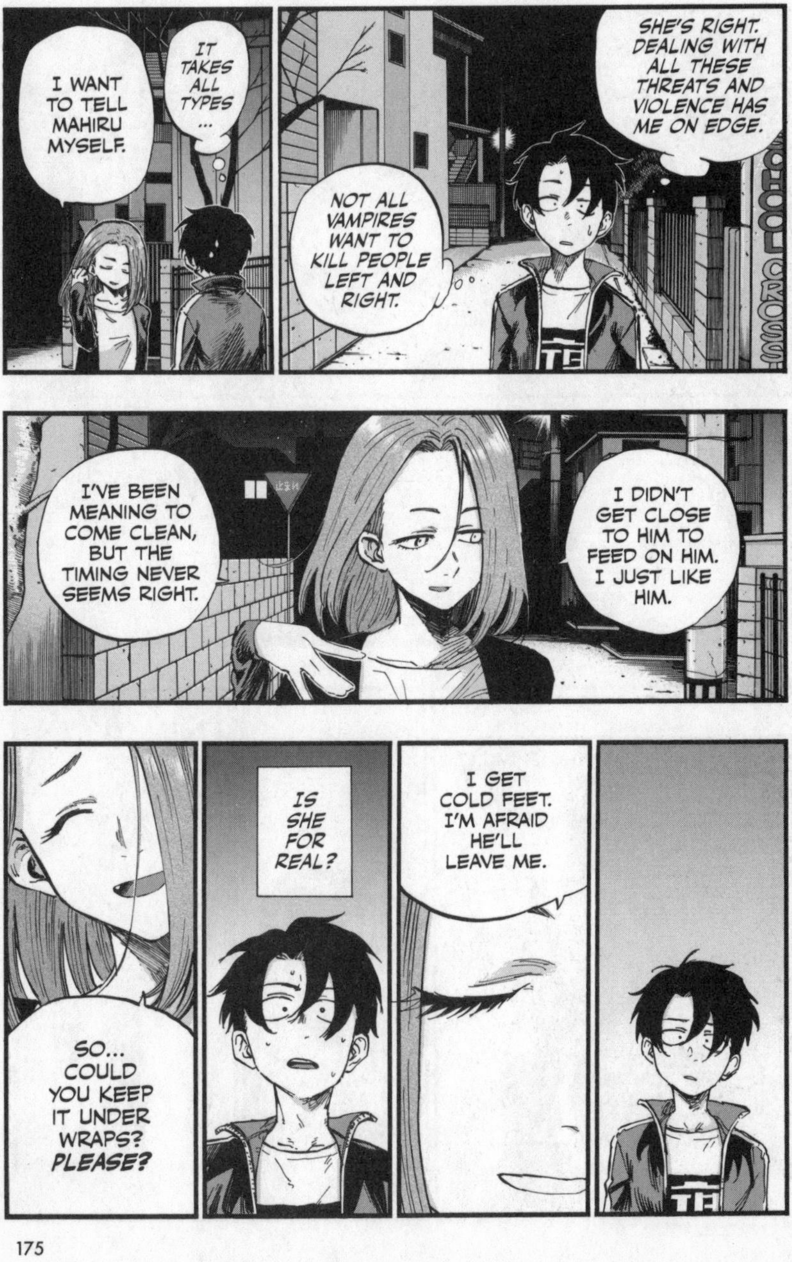
SHE'S RIGHT. DEALING WITH ALL THESE THREATS AND VIOLENCE HAS ME ON EDGE.
NOT ALL VAMPIRES WANT TO KILL PEOPLE LEFT AND RIGHT.
IT TAKES ALL TYPES...
I WANT TO TELL MAHIRU MYSELF.
I DIDN'T GET CLOSE TO HIM TO FEED ON HIM. I JUST LIKE HIM.
I'VE BEEN MEANING TO COME CLEAN, BUT THE TIMING NEVER SEEMS RIGHT.
I GET COLD FEET. I'M AFRAID HE'LL LEAVE ME.
IS SHE FOR REAL?
SO... COULD YOU KEEP IT UNDER WRAPS? *PLEASE?*

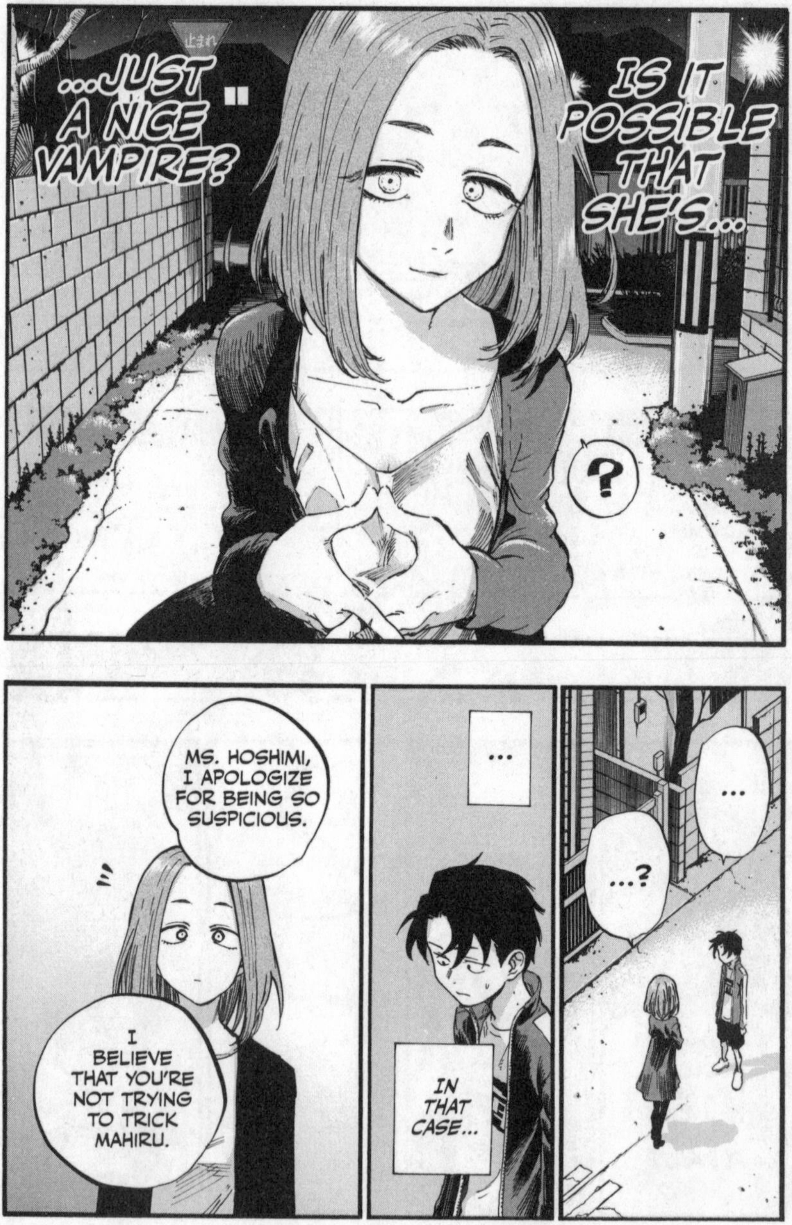
止まれ
IS IT POSSIBLE THAT SHE'S...
...JUST A NICE VAMPIRE?
?
...
...?
...
IN THAT CASE...
MS. HOSHIMI, I APOLOGIZE FOR BEING SO SUSPICIOUS.
I BELIEVE THAT YOU'RE NOT TRYING TO TRICK MAHIRU.

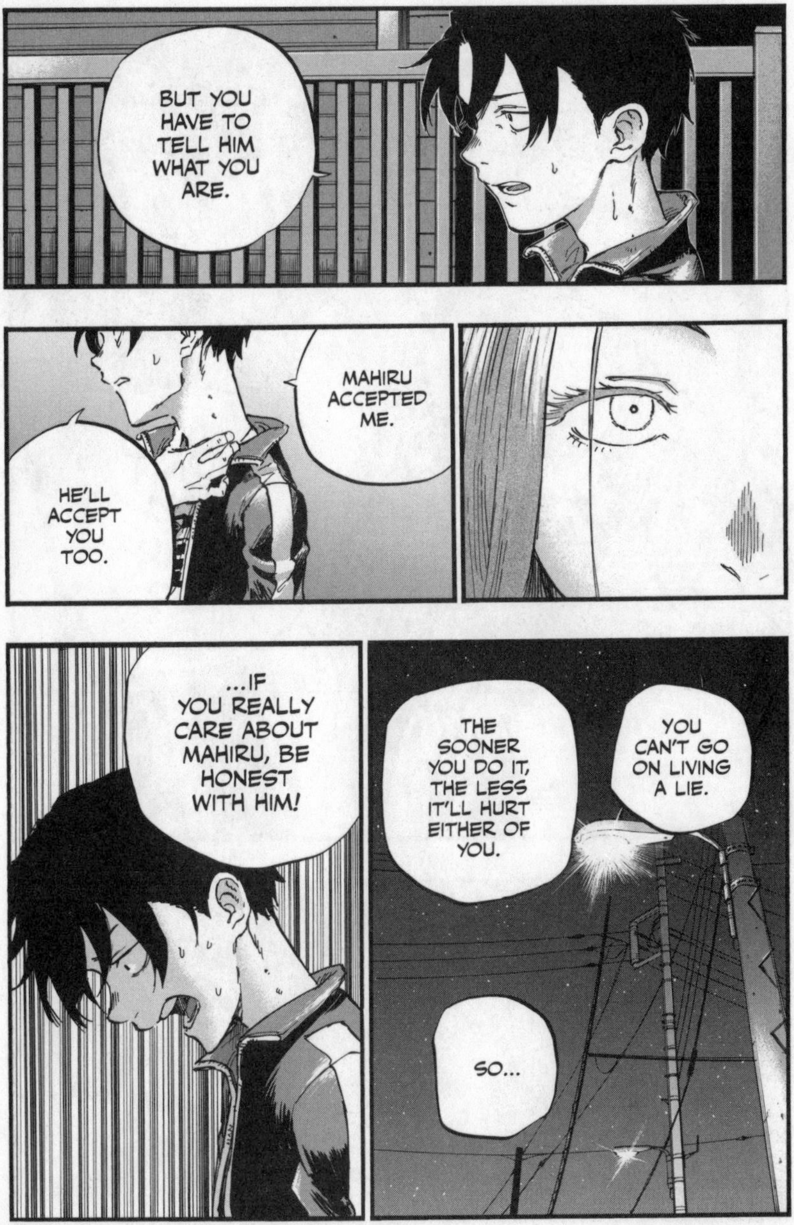
BUT YOU HAVE TO TELL HIM WHAT YOU ARE.
MAHIRU ACCEPTED ME.
HE'LL ACCEPT YOU TOO.
YOU CAN'T GO ON LIVING A LIE.
THE SOONER YOU DO IT, THE LESS IT'LL HURT EITHER OF YOU.
SO...
...IF YOU REALLY CARE ABOUT MAHIRU, BE HONEST WITH HIM!

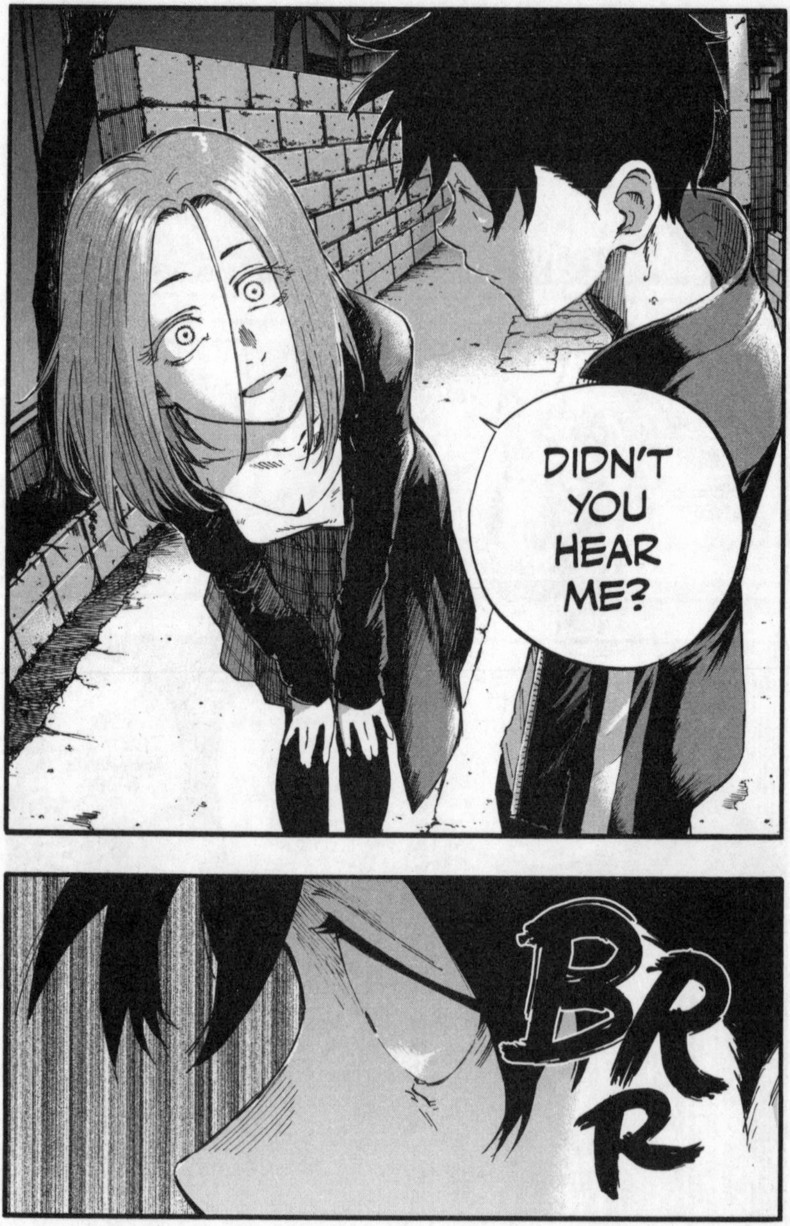
DIDN'T YOU HEAR ME?
BRR

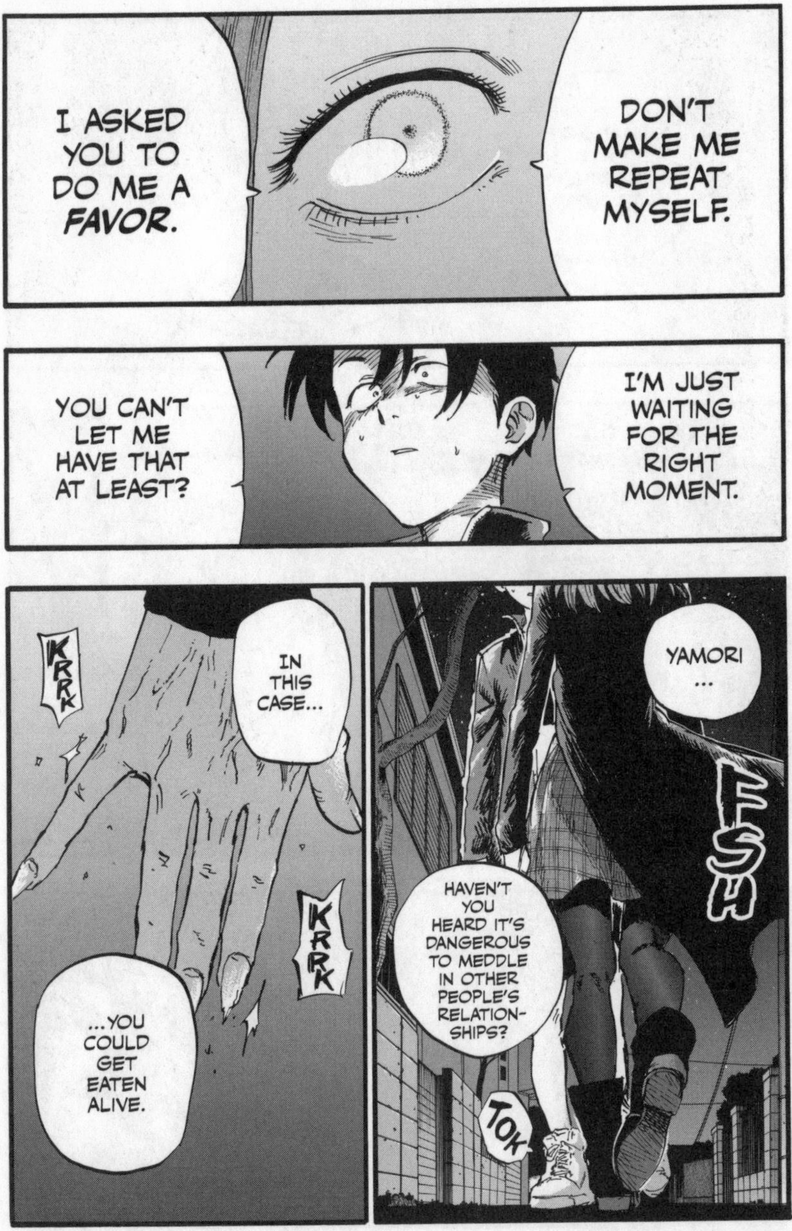
DON'T MAKE ME REPEAT MYSELF.
I ASKED YOU TO DO ME A *FAVOR*.
I'M JUST WAITING FOR THE RIGHT MOMENT.
YOU CAN'T LET ME HAVE THAT AT LEAST?
YAMORI ...
FSH
HAVEN'T YOU HEARD IT'S DANGEROUS TO MEDDLE IN OTHER PEOPLE'S RELATION-SHIPS?
TOK
KRRK
IN THIS CASE...
KRRK
...YOU COULD GET EATEN ALIVE.

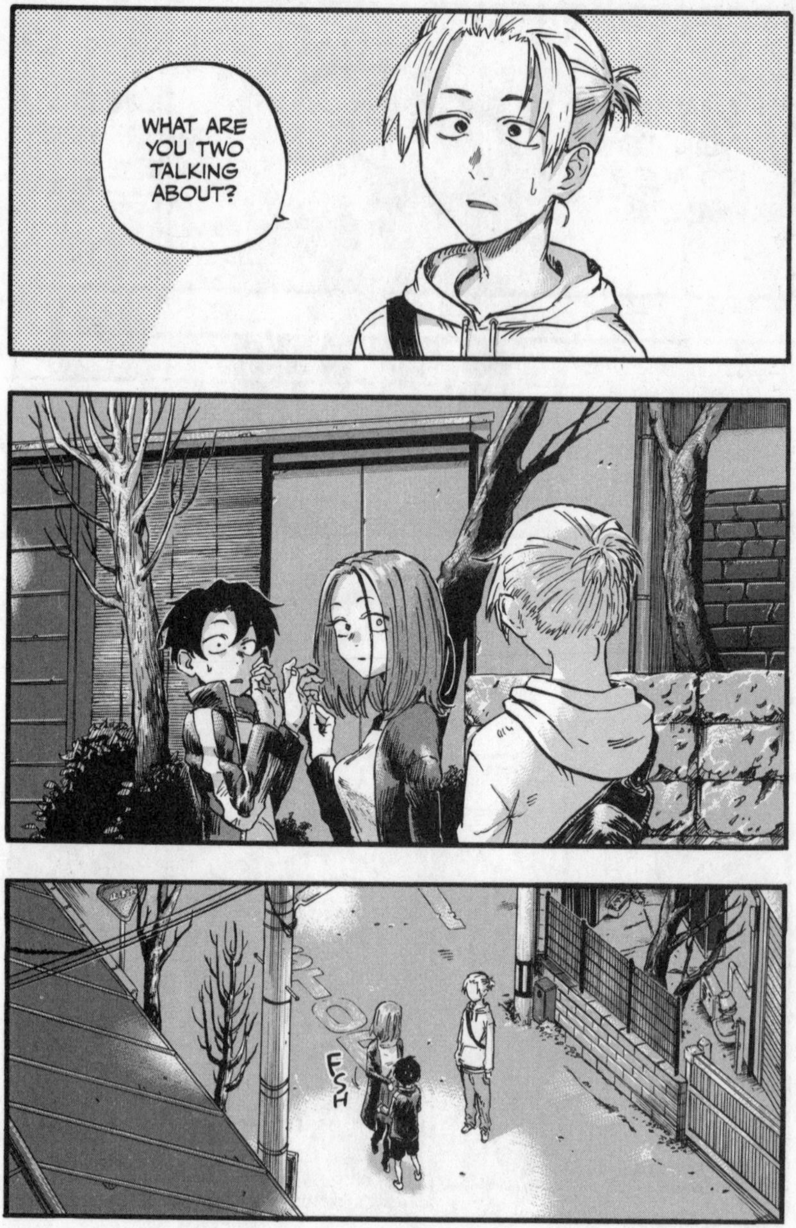
WHAT ARE YOU TWO TALKING ABOUT?
FSH

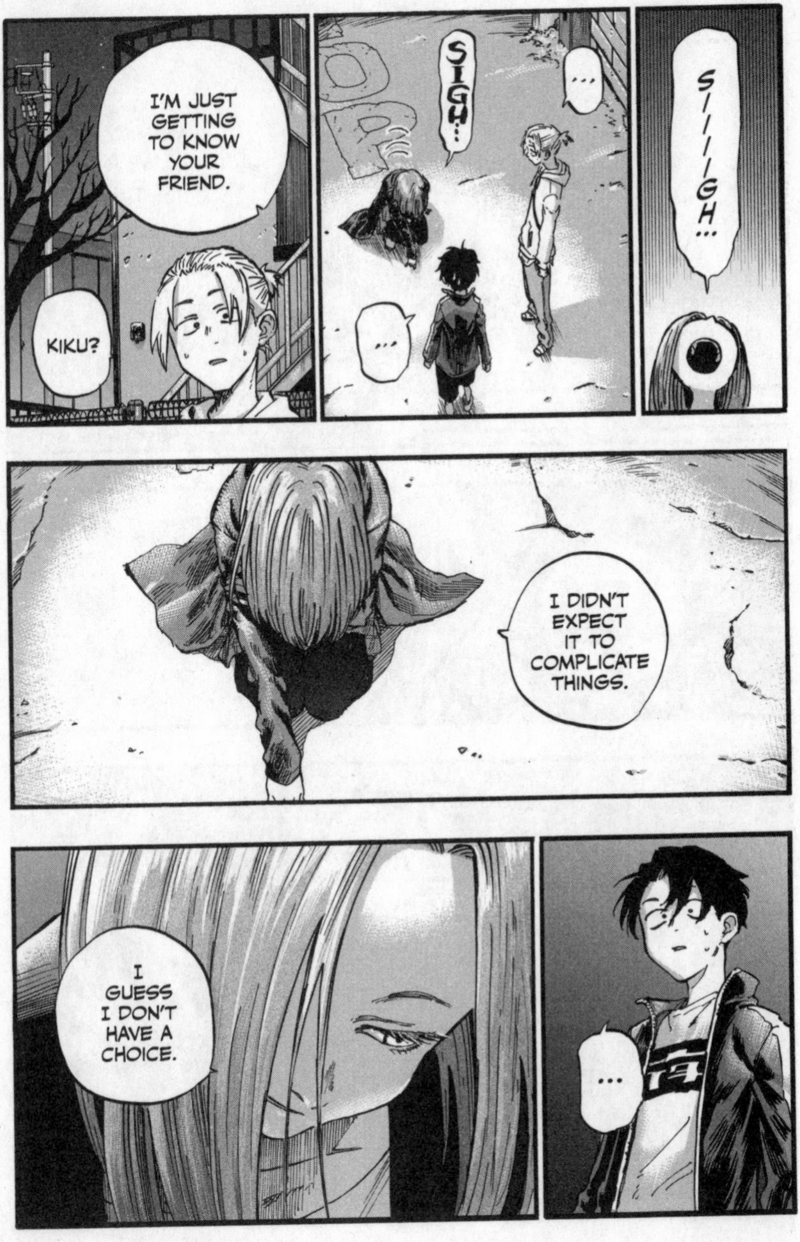
SIIIIGH...
...
SIGH...
...
I'M JUST GETTING TO KNOW YOUR FRIEND.
KIKU?
I DIDN'T EXPECT IT TO COMPLICATE THINGS.
...
I GUESS I DON'T HAVE A CHOICE.

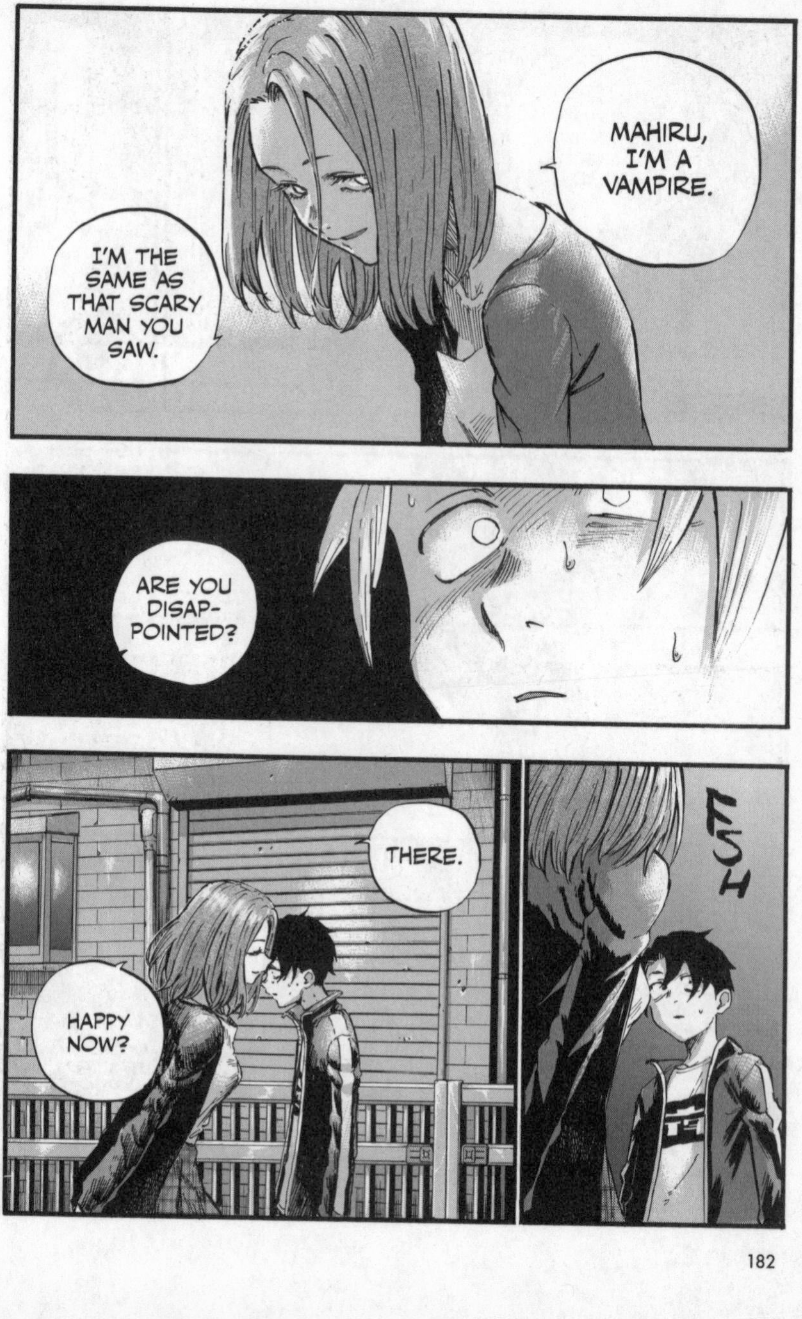
MAHIRU, I'M A VAMPIRE.
I'M THE SAME AS THAT SCARY MAN YOU SAW.
ARE YOU DISAPPOINTED?
FSH
THERE.
HAPPY NOW?

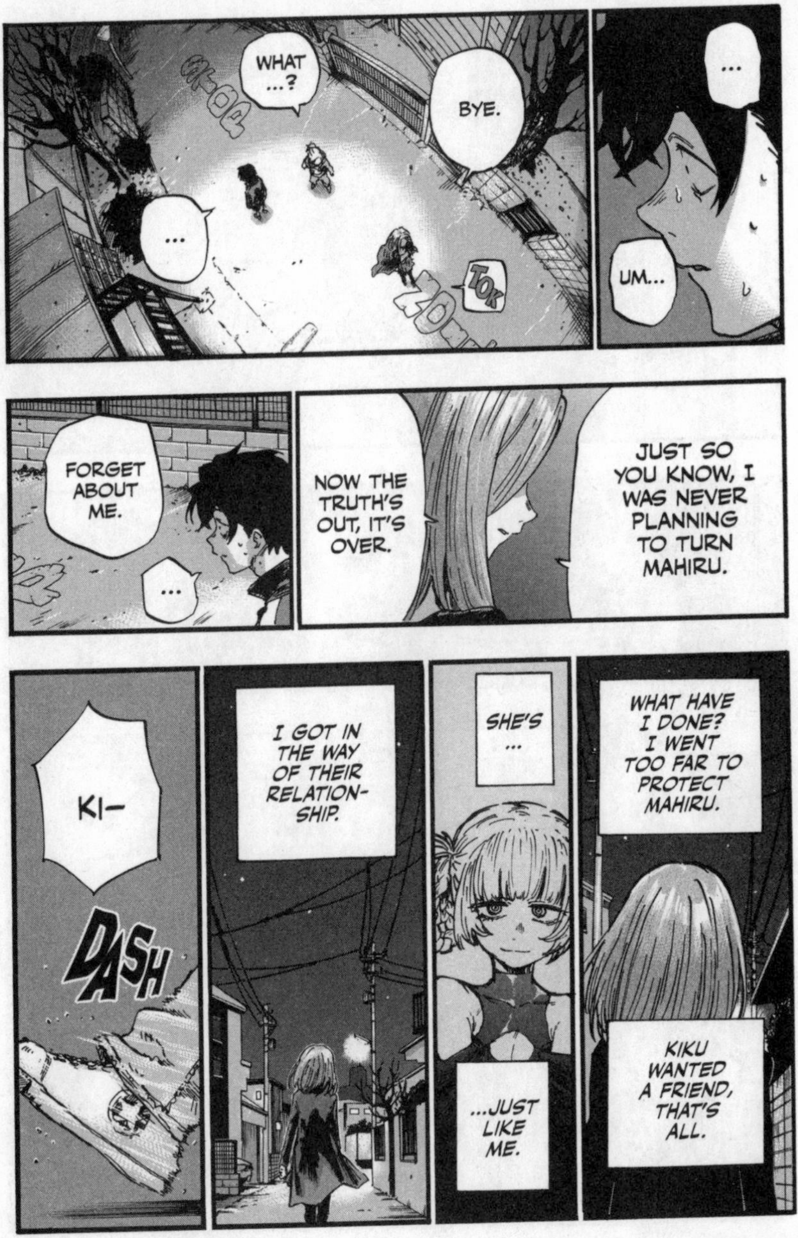
...
UM...
BYE.
WHAT ...?
...
TOK
JUST SO YOU KNOW, I WAS NEVER PLANNING TO TURN MAHIRU.
NOW THE TRUTH'S OUT, IT'S OVER.
FORGET ABOUT ME.
...
WHAT HAVE I DONE? I WENT TOO FAR TO PROTECT MAHIRU.
KIKU WANTED A FRIEND, THAT'S ALL.
SHE'S ...
...JUST LIKE ME.
I GOT IN THE WAY OF THEIR RELATION-SHIP.
KI-
DASH

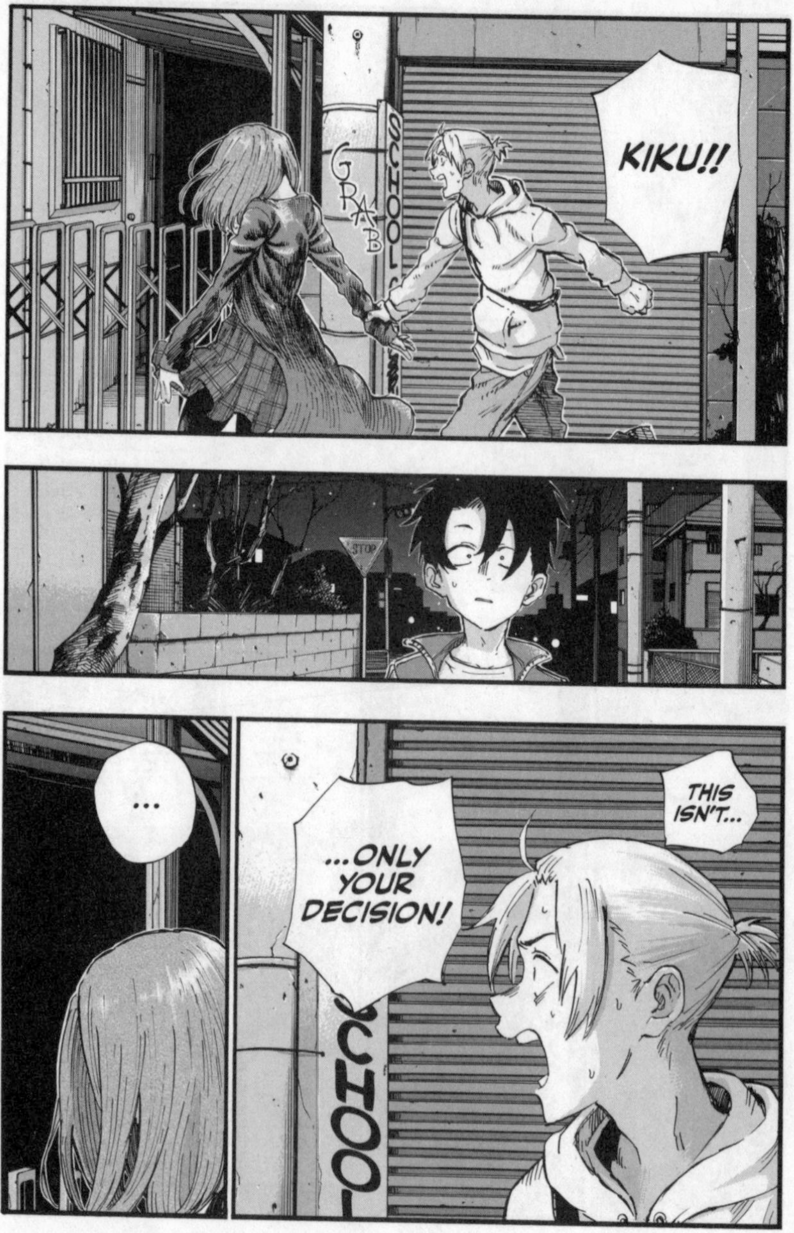
KIKU!!
SCHOOL
GRAB
THIS ISN'T...
...ONLY YOUR DECISION!
SCHOOL
...

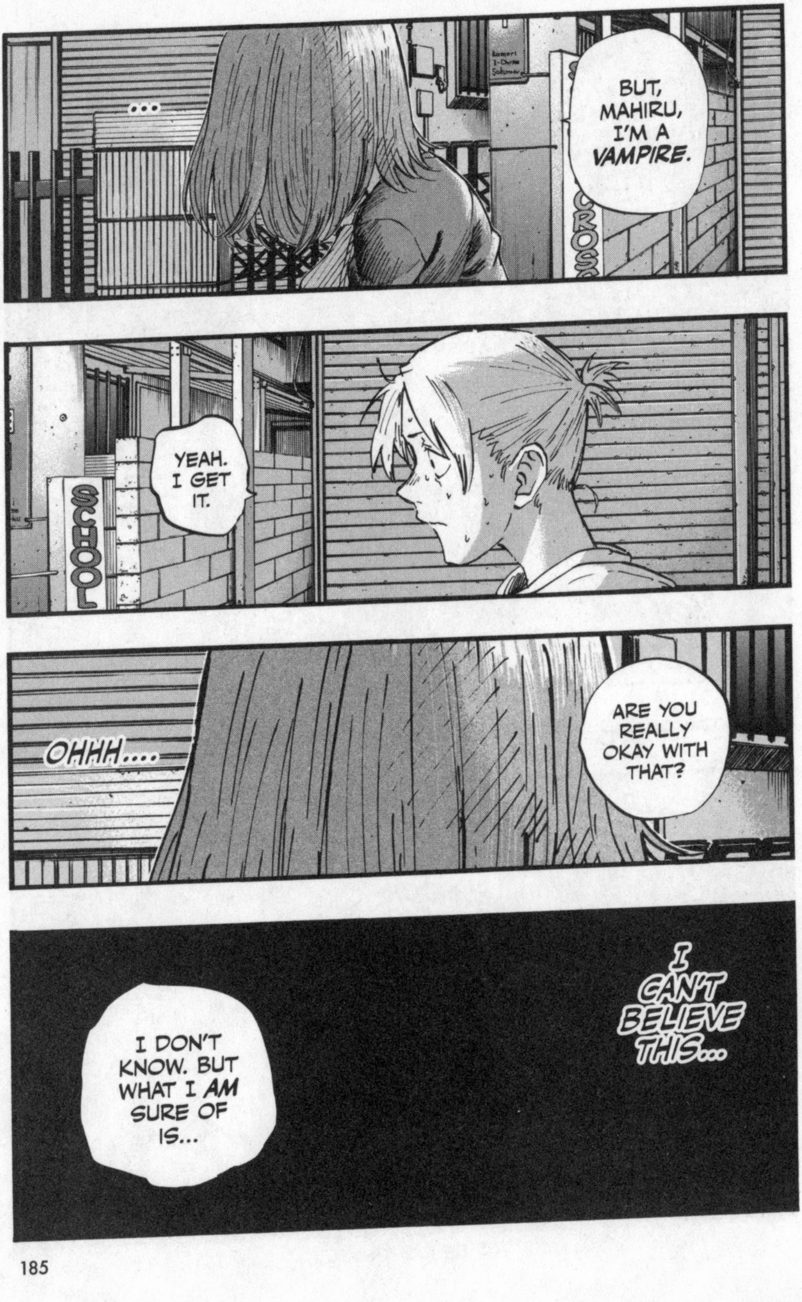
BUT, MAHIRU, I'M A *VAMPIRE*.
...
YEAH. I GET IT.
SCHOOL
ARE YOU REALLY OKAY WITH THAT?
OHHH....
I CAN'T BELIEVE THIS...
I DON'T KNOW. BUT WHAT I *AM* SURE OF IS...

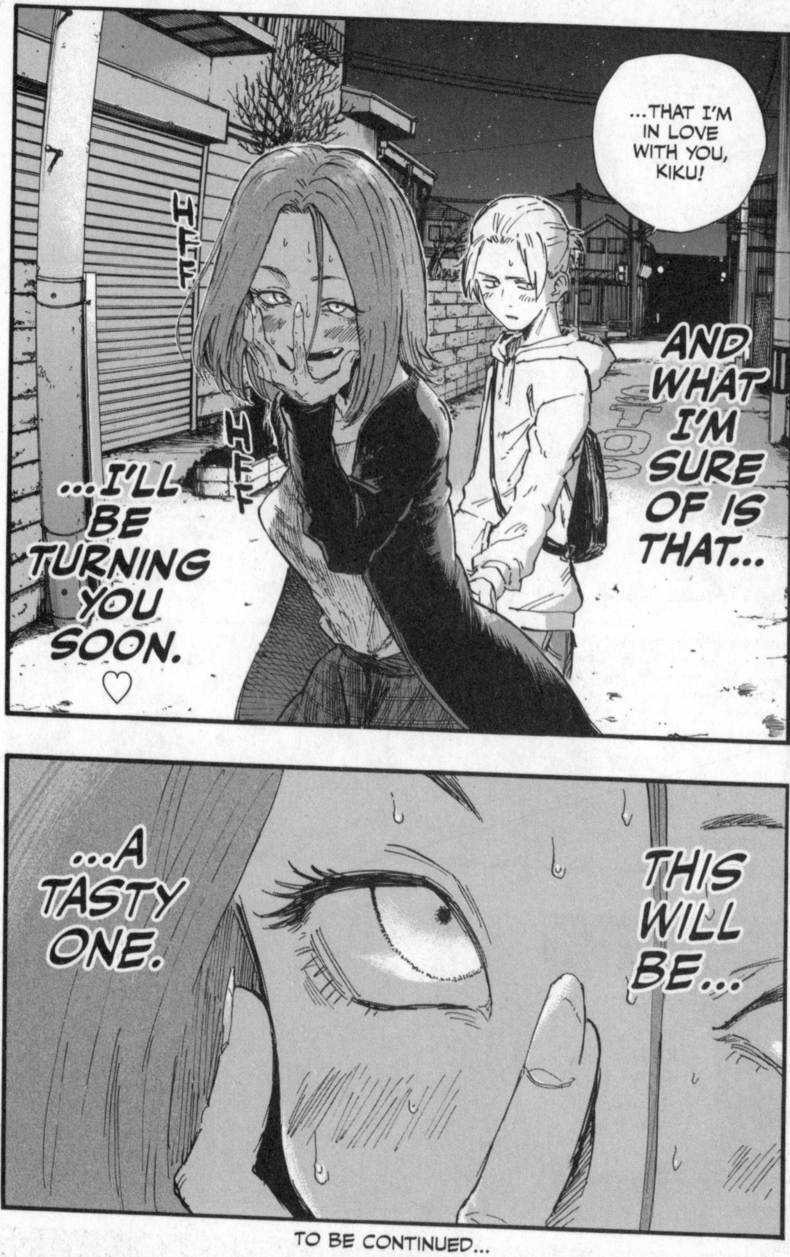
...THAT I'M IN LOVE WITH YOU, KIKU!
AND WHAT I'M SURE OF IS THAT...
HFF
HFF
...I'LL BE TURNING YOU SOON. ♡
THIS WILL BE...
...A TASTY ONE.

TO BE CONTINUED...

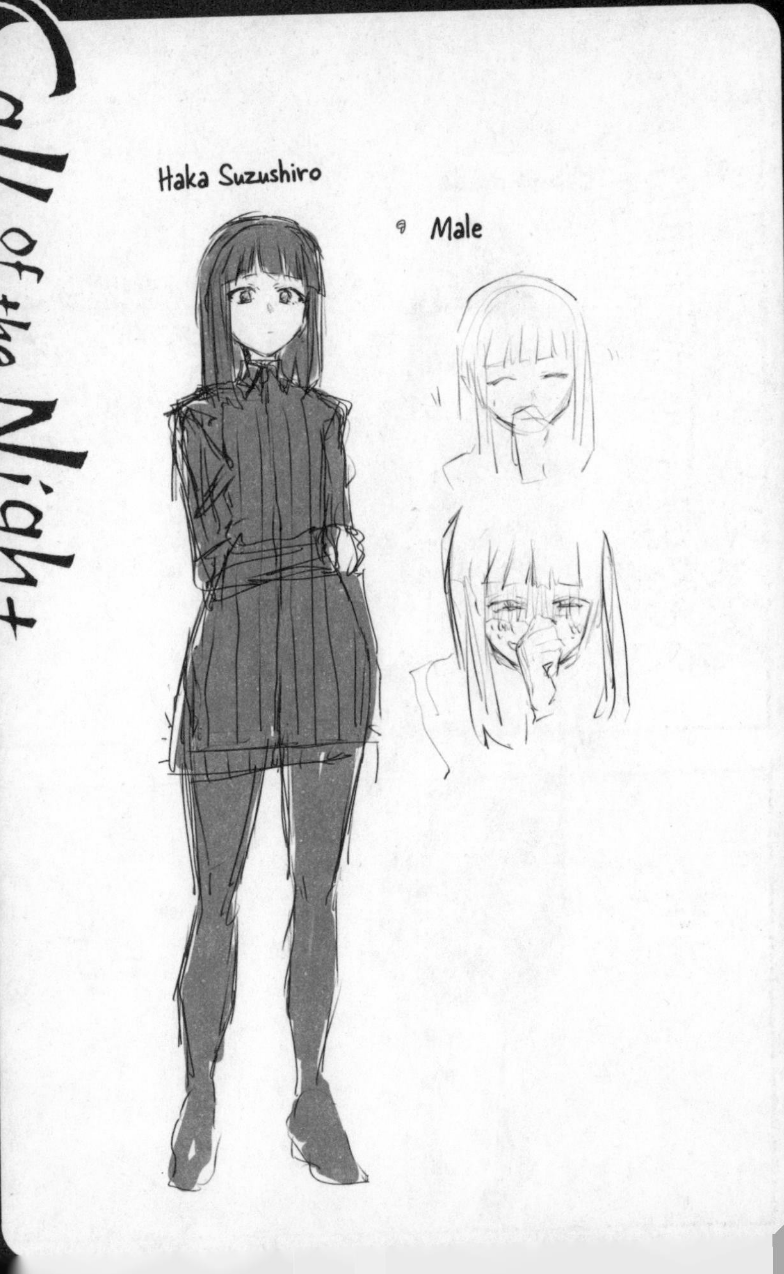
Haka Suzushiro
Male

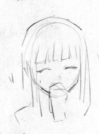

Call of the Night

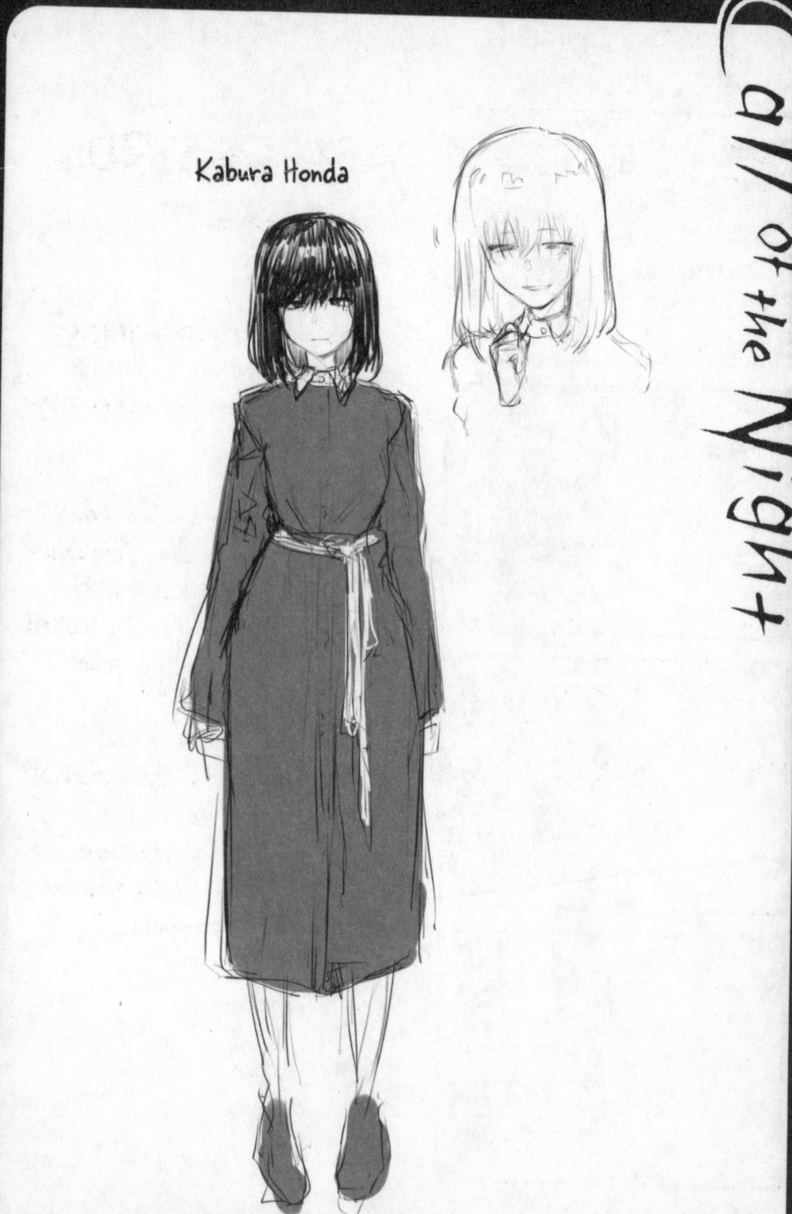
Kabura Honda

Character Model Sheet #Kabura

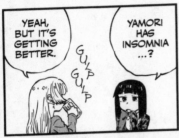

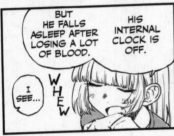

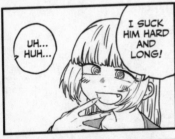

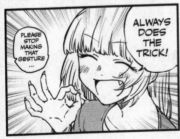

AFTERWORD

Welcome to volume 5!
Kotoyama here.

I've been lazy. After a year of not cutting my hair, I finally went to a barber the other day. Yayyyy!

Have you seen the promo video I did with the rock duo Yorushika? Wasn't it great? I was a little weirded out by how cool I looked. Thank you so much, everyone!

Now we're at volume 5 and getting to some of the material I've been longing to draw. There's plenty more to come, so I'll keep it up. Thank you for your continued support!

See you in volume 6!

KOTOYAMA

YAMORI HAS INSOMNIA ...?
YEAH, BUT IT'S GETTING BETTER.
GULP GULP
HIS INTERNAL CLOCK IS OFF.
BUT HE FALLS ASLEEP AFTER LOSING A LOT OF BLOOD.
WHEW
I SEE...
I SUCK HIM HARD AND LONG!
UH... HUH...
ALWAYS DOES THE TRICK!
PLEASE STOP MAKING THAT GESTURE ...

I don't know how to
draw braids. That's what I say as
I am drawing them.

—KOTOYAMA

KOTOYAMA

In 2013, Kotoyama won the Shonen Sunday Manga
College Award for *Azuma*. From 2014 to 2018,
Kotoyama's title *Dagashi Kashi* ran in *Shonen Sunday*
magazine. *Call of the Night* has been published
in *Shonen Sunday* since 2019.